WOMEN EMPOWERMENT THROUGH ENTREPRENEURSHIP DEVELOPMENT

Women Empowerment Through Entrepreneurship Development

E.D. Setty
P. Krishna Moorthy

ANMOL PUBLICATIONS PVT. LTD.
NEW DELHI - 110 002 (INDIA)

ANMOL PUBLICATIONS PVT. LTD.
H.O.: 4374/4B, Ansari Road, Darya Ganj
New Delhi-110 002 (India)
Ph.: 23278000, 23261597
B.O.: 1015, Ist Main Road, BSK IIIrd Stage
IIIrd Phase, IIIrd Block
Bangalore - 560 085 (Karnataka)
Ph: 080-517 3429, Tel/Fax: 080-2672 3604
Visit us at: www.anmolpublications.com

Women Empowerment Through Entrepreneurship Development

First Published, 2007

ISBN 81-261-3117-9

PRINTED IN INDIA

Printed at Mehra Offset Press, Delhi.

Contents

Preface

The volume in general speaks of humanistic and constitutional need in terms of empowerment of women detailing the various government orders and institutional building and measures initiated by various departments in empowering womenfolk.

One could see the measures comprising economic, social, educational more importantly entrepreneurial in providing opportunities especially to the women below poverty line.

Chapter 1 gives a brief historical and constitutional background in terms of the efforts towards empowerment of women. It traces the measures initiated right from attainment of independence and upto the recent times.

As mentioned above, Chapter 2 focuses on legal measures in terms of empowerment of women. Similarly, Chapter 3 briefly expounds the policy formulations with the objective of empowerment of women.

As the title of the Chapter 4 indicates the focus of this chapter is empowering women to economic development. The chapter also focuses key indicators of women's social status in a few selected countries and continents over the globe. This highlights the need for empowerment of women developing their capabilities providing relevant opportunities to them. This chapter brings in a brief comparison amongst East Asia, South-East Asia, Oceania, Latin America & Sub-Saharan Africa. This chapter focuses mainly on role of women and their establishing what is called the Self-employed

Women's Association (SEWA) in India. SEWA has been tremendously successful in respect to establishing Banks and assisting thousands of poor women engaged in a variety of mini and small scale enterprises. Some of them established at their own residences.

Chapter 5 speaks of socio-psychic elements pertaining to individuals the way the prospective entrepreneurs are to overcome certain inhibitions and motivate themselves and gain confidence and venture into some enterprise with a vision and strong determination.

Chapter 6 highlights the relevance and importance of developing entrepreneurship among women, briefly touching upon the significance and the history of creating a respectable place and status for women folk. It briefly points out the potential women clientele who are to be encouraged to move into entrepreneurial activity.

Chapter 7 in general, presents a model for developing agro-enterprises among farm women.

Chapter 8 briefly describes the role of women, the hidden and signifiant part they play in the sphere of economic development.

Chapter 9 is an illustrative and comparative model from Bangladesh in organizing poor women into groups and helping them to become self-reliant. The Bangladesh Rural Advancement Committee (BRAC) has been for the past several years mobilizing and organizing poor women into groups helping them financially, training and guiding them in starting small-scale enterprises and facilitating the marketing of the products produced by the groups. The BRAC efforts serve as an effective model in organizing the poor women motivating and assisting them to operate as mini-entrepreneurs

Chapter 10: Though the title speaks of extension in aid of

agricultural marketing, it could be taken as the marketing strategies for the products of small-scale enterprises. It illustrates the extension methods that are to be employed in generating awareness and securing the means to venture into entrepreneurial activities. Entrepreneurship development in a larger sense is an educational process. The chapter explains the ways to market agricultural products. Of several problems which may be called factors in the entire field of entrepreneurship development, marketing of products in a competitive world appears to be really a challenging one.

Chapter 11 which is rather comprehensive focuses on the ways in which small-scale and cottage industries are being promoted in Asia. Further, it lays emphasis on the need for rural industrialization and on the economy related to cottage and small scale industries. It highlights the fact that the future prosperity of agricultural countries in the Asian region lies in the working hands of the villagers who are a hidden resource which needs to be mobilized. The chapter further focuses and brings out the advantages and disadvantages in respect to the large-scale and small-scale industries and highlights the role of industry in integrated rural development.

Chapter 12 which is rather elaborate briefly covers the industrial development policies promulgated by the Government of India during the past six decades in promoting small-scale enterprises providing incentives to the neo-entrepreneurs and making reservation of items for manufacture in the small-scale sector. In order to translate the industrial policies, issued periodically, the chapter lists out the institutional framework that has been established both at the national and state level.

Chapter 13 may be considered, as a key chapter which details the approaches to development of entrepreneurship highlighting the sociological aspects, physical conditions, cultural patterns and human resources in promoting entrepreneurship in a given community. It speaks of the kind of barriers and stimulants in promoting entrepreneurship. It spells out four principal factors that matter in EDP namely, organization, infrastructure, resources and entrepreneurs himself. It draws the attention of EDP promoters to the need for a successful utilization of EDP promoters to the need for a successful utilization and blending of these factors which promote entrepreneurship. The different phases that one has to go through in promoting entrepreneurship are detailed in this chapter.

Chapter 14 is of a general nature describing women in society and their participation in development activities. It lays emphasis on empowering women enabling and facilitating them to participate in all development programmes which of course, is a stupendous task.

Chapter 15, in brief, details the manner in which the DWCRA programmes are being helped by different institutions and the way in which the self-help groups carry on the mini-enterprises and the kind of products they make and the way they go about improving their standard of life. This chapter concludes with an illustrative case study from the district of Warangal in Andhra Pradesh, entitled "Empowering Women through Self-Help Groups".

Chapter 16 briefly describes the programmes related to empowerment of women and self-employment in the State. With a twin objective, protecting existing forests and also contributing to afforestation, at the same time helping people bordering forest areas, the Government of Andhra Pradesh has constituted Vana Samrakshana Samithis (VSSs) which are of group nature.

Chapter 17 speaks of the key features of DWCRA Programme and its objectives, the way in which the beneficiaries are identified and formation of SHGs and the kind of assistance extended to them and the way in which these women self-help groups are being trained so that they could become effective micro-entrepreneurs.

Chapter18 in brief speaks of the efforts made by Non-Governmental Organizations (NGOs) such as Hindustan Lever Limited (HLL), Padmavathy Sangam, Rashtriya Seva Samithi (RASS) and Swayam Krushi Mutually Aided Cooperative Thrift Society in encouraging and helping women below poverty line to get self-employed. The Hindustan Lever Limited under its Project Shakti helps marketing of its products by the women, thus paving the way for individual and group entrepreneurial venture on the part of the poor women. It only indicates that not only the government but also the NGOs in their own self-interest and also to help the society could pave the way and lead the poor segments of population towards better way of life through economic pursuits.

Acknowledgment

We would like to express our deep appreciation and sincere thanks to Mrs. E. Vishalakshi for her sharing with us pertinent and relevant issues and needs related to women in general. In a sense, she has been a partner in accomplishing this volume on "Empowerment of Women through Entrepreneurship Development".

We express our deep and sincere thanks to Sri S. Ramakrishna who has prepared the entire manuscript in a meticulous way. Our sincere and grateful thanks to M/s Anmol Publications Pvt. Ltd., New Delhi for undertaking publication of this volume as they did, in an excellent way, the earlier volumes:

—**Authors**

Introduction

For the past several centuries, there have been attempts to ameliorate the status of women in the society. The privileges or the status accorded to and enjoyed by women differ from culture to culture and from age to age. Sporadic political, social and religious attempts have been there to elevate or treat women as equal to man. We have not so far succeeded in bringing about the equality of sexes. One may write volumes and speak at length on the need for empowerment of women, but in reality and practice it may end as a wishful thinking. The importance that she enjoys at home is different from the way in which she is treated outside. Whether it is political emancipation or ensuring of social equality, it has been in the process for several centuries. One significant and potent factor that would empower women is through their economic contribution. We find a very close relationship between women empowerment and women taking to self-employment or some entrepreneurial activity. Here we emphasize some economic activity exclusively in the domain of women and managed by women. It could be one of the surest ways of bringing about equality between man and woman.

One can think of several approaches to remedy the gender inequality and imbalances in development, but one substantive approach could be promoting self-employment and assisting women to take to some micro-enterprises. The usefulness of this approach depends on how seriously and faithfully it is translated into action. Unless there is something exclusive answering the cause and improving the economic conditions of women, any grand designs, formulation of policies and diluted approaches in the name of women development will hardly bear fruits.

Various conferences and seminars have brought out the point forcefully that integration of women in all sectors of economic and social development is necessary for national development. One could see some kind of reluctance, hesitation and unwillingness and prejudices in respect to encouraging women going in for productive economic activity. There is a need to bring about a change in the attitude of people and the state has to make special efforts to create a facilitating situation to gradually encourage women to move into a state of self-reliance. These approaches are to be from several angles political, economic, social and religious but one solid effort could be motivating and facilitating women to take up some enterprises. One may speak volumes on why women are to be brought into the entrepreneurial activity. There is a need. If you are to treat them and make them equal to man the more effective means is through economic pursuits.

Different societies and cultures are deeply rooted in discriminatory values and prejudices in respect to women. To cross these social attitudinal barriers is a very difficult task. But we have to make a beginning. Elsewhere and even in the context of India, we had made some beginning. It is worth noting that the Government of Andhra Pradesh is marching forward towards social and economic empowerment of women through better access of women to economic resources, increased mobility, awareness, assertiveness, confidence, self-respect, self-esteem and gender equality. Net-working of SHGs at village, cluster and mandal level are emerging with the pro active role taken by the Government by way of introduction of MACTS Act, 1995 which is encouraging Women's Cooperative Thrift Societies. In the last 5-6 years the Government has been involving the women as active partners in the development process.

Savings and credit or income generation requires a holistic approach to human development, which ultimately leads to community development. The approach towards poverty alleviation should be self-help. Savings plus credit is a good starting point for group formation. Now in Andhra Pradesh the Self-Help Groups (SHGs) have become a forum for the collective unit of the poor against common expression and explanation, to understand individual and common problems and to improve their skills and capabilities to manage resources.

In a relative vacuum and rarity of interest, initiative, knowledge, skills and resources material and human on the part of the downtrodden women folk, the Self-Help Groups function as educational and enabling instruments to gradually elevate the life of the poor to minimum meaningful standard of life. This development is a journey and the destination will be moving forward on and on. The way in which the programmes are being carried on serves as training for the women folk. Entrepreneurial activities being carried on with assistance from different quarters, it is hoped that it would play a contagious role drawing people from other segments of the population. Here, we may presume though, the self-help groups are functioning collectively, over a period of time, individuals within the group are likely to graduate into successful independent entrepreneurs.

Though we speak of empowerment of women especially through promoting entrepreneurship among them, we may have to consider two vital factors. Age old attitude of men towards women and vice-versa. One may bring in constitutional, legislative, administrative and social changes in favour of empowerment of women, but women for centuries together largely were used to and subjected to subordination and secondary roles, normally will be hesitant to move on to the threshold of business enterprises. It does not mean that there are no women folk world over who have proved to be effective and successful leaders in the field of entrepreneurship development. On one hand, the man has to change his attitude and encourage the women folk and simultaneously the women too have to girdle up and assume initiative and move forward and avail themselves the opportunities that are offered to them by several means. In a sense, the success of empowering women is a two way approach. Men on one hand and the women on the other. Entrepreneurship by itself may not bring in the anticipated power to the women folk especially in taking lead, initiating projects and managing them effectively and successfully. Here, we mention entrepreneurship development is not a single factor, but it is a composite system of management. Several significant aspects such as vision, creativity, expansion, diversification and adaptation of appropriate of modern technologies and most importantly the new ways of making use of resources and expanding the market for a particular produce or service. We believe promotion of entrepreneurship will play a vital role in empowering the women folk.

1

National Efforts Towards Empowerment of Women

Women all over the world are overwhelmingly concerned with the issue of gender equality through women's empowerment. The results are periodically assessed in world conferences, of which we have had four since the Mexico Conference, the last one being in Beijing in July 1995. In the intervening period; national and international conferences deliberated on women's issues including gender equality.

In terms of constitutional, legal and administrative measures as well as enabling support to improve the working and living conditions of women, many initiatives were taken since 1947. Prominent among them are the constitutional mandates for gender equality and justice, enactment of very many new laws and amendment of existing laws to protect and promote the interests of women, setting up of women-specific administrative and economic structures like separate Women and Child Development Department at the union and State Government levels, constitution of the National Commission for Women and also Commissions for Women in several States, State Women Development Corporations, orientation in plan strategy to include women specific and women related programmes, launching of special schemes like Rashtriya Mahila Kosh, Indira Mahila Yojana and Mahila Samridhi Yojana and the foremost among them all, the provision to reserve for women, one-third number of seats to be filled by direct election in Panchayats and urban local bodies and also offices in specified rural and urban local self-government institutions, initiaing introduction of the 81st Constitution (amendment) Bill for reservation of seats in Lok Sabha and State Legislatures.

Thus, we have enacted useful legislations to curb indignities on women and provide safety and security and harmony in family and society while some countries are still struggling for the emancipation of women. What we find is that these social legislations, such as those on dowry prohibition, equal remuneration and like, lag behind implementation because the society has not kept pace with the rapidity of legislations, fast changing societal norms and dynamics of human behaviour and the need of human rights prerogatives. Our culture accords a high position to women. We venerate women and we accord the highest place for the mother in the family, yet women are denied equality of status, contradictory and strange are the human motives. In this context, we are reminded of what A.C.Pigou said in his Welfare Economics. "When we elect to watch the play of human motives, that are ordinary, that are dismal and ignoble, our impulse is not the philosopher's impulse - knowledge for the sake of knowledge but rather the physiologist's knowledge for the healing that knowledge may help to bring". We need remind ourselves that the knowledge that we may gain through conferences and other means must be utilized to heal the ills of society and to bring about sober and sound systems that make the home, the society and the country a place worth living.

Governance is an omnibus phrase. It encompasses social, political and economic empowerment. Gender equality, as in many other areas, is a relative term. While in a female-headed household or matriarchal system, the women may have equality to a large degree, but when it comes to the society, the social status varies considerably from community to community. In general, women lag behind in the equality status. The society and the Government have not been able to shed their inhibitions and reservations in according an equal status to women, notwithstanding very many progressive elements found in many of the religions of the world as well as the Constitutions of various countries.

When it comes to economic empowerment, while women work along with men equally hard if not harder, their work is neither recognized nor taken into account in computing income. The statistics in our country, so also in very many others, show that the number of women in employment of a regular nature has been increasing and women are now to be found in a variety of jobs once considered to be the preserves of men. It is a universal truth that if real empowerment is to be had, women must be economically independent. Many family discords occur mainly because of glaring unequal economic status of couples. It is also essential that the title of property owned should at least be, in the joint names of the couples if not exclusively in the name of female especially if the property was acquired through money brought from parental home. The role of women in taking decisions in the family affecting economic areas must also be a joint effort of husband and wife, father and mother, daughter and son, brother and sister and so on, involving equally the male and female members. Then alone can harmony be built. As somebody put it, a happy home is heaven in advance.

In our country, the main obstacle for empowerment is the dismal female educational level.

The gender disparity that vitiates the development process has its origin at the most vulnerable point in a woman's life, viz. girl-child growing up in a family. Education of the girl-child is the best remedy to correct the imbalance and no cost is too high to achieve it. In respect of girls' education, we may not be wanting too much in theoretical formulations and planning strategies, our major weakness seems to lie in the lack of sincerity in execution and vigour in implementation.

Women in Decision-making Process

In the empowerment route, participation of women in decision making at all levels has special significance, especially in a democratic set-up. It is unfortunate that some countries in the world have yet to confer full voting rights to women.

The empowerment of women and the achievement of equality should not be considered in isolation. The realization of these goals is the only way to build a harmonious, just and balanced society. Let us pledge ourselves to actively pursue the essential requisites for the good of humanity.

Empowerment of Women Through Various International and National Agencies

Poverty eradication assumes great significance in this context. Poverty eradication and empowerment of women are now at the centre stage of development.

A nation can ill afford to leave behind half of its population in its march towards progress and prosperity.

Equality between women and men is a condition for social justice and is also a necessary and fundamental requisite for equality, development and peace.

Babu's Concern for Women

Mahatma Gandhi, who was instrumental in bringing hundreds of thousands of women out of their homes to fight in the freedom struggle, did not equate legal equality of sexes with equality of occupations. He believed that there was a basic difference in the roles and functions of men and women but they were complementary. He further asserted that they were not inferior to men and that men and women were equal in law. The amelioration in the condition of women was a necessary precondition to the regeneration of Indian society. So he mobilized women into the national movement, apart from working for their emancipation.

Representation of Women in Governance

In the annals of evolution of local self-government in the country, June 1, 1993 occupies a prime place. It was on that day a constitutional status to municipal administration in India was accorded by bringing into force the Constitution (Seventy-Fourth Amendment) act. 1992. It is well known that earlier the Constitution did not make local self-government in urban areas a specific constitutional mandate. While the Directive Principles of State Policy refers to village panchayats, there was no specific reference to municipalities except implicitly in Entry 5 of the State List which places the subject of local self-government as a responsibility of the States.

Urbanization is a natural consequence of the economic changes that take place in a country.

Empowerment Through Grass Roots Democracy

Everything must start from the beginning. So also is the case with progress and development for these to be meaningful. Moreover, it must involve both men and women, from the lowest possible levels - grass roots level, as we often refer to them, to enable their total involvement and participation. Unless we the people help ourselves and thereby strengthen the hands of the nation towards peace, plenty and prosperity, there can be no future at all for this nation nor for the suffering millions. While eradication and total abolition of poverty, illiteracy and disease must be the main plank for us to commence our programmes and policies, what needs to be worked out is the modus operandi for successful implementation of these schemes and programmes. In any of the multi-pronged phases involving integrated rural development with its composite, package of potable water, housing, fuel and electricity, health, education and introduction of innovative appropriate technologies, all of them perforce have to deeply involve committed villagers of both the sexes.

Then and then alone can we see the beginning of great future for this great nation with its grand manpower of skilled, trained competent band of administrators and scientists. We do not have a dearth of either technologies or people to transmit these technologies to the relevant strata of society, making them the beneficiaries of the fruits of a grand endeavour. The lacunae must be identified and the gaps filled without any further delay in order to enable both the village and urban level populations subsisting at village on the fringes of big metropolitan cities.

To this end we must set up task forces involving as many people at various levels, as possible including recently retired officers of the Government to enrich the programmes with their excellent experience. While men at all levels must be drafted into these schemes, since women form often more than 50% of any population be it rural or urban or even semi-urban, success will be assured to most programmes by their active involvement and achievement. But many of the women are either hesitant or even reluctant to enter these programmes although several of them have already been drafted into them by various processes of mediation, awareness of their own potential and actual gains for themselves individuals as well as for the whole family and village at large. Despite lack of formal education, many of these women have a native intelligence quotient rather of a high order and are able to master the three R's (i.e., reading, writing and arithmetic) rather rapidly particularly the arithmetic part of it including computing, etc., of accounts. Better roads and commuting facilities, lighting, availability of fuel for cooking, will free them from unnecessary drudgery of long and arduous chores, and make them available for work for society, village and the nation.

Benefits of modern science and technology must reach the masses in various appropriate levels and phases. This is an ongoing process and many women have adopted and adapted to these facilities. The stress and emphasis on Panchayati Raj and the 33% reservation for women is a great and laudable step in this direction. There is a general feeling that village men folk not only discourage their women to participate in the great national adventure, they also prevent and condemn their involvement. While it is so in some cases it has been observed that by motivating the men and impressing on them the benefits for the whole family would accrue because of such scheme many men are willing and what more, are even glad to have their womenfolk enter all arenas. This is nothing new. The men have been working shoulder-to-shoulder in the fields and have taken it as a matter of fact and necessity. By persuasion and coaxing of men it is easier to ensure the smooth transition into other fields also, mainly political which would then usher in an era of politics and socio-economic progress.

Political Empowerment of Women

This brings us to the question of political empowerment, a very crucial issue in many of the ongoing debates and concerns throughout the length and breadth of the country. Where do we begin to enable active participation of women in the decision making levels? Understandably it must be at the grass- roots level of the Gram Panchayat and to repeat, the 33% reservation for women at all tiers of Panchayat has made a significant beginning and a major contribution. In order to get the elected women to function effectively and safeguard the interests of the village and in particular of women and children adequate training and authority have to be provided to them, by continuous motivation and awareness procedures of the rich dividends inherent in such empowerment. The constant and beneficial interaction of women with bureaucracy will usher in an era of new perception and comprehension for the women, who thenceforth will need no further guidance. Most of them are quick learners and the spirit of enthusiasm and optimism will affect the entire village population especially the women, most of whom are already in a socially cohesive group, due to the great vision and mission of the Father of the Nation Mahatma Gandhi, who spread the concept and message of cooperative farming, cottage industry benefits, etc., which have grown into small industries.

In this context the 73rd and 74th Constitution amendments which apart from providing a statutory framework for a decentralized democratic polity are intended to ensure the smooth functioning of the three-tier structure. It is now for the Gram Panchayat bodies to take full advantage of this opportunity and through elected men and women start regulating and governing themselves. The women must take full advantage of the 33% representation and without hesitation or fetters of Ghoonghat (Veil) forge ahead, in this great effort to enable these women to come forward and acquire and sustain their rights and contribute to the development of the nation. Political empowerment is both a weapon and device in the struggle of women for emancipation from poverty, disease and illiteracy, for by active involvement in the decision-making machinery of the country at all levels will ensure and carve a place for themselves and their girls, daughters, the future citizens of this nation.

A development strategy committed to equity and participation must also give priority to the raising of the social and economic status of women.

Whenever we talk of partnership, we would first see partnership in changing the mindset of man. "Gender Revolution" is the only way of ending the subjugation of women. In India we have achieved grass roots solidarity like the Sathins of Rajasthan, women in chipko movement, women in prostitution, Self Employed Women's Association or SEWA, women in agriculture, women entrepreneurs, women in the anti alcohol movement.

Enlightenment: Key to Progress

Our Constitution and our laws give Indian women a number of "Rights" and "*Guarantees*": protecting women's liberty, equality and freedom. Unfortunately the gap between legal "*Guarantees*" and "*Ground Realities*" is, vast.

LEGAL AWARENESS AND HUMAN RIGHTS

Fifty Years of Independence and Status of Women

We are now recognizing that if women are healthy and educated their families do better. If they are free from violence their families do better. If they have the opportunity to earn and work as equal partners in societies those families do better. Needless to say when those families do better then the communities and nations of which they are part also do better.

Institutionalized Mechanisms for Gender Equality

Institutionalized mechanisms in a democracy for gender equality would naturally include micro and macro level strategies and initiatives. At the micro level, India's record of initiating social legislations and positive discrimination through quota system in local self-government institutions are unparalleled. At the macro level, policy prescriptions for compulsory education, State policies on women, health policy, special dispensation for weaker social groups are too, well known. It may be added that our national policy on women is yet to be officially adopted. Indeed, in a democracy, impediments en route to realizing the goals of gender equality and gender justice could stem from the nature of government, whether it is secular, whether it is truly representative, whether it is one party or coalition and so on. In this matter, we are fortunate in that we have a national Government with wide representation of different shades of public opinion and a common, minimum programme, committed both by the constituent parties election manifestos and through public pronouncements of leaders. Their adherence to empowerment of women is a significant aspect which cannot escape notice. It is a different matter that for some unclear internal differences of some constituents of the United Front Government, some of the measures, such as the 81st Constitution Amendment Bill aimed at providing 33 1/3 per cent seats for women in State Legislatures and Lower House of Parliament (Lok Sabha) have not been acted upon till now, but the bill to this effect is likely to be introduced in the winter session of 2003. We are all sure that this will be done through the support of women's commission, women's council, women's board, etc,. constituted by the Government, apart from those of the independent NGOs working in various fields. It should, however, be admitted that balanced and sustainable development is not a simple matter of Government alone. It is in this context that the relevance of various specialized institutionalized arrangements rendering requisite inputs are recognized and appreciated.

"Poverty affects women more severely. Already suffering from societal bias, they are more vulnerable than men and bear a heavier burden when poverty strikes. Poverty and gender are inextricably linked - gender inequality is strongly linked to human poverty. Generally, the face of poverty is changing, but female poverty continues to remain a constant factor".

Women Sustain the Community

Women's place in every community is vital to the well-being of that society; without them both in the formal sector and in the family, most communities would not survive. It is now well recognized that enhancing women's status and enforcing their rights on an equal basis with men will do much to achieve the objectives of Equality, Development and Peace adopted at the Fourth world Conference on women held in Beijing in September, 1995. These are the guideposts for nations and movements to take note of and act upon.

The UN Perspective for Women's Development

The areas identified are:

(1) The persistent and increasing burden of poverty on women,

(2) Unequal access to and inadequate educational opportunities,

(3) Inequalities in access to health and related services,

(4) Violence against women,

(5) Peace and conflict resolution and their impact on women,

(6) Gender equality in economic structures and employment,

(7) Participation in decision-making at all levels,

(8) Mechanisms to promote advancement of women,

(9) Women rights as human rights,

(10) Access to communication,

(11) Women and environment, and, lastly

(12) Survival of the girl child.

Education of the girl-child is the best remedy to correct the imbalance in development process vitiated by gender disparity. Indeed, no cost is too high to achieve it. "Destiny of India is now being shaped in her classrooms", declared the Education Commission (1964 - 66) in their report. It is unfortunate that female members constituting almost half the population of the country have missed their "tryst" with destiny. Even after a quarter of a century, since the stirring assertion of the Education Commission, the female literacy rate, according to the 1991 Census is only 39.19 per cent as against 64.20 per cent for males. In respect of female education in our country, we may not be wanting too much in theoretical formulations and planning strategies. Our major weakness seems to be lack of sincerity in execution and vigour in implementation.

"The web of poverty is too frail to bear the weight of gender". Someone had remarked that "women are like rails, they carry the burden but if they are moved then it means society will be derailed and there will be chaos". Women are important economic agents. Women's income in the poverty groups is critical for household survival. There is an urgent need to ensure timely and effective economic resources like credit, skill upgradation and skill formation, organizational support, marketing facilities, working atmosphere and generally an appreciative outlook towards women in economic activities both in rural and urban areas.

Rights and equality: how to attain

Women's rights and women's equality cannot be achieved unless women in large numbers are visible and active. With this end in view, the national Commission for Women has been advocating distribution of tickets for more women candidates and further have been lobbying for this with the various political parties on the eve of the Lok Sabha elections.

It would be appropriate at this moment to recall what the Universal Declaration of Human Rights states on the subject: "Everyone has the right to take part in the government of his/her country". The United Nations Economic and Social Commission endorsed a target of 30% women in all levels of decision-making by 1995. In spite of this, globally women constitute ten per cent of legislative bodies and less in parliamentary positions.

In some of the State Legislature of India, we had as high as 18 per cent women members.

Representation of Women in State Legislatures

States/UTs	*Year*	*Total*	*Women*	*Year*	*Total*	*Women*
Andhra Pradesh	1957	252	11	1994	294	9
Karnataka	1957	179	18	1994	224	7
Kerala	1957	127	6	1991	140	8
Madhya Pradesh	1957	218	26	1993	320	12
Punjab	1957	101	5	1992	117	6
Rajasthan	1957	136	9	1994	200	9
Tripura	1957	30	0	1992	60	2
Uttar Pradesh	1957	341	24	1993	425	12
West Bengal	1957	195	11	1991	294	18
Delhi	1972	56	3	1993	70	3

Government Commitment to Empowerment of Women

As observed earlier, we as a nation are committed to the empowerment of women. In clear terms, country's approach paper to the Ninth Five Yea Plan (1997-2002) commits:

An integrated approach will be adopted towards empowering women. This underscores harmonization of various efforts on different fronts, viz., social, economic, legal and political. Further, a special strategy of earmarking of funds as 'women's component' will also be adopted with a close vigil to ensure a flow of adequate share of resources and benefits for women from all development sectors both in the Center and States. To this effect, the Ninth Plan recommends expeditious adoption of the 'National Policy for Empowering Women's along with a well defined Gender Development Index to monitor the impact of its implementation in raising the status of women from time to time.

In the political and administrative spheres, the proposed strategy of quota system for women both in Parliament and State Legislatures and also in Services will be adopted so as to strike a gender balance in decision-making.

For capacity building of women, it is essential that attention is paid to their health, especially the reproductive health and their access to health care services. A life cycle approach to women's health with a special focus on reproductive health and choices will be adopted.

Economic empowerment of women is based on their participation in decision-making process with regard to raising and distribution of resources, i.e., income, investments and expenditure at all levels. The entire effort of empowering women is to help them to exercise their rights in decision-making at all levels and in every sphere both within and outside the household as equal partners in the society.

In civil services, many provincial governments have legislations providing for 30 per cent reservation for women.

India had made five commitments at the Beijing Conference.

These were:

(i) Formulation of a National Policy on Women

(ii) Increased investment of 6 per cent GDP on education by 2000 .A.D.

(iii) Universalization of mother and child care programme

through the Integrated Child Development Services (ICDS) Schemes; and

(iv) Setting up of Commissioner for Women's Rights

As a follow-up to this commitment, a National Policy for the Empowerment of Women has been drafted after wide ranging consultations throughout the country. The proposed National Policy will continuously guide and inform action and policy in every sector, by incorporating a gender perspective into all plans, policies, programmes, budgetary allocations, appraisals, monitoring and evaluatory exercises.

As a part of support services we have committed to universalizing child care services. We have since done that by sanctioning ICDS projects in the whole country which include 5291 Community Development Blocks and 310 major urban slums in the country. The scheme had been operationalized in nearly 4000 blocks and preparatory work has been started in the remaining areas. We are in the process of finalizing Gender Development Indices and situational profiles of states and districts. This is expected to channelize Social Development programmes with greater intensity in the areas where low levels of development are indicated.

EMPOWERMENT OF WOMEN

While dealing with a complex issue like empowerment of women, it has to be conceded that the life of a human being is many sided. There is an economic aspect, a legal aspect, a political aspect, an aesthetic aspect, a personal aspect, a religious aspect and so forth, but blending into them all is the social aspect. Society is the marvelously intricate and ever-changing pattern of the totality of these relationships. Empowerment of women is influenced and determined to a very great degree by societal attitudes towards gender issues.

When we are to deal with empowerment which has close social relationships, we must discriminate their specific forms, varieties and patterns. We must observe how they crisscross and how they combine. We must note their responsiveness to changing conditions, changing demands and changing needs. These will enable us to adopt acceptable strategies.

Women's issues cannot be considered in isolation. It is the society which liberates and limits the activities of human beings, sets up standards for men to follow and maintain whatever the imperfections and tyrannies it has exhibited in human history, as it is a necessary condition of every fulfillment of life. Society is a system of usages and procedures, of authority and mutual aid, of many groupings and divisions, of controls of human behaviour and of liberties. It is the web of social relationships. And it is always changing.

We are aware that many social legislations aimed at improving the status of women are not really implemented for want of social acceptance e.g., Dowry Prohibition Act, Child Marriage Restraint Act., etc., Our endeavour should be to inform and influence the society about the need to enlist men and women in partnership towards progress of every section of people - men, women and children. There is too much of violence against women but the society remains a silent spectator. Men oppress women not because of their biology, nor because they are innately more aggressive, they do so because they benefit from doing so. This is the origin of 'class' legislation creating and upholding an insurmountable difference between the sexes.

Participation of Women in Public Affairs

Women's deprivation has many facets. These encompass not only denial of social and economic rights, but civil and political rights as well. In every society, women are denied opportunities which can be economic, political and social in every field, be it access to health and basis education, employment, information and technology, access to productive assets, access to shelter and so on.

One of the main reasons impeding the march of our Indian women to progress and equality is the essential structure itself,. Unless the archaic patriarchal attitude towards women is altered, no positive changes can happen in the affairs of any nation.

The female character should possess the mild and retiring virtues rather than the bold and dazzling ones, great eminence in almost everything is sometimes injurious to a young lady; whose temper and disposition should appear to be pliant rather than robust; to be ready to take impressions rather than to be decidedly marked, great apparent strength of character, however, excellent is liable to alarm both her own and the other sex, and to create admiration rather than affection".

A deep concern with the status of women and the recognition that the progress of the nation is integrally linked with the advancement of women, have underpinned Indian approach to planned development since Independence. Mahatma Gandhi was a champion of women's rights. He emphasized that, "subjugation and exploitation of woman was a product of men's interested teachings and woman's acceptance of them." The leaders of the nation recognized that freedom gained without the active involvement of women would be a hollow and fragile freedom. The Constitution guarantees equality to women, it also empowers the State to adopt special measures of affirmative discrimination in favour of women. The Constitution further imposes a fundamental duty on every citizen to uphold the dignity of women.

It is ironical that in matters of deprivation and gender discrimination there is a certain amount of uniformity. Lack of education and training and absence of awareness intensify deprivation. In such a situation, women of all groups are excluded not only from political and social and economic power but also from the power of knowledge as well, while comprising half of humanity contributing two-thirds of the world's workforce, they earn only one-third of the total income and own less than one tenth of the world's resources. The objectives of development are to enlarge people's choices for a reasonable living and increase people's capabilities to exercise such choices. When fruits of development reach the intended groups, human rights violations are also curbed, as a consequence. Nowhere are these challenges more stark and daunting than in case of poor women. The situation is aggravated due to a general societal inability and apathy to be able to discern these inadequacies of the development response. Many women are often conditioned into insensitivity and unquestioned submission to biases and discrimination, which they view as socially ordained and irrevocable. It is this ideology of patriarchy and the accompanying culture of silence which needs to be challenged and broken if development is to touch the lives of women, no matter to which diversified groups they may belong to.

It is the empowerment strategy which is today emerging as a unique Indian response to the challenges of gender justice, sustainable development and human rights guarantees. If women are to be empowered, it is necessary to provide support services. If women are to be economically empowered, they are to be provided with additional channels of credit, training, employment, management skills and social security. And if women are to be politically empowered, the imperative is to resort to different forms of affirmative discrimination, such as quotas of reservation in various political apparatus, to enable them to participate in decision-making process. Women have to be given access to knowledge, power and resources. If women are to be persons in their own right, they must be in control of their own bodies. In India we have moved a long way in all these fronts and the results are not disappointing. A strong women's movement supported by NGOs and national machinery keeps a vigil to ensure gender equality and justice.

It is noteworthy that the last decade of the 20th century has seen the emergence of gender as one of the basic issues of human progress. Concern over the status of women has permeated both thinking and rhetoric. The immediate need to capture women's insight for solving basic problems of poverty, illiteracy, environmental degradation and violence is being felt increasingly and at different levels. The challenges before us is to use this concern and this increased awareness to break the stereotypes and move towards a new generation of men and women working in partnership to build a better world for all of us and posterity.

(Source:- Partly adopted with grateful thanks from "Women and Development" - Perspectives from Selected States of India, Volume-2 - Edited by P.R. Reddy, P. Sumangala, B.R. Publishing Corporation, New Delhi, 1998.)

2

Women Empowerment Through Legal Measures

The question and process of women empowerment is a stupendous task which had several attempts in the annals of Indian history. The question of women empowerment is not simply unique to India but it is a global question. Attempts and the degree of empowerment of women vary from century to century and from culture to culture or from nation to nation. One may know of formal legislative attempts and through informal kind of learning about the changes in the ethos of behaviour of people vis-à-vis women. One may try to bring in social change in respect to according equal and respectable status to women in an informal way. But once you bring in legislative measures which operate as civil law will have the force in bringing about equality and enhancement of status of women. Before we look into the kind of measures or schemes that are initiated by the government of Andhra Pradesh and some non-governmental organizations (NGOs), we may have a brief look into the legal process that has gone so far in the process of empowerment of women. In this context, the material that follows throws some light of what has gone until now.

The contemporaneous juristic orientations, legislative projectiles and societal attitudes apparently accord wide spectrum of immunities, privileges and rights to women. But the gulf between the principles and pragmatism has transmuted into reality her inferior status. In spite of continuing resurgence of feminism and heightened awareness of the task of socio-economic emancipation of women, malefic deficiencies and distortions in the policy making and programme implementations kept Indian women in impoverishment of body, mind and soul and in continued suppression, subordination, and super-ordination by men. Institutional and attitudinal impediments continue to defy her human worth and dignity and mock at the credibility of Rule of law. Inherently, patriarchal societal system which has been approved by all the major religions was a dominant wherewithal for gender discrimination. Her qualities of softness and suavity, her physical and psychological dependence during the long periods of carrying, nursing and feeding the child, her contradicting roles at home and work and lack of interest and time to participate in the political decision making process may be added factors for her continued degradation and servitude.

Yet, there is a relative and discernible change and gradual evolution in the empowerment and entitlement of women. The processual transformation of society from ancient, medieval to modern age of development variegated ameliorating spells in her status. After all, social systems never change overnight, though the change is inevitable. Change always will be uneven and partial and extremely slow when religious ordinations and societal psyche oppose it or are unwilling to accept such change. Law ought to adopt, adjust and supplement to the needs of the society and it is supposed to generate, activate and accelerate ordered social change. Arthur T. Vanderbilt observed,

> "dissatisfaction must inescapably result if the law fails to keep pace with economic, scientific, political and social changes".

Law as an instrument of social change aims at achieving equilibrium by orderly regulation of social relationship, removing social "irritants", manifested by objectionable, unjustifiable, indiscriminate, inequalities and positively providing for the welfare and security of all the subjects. The quality of a polity is estimable by gauging the speed and frequency at which rational, reformative changes are brought about through the instrumentality of law. One can judge a society by the way it treats its weaker members. India inherited from the past the menacing, cankerous malady of discrimination of women which is sought to be obliterated through the instrument of law.

Legal Status of Women at Different Stages in Indian History

Legal Status of Women in Ancient India

This period can be approximately considered to be 4000 B.C. to 1300 A.D.

Vedic Period

Vedas or Srutis are considered to be most ancient and paramount source of Hindu system of jurisprudence. During this period (4000 - 1000 B.C.) women were treated relatively equitably and with a fair deal. Women were allowed to recite Vedic verses and perform *Yagna*. It is said that there were 32 women compilers of *Rigveda* who expounded or expanded the Vedic literature. There were no child marriages during this period and women were free to marry anyone irrespective of caste. However, there were indications in many verses of male members having domination or proprietary rights over women. *Taittiriya Samhita* speaks of women as "destitute of strength" and so, unfit to have the portion of the property, though she was given position of respectability in the family. Rigveda (IX: 85) mentions,

> "Be thou mother of heroic children, devoted to the Gods, be thou queen in the father-in-law's house. May all Gods unite the hearts of us two into one".

Throughout the Vedic period the marital union was considered sacramental and indissoluble union and polygamy was not acclaimed. Srutis ordain that he shall not leave the wife in discharge of dharma. The principle of exogamy was followed in marriages. The Vedic literature gave importance to an aurasa son (natural born legitimate son) for spiritual benefit and continuation of family and in his absence, one can find references to, Kshetraja (soil born), putrika putra (daughter's son), Kanina (modern born), Dattaka (adopted) sons, though *Rigveda* clearly mentions "Oh! Agni, no son is he who springs from others". Patriarchy was followed and head of the joint family (Karta) was to be a male.

Smriti Period

This is a period (800 B.C. - 200 A.D.) of marked deterioration in the legal status of women. Manu smriti (200 B.C.) in particular was very harsh towards women and sudras. During this period her status was apparently eulogized and she was given a respectable position as a queen of the house. It was ordained that where women are honoured, there the Gods are pleased. He only is a perfect man who has his wife himself and his offspring (Manu IX: 46). It was also said that only those who have wives can fulfill their due obligations in the world (Mahabharat, Adi: 74). In Ramayana, the wife is considered to be the very soul of the husband (Ramayana 11, 37, 23-24). However in practice she lived in servitude. Male chauvinism is manifest in the following observations in Smritis. It was said that the wife should ever treat the husband as God, though he be characterless, sensual and devoid of good qualities (Manu V: 154). There is no higher world for a woman than that of the husband (Vasishata XXI: 41). None should eat the food offered by a woman who disobeys her husband.

A Hindu marriage was a sacramental indissoluble union to beget a *son* for salvation. Hence, no widow remarriage was recognized and she was supposed to maintain her purity and chastity even after the death of her husband (Manu V - 160 - 161). Husband was allowed to have concubines (*Avurdhasthri*). Adultery by the wife was considered as greatest sin. Inter *varna* marriages were disapproved. *Sapinda* marriages were prohibited. Though by implication the age at marriage for a male could be fixed as attainment of majority no such indication can be arrived at with regard to age at marriage for a female. Child marriages were prevalent and were validated. In the recommendatory conditions of marriage it was mentioned that she must be beautiful, younger in age and shorter in stature than the husband. *Sati* found its sanction during this period.

> "Let the sonless widow keeping unsullied the bed of her husband and abiding with her venerable protector enjoy with moderation the property until her death". This constituted women's estate. Though she was entitled as a matter of right, maintenance from the joint family, she could not be the head or *karta* of the joint family and she could not become a coparcener. However, throughout this period she was entitled for *stridhan* for which she had absolute powers as an owner and it could become her fresh stock of descent capable of being inherited.

The smritis were subject to further analysis, systematization and classification in the subsequent period (700 A.D. to 1760 A.D.) and many digests and commentaries were written. The authoritative texts that were prevailing in South India brought certain liberal construction in favour of women. For instance Vasista's text requiring husband's consent for adoption was interpreted as the consent of nearest *sapindas* of the husband and hence a widow was able to adopt.

Status of Women during Mauryan Period

Kautilya's Arthasastra conferred certain rights on women like right to remarriage, subject to surrender of deceased husband's property to the relatives and children if any; abandonment of husband when he was of bad character, went abroad for a long period, or where he was a traitor, lost virility or fallen from his caste or endangers wife's life; women's right to earn an independent livelihood; right to maintenance. However, right to remarriage was limited to the brother or near relative of the husband. Megasthanese recorded child marriages during this period, especially in peninsular India. This period was also marked with the development of *Sulka* which should be settled on the bride by her parents.

Though Buddhism which flourished during this period, approved patriarchy, it gave women a fair deal by allowing them to join in Bikshu sangha. Only grown up girls were considered competent to marry and it secularized the marriage. Sati was checked.

Legal Status of Indian Women During Medieval Period

With the recurrent attacks of foreign invasion and establishment of Muslim rule, the elders of Hindu society started imposing more vigorous restrictive regulations on Hindu women, ostensibly in the interest of her own preservation of chastity, prestige and honour of the race. Child marriages and the evil of Sati (self immolation of the wife on the death of her husband) were widely prevalent, practiced and enforced. Female slave trade and female infanticide was also in practice. Polygamy was widespread among both Hindus and Muslims. "Purdha" system was grafted into Hindu system especially among the upper caste. The status of Muslim women was no better as they suffered easy talak, female infanticide etc. There was a sigh of relief during the period of Akbar as he abolished sati. But, the status women was at its lowest during the period of Aurangzeb.

Legal Status of Women During the British Period

History records traces of women patriots like Ahalyabai and Lakshmi bai of Jhansi. However, their contribution to the emancipation of women was not much. Albuquerque (1510), Portuguese Viceroy prohibited *sati.* The last Peshwa, Bajirao was also against *sati.* However, East India company and subsequent British rulers adopted the principle of 'non-interference', 'slow', and 'cautious' approach in changing the personal, legal status of natives. Warren Hastings declared in the year 1772 that in all the matters regarding inheritance, succession, marriage, and caste and other religious usages, the law of Kuran with respect to Mohammedans and those of the Sashtras with respect to Hindus shall be invariably adhered to. However, at the instance and insistence of native Indians and because of public upsurge, some fragmentary reformative legislations were passed during this period. As a sequel to the public movement headed by Raja Ram Mohan Roy, Abolition of Sati Act of 1829 was passed during the period of William Bentick. Besides prohibiting Sati, it was provided that the persons helping in any way even in voluntary sati were liable under culpable homicide. Keshav Chandrasen was instrumental in getting Native Marriages Act, 1872 which abolished early marriages, polygamy and allowed widow remarriages and intercaste marriages. Pandit Ishwara Chandra Vidyasagar and Prof. Karve were instrumental in getting Hindu Widow Remarriage Act, 1856 passed. Caste Disabilities Removal Act, 1850; Parsi Marriage and Divorce Act, 1865 in which monogamy was enforced and divorce was allowed; Christian Marriage Act of 1872, the Legal Practitioners (women) Act of 1923; Child Marriage Restraint Act, 1929, Arya Marriage Validation Act, 1937; Hindu Women's Right to Property Act,

1937; Hindu Women Right to Separate Maintenance and Residence Act, 1946; Hindu Marriage (Removal of Disabilities) Act, 1946, were other fragmentary reformative legislations which granted women certain entitlements but created some more problems. For instance her proprietary rights have repercussions on joint family system, clamouring for reforms and the need for adopting archaic Hindu Law to the modern needs, resulted in the establishment of Hindu Law Committee in 1941 which recommended the gradual codification and rationalization of Hindu Law. This committee was revived in the year 1944 under the chairmanship of Sir B.N.Rao which submitted its report in the year 1946. Based on these recommendations, four legislations covering major portion of Hindu Law could be passed in the years 1955-56.

Dr. Annie Besant lectures of "Wake up India" worked as cementing force for the unity of Indian Womanhood in 1914. Gandhiji's call for non-violent participation of women in freedom struggle worked miracles towards awakening of women and their emancipation. In the year 1927 the first All India Women's Conference was held at Pune which discussed the need of education, problems of early marriages and women discrimination. The Government of India Act of 1935 provided Franchise and Civil services under the Crown for women also. The period of freedom struggle can be considered as dawn for women resurgence. It gave an impetus to women's movement as well, wherein the women could come out of their reclusion, unite and voice their grievances, though with limited success.

Protection of Women Under the Indian Constitution

Indian constitution is a fundamental social document designed to achieve planned social change. The political revolution completed by the attainment of independence and assurance of political justice irrespective of sex, creed, race or caste, through the principles of the constitution is sought to be strengthened and supplemented by social and economic revolutions constitutionally planned especially through Part III, Fundamental Rights and Part IV, the Directive Principles of State Policy which are considered to be the core and conscience of the constitution. It may be noted that by the time Indian Constitution came into force at international plane, universal declaration of Human Rights was already adopted in 1948 and India was a signatory to it. Among other things, it guaranteed equal status for women. Adoption of the constitution on 26th November 1949 and its coming into force on 26th January 1950 can be considered as a remarkable achievement especially towards emancipation and empowerment of women.

Status of Women Under Personal Laws

Legal Status of Muslim Women

Quran, the paramount source of Islamic Law says "O! men, fear your Lord, who hath created you out of one man, and out of him hath created his wife..." (Ch. IV). Under Mohammedan Law, marriage is a civil contract which has for its design and object the right of enjoyment and procreation of children. The legal capacity of a wife is not lost, on marriage and she retains the same powers of dealing with her property, entering into contracts, to sue or being sued. Consent of the woman in marriage is vital and if it is not obtained, consummation against the will of the woman would not validate the marriage. Two male witnesses or one male witness and two female witnesses are required for a marriage agreement. Conferment of dower on women is an essential aspect of Muslim marriage. Polygamy upto four wives living is recognized under Mohammedan law provided the husband can treat them equitably and justly (Quran IV - 3) and it does not permit polyandry. Attainment of puberty is another requirement of marriage. Guardianship in marriage (Jabar) manifests patriarchal element, as the mother can become a guardian in marriage only in the absence of the father and other paternal relations.

Status of Women Under Codified Hindu Law

Hindu law was subject to fragmentary reformative legislations during 50's as noted hereunder:

- Hindu Marriage Act, 1955
- Hindu Adoptions and Maintenance Act, 1956
- Hindu Minority and Guardianship Act, 1956
- Hindu Succession Act, 1956

The Hindu marriage Act of 1955 mostly secularized the institution of marriage, though Hindu marriage still partakes the character of sacramental nature because customary ceremonies of either party to the marriage are still prerequisites (S - 7). Monogamy is strictly enforced (S - 5). There is no bar for widow remarriage. The age at marriage is prescribed at 21 and 18 for the bridegroom and bride respectively. However, child marriages continue to be valid even though the parties responsible to them are punishable. Consent of the woman is implicit in the provisions relating to marriage (S - 5) (ii) and S - 12 (c). Wife is entitled to annul marriage and obtain divorce on diverse grounds including husband's adultery, cruelty, desertion, insanity, leprosy, venereal disease, conversion, renunciation of the world, and presumption of death; non-resumption of cohabitation after judicial separation or after the decree of restitution of conjugal rights. Wife has certain special grounds in addition to above grounds namely, husband's pre-Act polygamous marriage, unnatural offence, non-resumption of cohabitation after a decree of maintenance, repudiation of child marriage. Divorce by mutual consent is another important matrimonial remedy (Ss - 13, 13A, 13B).

Hindu Succession Act of 1956 can be considered as a milestone in the direction of economic emancipation of women. She has become class I heir in various capacities, if a male Hindu dies intestate after the commencement of the Act.

II

> "There will never be a generation of great men until there has been a generation of free women or free mothers".
>
> —*Ingersoll.*

Indian civilization seems to have given the woman a place in the society where she could exercise her ability, her judgment without having to forfeit any of her essential femininity. Though historical events and ideas disfigured some of this structure, twentieth century as well as the breakthrough given by the freedom struggle removed some of the disabilities in one rapid sweep.

Law and Social Change

Social Legislations for Women - Dialects and Dynamics

Socio-economic justice of our country can be achieved by providing equality to women along with men in all fields, and special protection in needed areas. Not only at home but also in the community which needs the hands and talents of women for development. In the modern world the role of women extends much beyond home and now she is adopting a career of her own and sharing equally the responsibility for the development of society in all aspects.

The term 'social legislation' is used by legislators, academicians, lawyers and others very frequently, but no adequate efforts appear to have been made to define it precisely. It may be used to name the collection of social norms which are generally directed towards fulfillment of desired social goals in a given society. The social legislation also enables action to prevent social ill-health and to preserve and promote social health.

Conclusion

In its advance the above analysis clearly shows that the transformation in the legal status of women has been slow and sluggish and the legislative field is marked with wide gaps still to be abridged. The frail packages of Legislative hieroglyphics towards emancipation and entitlement of women often met with operational pitfalls and implementation failures due to administrative lax. The distance between social realities of status of women and legislative dilettantism defied the solution to the women's problems. It is a ground reality one has to confess to with sorrow and indignation that social change occurred at high speed with necessary changes in law in all the walks of human life except with regard to the facet of status of women which still remains bleak. Though transformation of patriarchal society requires attitudinal changes, necessary legislative support may generate and activate such changes.

Adoption of uniform civil code is necessary as it is a constitutional mandate to the state under Article 44 and also is a vital link in the emancipation of women from the shackles of religious fanaticism manifested and perpetrated in the different personal laws. Some of the directive principles of the state policy enshrined in the constitution aiming at equalizing protecting women should be made as Fundamental Rights making them enforceable. There is no gain in saying that there are piecemeal legislations to implement the same, as they are ridden with deficiencies and inadequacies. Right to work may also be considered for making it as a fundamental right in so far as women are concerned towards meaningful economic emancipation of women.

In the same country women belonging to various religions

are treated variedly with varying degrees of discrimination. In a country which is secular, the people are supposed to be subject to secular laws uniformly by making territorial application of laws. Even if it is indicated that codification of different personal laws is a prelude to the adoption of uniform law, it may be submitted that those attempts were also fragmentary and half-hearted. Hindus are still governed by uncodified law relating to joint family partition, antecedent debt etc., which work to the disadvantage of women. The fragmentary legislation also manifests inherent male domination. So of the Hindu Marriage Act relating to archaic and brutal remedy of restitution of conjugal rights shall be abrogated in the interest of maintaining worth and dignity of women. With regard to guardianship female shall be recognized as the first natural guardian before father. The concept of coparcener property, backbone of patriarchal heritage has to be changed so as to make all class I heirs simultaneously eligible to such property as if it is a self acquired property.

In the property agenda Muslim woman requires protection against triple 'talak' which made the institution of marriage as a one sided engine of oppression. Her right to maintenance under S - 125 of the Criminal Procedure Code should be restored.

The law relating to marriage and divorce with reference to Christians still suffers from colonial hangover and requires a speedy legislation atleast to keep them on par with the other women.

Penal laws require continuous revision in view of recurrent high incidence of violence against women. Women are becoming the victims of violence not because of their misconduct but of misfortune and because of the state's failure to check it. The state is ostensibly responsible for such omissions and hence, the female victim must be suitably compensated and rehabilitated as a matter or right. Imposition of increased mandatory punishment can also be recommended for the offences against women.

Plethora of labour welfare legislations, in fact confer a wide spectrum of rights on women but still the need for reformation remains. As observed by National Commission for labour women continue to be discriminated in the payment of wages and the worst sufferers were those women who were ignorant, unskilled and semi-skilled unorganized workers in the lower strata. The recommendation made in the report on status of women of 1974 has met with only partial success. Extension of maternity benefit to those outside the ambit of the law; plugging of loop holes in the law; provision for crechery, enforcement of equal wages and minimum wages; vocational training, better payment for work done by home based women, betterment of working conditions in the unorganized sector, definite quota of reservation for women for training within the industry are some among those recommendations. It is in the interest of women if a comprehensive single code of labour welfare legislations is passed.

Dowry Prohibition Act of 1961 (as amended in 1983, 1984, 1986) is another piece of legislation which is respected more on its breach. Lack of psychological preparedness and subconscious hostility towards the law made it ineffective.

Some of the revolutionary medical advancements witnessed in the 20th century have their adverse impact on the status of women. Sex determination through amniocentesis with consequential termination of female fetus, surrogate motherhood threaten the worth and dignity of women and hence require special comprehensive central legislation to curb the same.

Legislation is one of the weapons in the armoury for social change. Struggle against patriarchy and gender hierarchy and attitudinal changes coupled with political will are the prerequisites towards total emancipation of women. Evolution of new norms of social life requires opposite levels of public opinion involving societal consciousness about the need of evaluation of new norms and psychological preparedness of the public to receive the same. Dominant public opinion automatically tends to become law. As rightly observed by Violet Alva

> *"We need a revolution within us for an evolution in society and unless that revolution comes about from within, social legislation, even though it expands in every field, will not achieve, results".*

This is true with regard to emancipation and entitlement of women. In the empowerment of women what has been done or accomplished, as a legal process has been minimal and sporadic. We have a long way to go. Even though, as is evident the law by itself does not operate. It is the people who have to understand respect and live up to the sanctions of legal measures. Empowerment of women is a long journey and we may have to pass through may be several ages, miles to cover to reach the destination where there is absolute equality between men and women. Once we look at the process of evolution and the growth of civilization we could be optimistic that we will reach that state of society where there will be no gender discrimination. All the states are working towards that end.

Source: Adopted with grateful thanks from 'Women, Law and Social Change', by T.V. Subba Rao, & V. Hemalatha Devi published in the book entitled "Women and Development" - Perspectives from Selected States of India, Volume-2 - Edited by P.R. Reddy, P. Sumangala, B.R. Publishing Corporation, New Delhi, 1998, pp.901 to 930.

3

Policy Towards Empowerment of Women

Introduction

In order to achieve the objective of Swarna Andhra Pradesh and Vision 2020, a Cabinet Sub-committee was set up to give their recommendation on the women empowerment policy. Consequent to the submission of this report, the salient features of the policy were placed before the Cabinet and the Cabinet has approved the women empowerment policy.

The main thrust of the policy is convergence of all the activities pertaining to the women in order to improve education, health, nutrition, and overall development of the social and economic indicators for women and children in the State. The strategy involves coordination with various departments of the State Government with a special thrust on awareness campaign on legal and legislative measures for the welfare of the women. The policy also calls for setting up a Women Development Agency at the District level in order to ensure that adequate focus is given on the women and child development activities and on gender sensitization.

Objectives

- Increasing gender sensitization.
- Addressing gender inequality in education and employment.

- Increasing gender sensitivity in case of health, welfare and economic programmes.
- Prevent atrocities against women.

Initiatives

In the last five years from 1995 to 2000 the Department has initiated various activities for the development of women and children by allotting budget of Rs. 440.61 crores under the following schemes:

- Integrated Child Development Services - a Project
- Children in need of Care & Protection (Child Welfare Institutions)
    -- Crèches
    -- Balwadies
    -- Children Homes
    -- Balavihars
    -- Shisuvihars
- Women Welfare Institutions
    -- Service Homes
    -- State Homes
    -- Working Women's Hostels
    -- Women's Technical Training Institute
    -- Home for Aged
    -- Home for Collegiate Girls
    -- Women Welfare Branches
    -- Rescue Homes
- Nutrition
- Women Education
    -- Girl Child Protection Scheme

-- Balika Sumrudhi Yojana

-- Kishore Balika Pathakam

Integrated Child Development Services

Under Integrated Child Development Schemes, children up to 6 years of age are covered. The scheme is implemented in 251 erstwhile blocks/urban slums. Under this scheme supplementary nutrition, women and child welfare centers, immunization, pre-school activities, referral service and health checkup have been taken up during 1995-2000 and an amount of Rs 65313.38 lakhs of budget is provided for benefiting 1,10,56,732, children and 26,01,584 women. During the year 2000-2001 a budget of Rs. 15940.57 lakhs is provided.

The infant mortality rare has come down in Andhra Pradesh from (1981 to 1991) 86 to 66 for every 1000 births. And it is proposed to reduce the IMR from 66 to 15 per every 1000 births by 2020 in Andhra Pradesh state.

The maternal mortality rate has come down from 4.36 to 3.8 for every 1000 live births. The information on maternal mortality rate collected during the end line survey indicated that the overall maternal morality rate was less (330/100,000 live births) than the State average of 450. The common causes of maternal deaths were difficult labour or tetanus. And it is proposed to reduce the incidence of 3.8/1000 to 0.5/1000 by 2020.

No. of Projects started and beneficiaries covered year-wise are:

TABLE I

Year	Projects	No. of Anganwadi Centers	Beneficiaries	
			Women	Children
Phase I				
1995-1996	209 Projects	29615	473840	2013820
1996-97	209 Projects	29615	473840	2013820
1997-98	209 Projects	29615	473840	2013820
Phase-II				
1998-99	251 Projects	36877	590032	2507636
1999-2000	251 Projects	36877	590032	2507636

In these projects in Phase-I, 1050 Anganwadi Centers were constructed with budget provision of Rs. 13.62 crores and in Phase-II ICDS 7082 Anganwadi Centers, 30 Child Development Project Officer buildings and 4126 handpumps were drilled with an amount of Rs. 127.00 crores.

1. *Crèches*

In these crèches food, clothing and non-formal education is provided to the children in the age group of 0 to 6 years who belong to low-income group families. There are 229 crèches functioning all over the state. During the period 1995-96 Rs. 1441.61 lakhs was provided benefiting 6870 children every year.

2. *Balawadies*

In these institutions children of 3 to 6 years belonging to urban slums and backward rural areas are enrolled and non-formal pre-school education is imparted through 166 institutions. During the period 1995-2000 Rs.874.08 lakhs was provided, benefiting 4980 children every year.

3. *Children Homes*

They are residential educational institutions oriented for the girls in the age group of 6 to 15 years through 81homes.

During the period 1995-2000 Rs 1530.64 lakhs was provided benefiting 5050 girl children every year.

4. *Balavihars*

These are recreation centers for school children and school dropouts from the low-income groups and socially backward classes for whom recreation activities are not within their reach. Throughout the State there are 28 Balavihars for the benefit of 840 beneficiaries every year. During the period 1995-2000 budget provided is Rs. 1699.99 lakhs.

5. *Sisuvihars*

In these centers abandoned infants and orphans below 6 years are accommodated. The infants are being given on legal adoption to child-less couples. There are three institutions in the state located at Hyderabad, Chittoor and Vijayawada accommodating 90 infants every year. During the period 1995-2000 budget provided was Rs.34.94 lakhs.

6. *Women & Child Welfare Centers*

These centers provide childcare facilities including pre-school education and snacks to women and school dropouts. Training is also imparted on nutrition and childcare education. There are 46 centers in the state accommodating 2760 during 2000-2001 an amount of Rs.5151.04 lakhs is provided to cover Crèches, Balwadies, Balvihars, Children Homes, Sisuvihars, which have been clubbed during 2000-2001 under services for children in need of care and protection.

Women Welfare Institutions

During 1995 to 2000 the Department has taken-up various activities for the welfare of the women by allotting budget of Rs.3588.38 lakhs under the following schemes.

1. *Service Homes*

These Homes are meant for destitute women, helpless widows and deserted wives, who are in the age group of 18-

35 years. Rehabilitation is provided through Job course and training cum production units. There are 5 Service Homes in the State for rehabilitation of 4200 needy women every year. During 1995-2000 an amount of Rs. 331.97 lakhs was provided to the Service Homes.

2. State Homes

These Homes are meant for women discharged from correctional institutions that are unable to protect themselves from adverse social forces and also for those women who voluntarily seek shelter. During their stay, skilled training is imparted to them for their livelihood after their departure from the Home. There are 4 State Homes in the State. During 1995-2000 an amount of Rs.270.27 lakhs was allotted to cover 2250 beneficiaries.

3. Working Women's Hostel

These hostels provide food, shelter and other facilities including security to the workingwomen who are away from their families, on payment prescribed by the Government. During 1995-2000, 18 hostels have been functioning in the state and an amount of Rs.429.55 lakhs was released to cover 4800 inmates.

4. Women's Technical Training Institutes

The institutes are meant for imparting 3 year Diploma Course in Engineering, Architecture, Computer and other technical trades. Especially inmates of the Departmental Institutes are given preferential admission. During 1995-2000 Rs. 195.18 lakhs was provided to train 2720 girl students. During the year 2000-2001 a sum of Rs. 60.63 lakhs was provided.

5. Home for Aged Women

These homes provide peaceful and comfortable living for old, destitute women. The Government provides free food, shelter and clothing for life. There are two old age

Homes in the state. During 1995-2000 Rs.42.31 lakhs was provided to shelter 400 old women.

6. Home for Collegiate Girls

The inmates of Children Homes who pass X class are admitted into these institutions to pursue higher studies of their choice. There are six collegiate Homes in the state. During 1995-2000 an amount of Rs.131.17 lakhs was provided to cover 1140 students.

7. Women Welfare Branches

These Branches are meant for women of 15 to 45 years of age group. Training in tailoring and other crafts is imparted to these women. There are eight Women Welfare Branches in the state. During 1995-2000 an amount of Rs.449.98 lakhs was provided for the benefit of 14400 women.

8. Rescue Homes

There is one rescue home at Hyderabad for rehabilitation of court-committed cases under the provision of Suppression of Immoral Traffic Act of 1956 and the convicted are kept in the Home. An amount of Rs.30.54 lakhs was provided during 1995-2000 to rehabilitate 150 women.

During 2000-2001 an amount of Rs.979.85 lakhs has been provided for Maintance of all women institutions.

NUTRITION

Nutrition programme and food security and better nutrition standards for improving the health of children, adolescent girls, pregnant and lactating mother and women in general, during the period from 1995-2000 an amount of Rs. 17587.64 lakhs was provided for 9300986 beneficiaries. During 2000-2001 6556.00 lakhs were provided for supplementary nutrition.

Women Education

The thrust area for women empowerment policy is women

education. Women Development and Child Welfare Department is launching a special Programme on literacy mission for giving them basic reading ability initially.

LITERACY RATE AND RANKS FOR SOUTHERN STATES

TABLE - I

State	*Male*	*Female*	*Total*	*Rank (in India)*
Andhra Pradesh	55.13	32.72	44.09	26
Karnataka	67.26	44.34	56.04	20
Kerala	93.62	86.17	89.81	1
Tamilnadu	73.75	51.33	62.66	12
India	64.13	39.29	52.21	--

In order to encourage girl enrolment and retention in primary classes upwards, the department has followed convergence approach and issued G.O. 49 jointly with Education Department. This G.O. provides linkages between Anganwadi and primary school, thereby bringing school dropouts and unenrolled girls back to the school. As on date 6,412 Anganwadi Centers are upgraded as Early Childhood Education Centers out of 8,042 Anganwadi centers. In addition to this, the Department provides education in all welfare homes for children in difficult circumstances and the following schemes are provided for educating the children as future mothers.

Girl Child Protection Scheme

Girl child protection scheme is introduced in the year 1996-97 to promote adoption of the small family norms, to benefit girl children in poor families by promoting Family Planning and to encourage enrolment of girls in schools to reduce school dropouts. During the period 1996-2000 Rs. 71.54 crores was provided for benefiting 143591 girl children.

During the year 2000 - 2001 an amount of Rs. 25.00 crores was provided to cover 41667 beneficiaries.

Kishora Balika Pathakam

Kishora Balika Pathakam was started in the year 1997-98 to generate awareness against child labour, to discourage early marriage and to achieve 100% elementary education especially for girls through.

- Bridge course
- Skill training programmes
- Workshops and exposure visits.

During the period 1997-2000 Rs.2.16 crores was provided for benefiting 69400 Kishora Balikas. During the year 2000-2001 an amount of Rs.1.73 crores was provided to cover 64000 Kishora Balikas.

Balika Samrudhi Yozana

Balika Samrudhi Yozana launched in the year 1997 by Government of India, New Delhi is a long-term strategy to change social attitudes and behavioral practices through the girl child while raising her status. During the period 1997 - 2000 Rs.4.24 crores was provided for benefiting 84742 individuals.

The women empowerment policy envisages the following strategy:

1. Women Literacy

It is proposed to increase female literacy rate from existing 32.72% to 52% by 2005 which requires about Rs.15 crores per year up to 2005. It envisages

- Compulsory Primary Education
- Rural Oriented Education
- Adult Women Education and
- Education through media and other means

2. *Girl Child Protection Scheme*

It is a novel programme and first of its kind in the country. It envisages fundamental change in the attitude of society that considers the girl child a burden.

3. *Kishore Balika Pathakam*

To achieve the following:

- 100% elementary education especially for girl.
- Discourage child marriages
- Equal opportunities for women

4. *Integrated Girl Child Labour Rehabilitation Programme*

- Withdraw girl below 14 years engaged in various occupations and their enrolment in schools. Education to be assured
- Sensitize community to stop child labour
- Girl Child labour rehabilitation by avoiding hazardous occupations

5. *Infant Mortality Rate*

- Improved neo-natal care
- Total coverage under immunization
- Reduction in low birth weights
- Reduction in the number of deaths due to diarrhea and acute respiratory problems.

Preventive Measures

- Pregnancy and birth care
- Avoiding frequent deliveries
- Proper nourishment
- Brest feeding
- Medical facilities

- Institutional deliveries
- Health education to would be mother
- Immunization

6. *Maternal Mortality Rate*

- Reduction of incidence from 3.8/1000 to 0.5/1000 by 2020
- Total ante-natal coverage
- All deliveries to be Institutionalized
- Emergency medical care
- Ambulance services for referral care

Strategies

- Targeting Nutrition and Health days
- Pregnancy care (early Registration of pregnant women, Antenatal checkup, identifying at risk)
- Planned interval in between pregnancies
- Proper nourishment and food security
- Institutional deliveries (Supervised, safe delivery)
- Medical facilities (Strengthening)
- Immunization (Universal coverage of Immunization Hepatitis)
- Awareness and Health Education and IFA availability
- Inter-sectoral co-ordination (Govt.-NGOs)
- Poverty alleviation programmes.

7. *Integrated Child Development Services - I C D S:*

- Supplementary Nutrition to 0 to 6 years, children, pregnant and nourishing mothers
- Immunization for pre-school children and pregnant mothers

- Health checkup
- Referral education
- Pre-school education
- Health and nutrition education

TABLE I

Phasing of I C D S Project from 2000-2004

Year	*No. of Projects*	*Anganwadi Center*
1999-2000	251 (209+42)	36877
2000-2001	286	42676
2001-2002	321	48744
2002-2003	351	53585
2003-2004	351	53585

TABLE - II

Coverage of Beneficiaries Under Six Components of ICDS Scheme

	1999-2000	*2000-20001*	*2001-2002*	*2002-2003*	*2003-2004*	*2004-2005*
Supplementary Nutrition Programme	3097668	3584784	4204036	461040	4610340	4610340
a. Children	2507636	2901968	3403332	3732180	3732180	3732180
b. Women	590032	682816	800704	878160	878160	878160
c. Pre school	1475080	1707040	2000760	2195400	2195400	2195400
d. Immunization	2802652	3243376	3803684	4171260	4171260	4171260
e. Health Check up	3097668	3584784	4204036	4610340	4610340	4610340
f. Nutrition & Health Education	590032	682816	800704	878160	878160	878160
Referral Services	Pregnant mother and at risk children required specialized treatment will be referred by the Anganwadi Center to Primary Health Center					

8. Nutrition

1. Expansion of coverage under supplementary nutrition Programme.
2. Medical interventional like providing Iron pholic acid and deworming tablets, etc.

3. Encouraging development of kitchen gardens
4. Improving standard of family diet.
5. Bringing attitudinal and behavioral changes.

TABLE - I

Supplementary Nutrition

The Nutrition Value of Food Provided to the Beneficiaries					
		Daily Ration		*Nutrition value*	
		Adult	*Child*	*Adult*	*Child*
CARE	Corn Soya Blend Soya Salad Oil	130 gms 16 gms	65 gms 8 gms	620cal 26 gms of protein	310 cal 13 gms of protein
RTE (Ready to Eat Food	Sweet Ready Mix/ Snack food	135 gms	80 gms	516 cal 17 gms of protein	304 cal

TABLE - II

Financial Requirements

(Rupees in Crores)

	1999-2000	2000-2001	2001-2002	2002-2003	2003-2004	2004-2005
General ICDS	84.69	84.69	88.13	96.94	106.63	178.20
WB ICDS	49.41	86.54	102.79	93.09	60.92	--
TOTAL	133.90	171.03	190.92	190.03	167.55	178.20

Compotent wise Allocation

Allocation for SNP	123.60	143.04	167.74	183.96	183.96	183.96
Pre School	5.83	9.70	14.00	17.25	17.25	17.25
Health Component	2.25	5.51	5.91	6.21	9.12	9.12

9. *Economic Support Programme*

- To Inculcate saving and banking habits among women groups

- To identify areas where women can be productively employed.
- To equip the women for sustainable long term remunerative activity

STRATEGY

Group Loaning

- Women below Poverty line
- Each group consists of 15 women
- Maximum loan facility Rs. 5,000/- each
- Savings Period six months for loan eligibility.
- Interest rate 6 ½% per annum.
- Recovery of Loan in 10 equal monthly installments

CMEY

- Each Group consists of 15 Women
- Minimum Thrift amount Rs. 5000/- accumulated over a period of 6 months.
- Margin money loan facility is 50 times thrift made by beneficiary,
- Maximum margin money eligibility Rs. 50,000/-

ACTION: PLAN

	Name of the Scheme			
	Group Loan		*CMEY*	
Year	*Financial (Rs. in lacks)*	*Physical (Groups)*	*Financial (Rs. in lacks)*	*Physical (Groups)*
2000-2001	1725.00	2300	1150.00	3600
2001-2002	2156.25	2875	1437.50	5750
2002-2003	2587.50	3450	1725.00	6900
2003-2004	3018.75	4025	2012.50	8050

2004-2005	3450.00	4600	2300.00	9200
TOTAL	12937.50	17250	8625.00	33,500

10. Training

- Training in employment and market skills to illiterates and semi-literate and literate women.
- Encourage women in self-waged employment.

STRATEGY

- Setting up of training centers at divisional level in a phased manner
- Setting up of mobile training units at village level
- Residential Programmes
- 200 to 300 women in each pranganam and 60 at divisional level
- Free hostel accommodation and training
- Qualified teaching staff
- Conduct field visits to gain knowledge
- Training in Entrepreneurship Development Programme
- Post training, follow-up for placement for self-wage employment
- Coverage of trainees under Rajarajeswari Insurance Scheme

ACTION PLAN

Year	*No. of Centers*	*No. of Beneficiaries*	*Budget (Rs. In lakhs)*
2000-2001	33	15,080	686.00
2001-2002	43	15,680	734.00
2002-2003	53	16,280	782.00
2003-2004	66	17,060	844.40
2004-2005	79	17,840	906.80
Total	274	81,940	3953.20

11. Reservation of 33 1/3% for Women

(a) Implementation of 33 1/3% reservation for women in employment by Government Departments, Corporations and Public sector undertakings.

(b) Implementations of carry forward system vacancies in employment and education.

(c) Monitoring of reservations in all departments & Institutions by Regional Deputy Directors and project Directors of W.D & C.W Department by inspections.

(d) Officers of Commissionerate comprising Commissioner, Joint Director, Deputy Director and Asst. Director may also be assigned with the inspecting powers to verify implementation of 33 1/3% reservations of any office, Department and educational Institutions in the State Level.

(e) Any Government Department or undertaking in the State making appointment for women to the extent of 33 1/3% should communicate copies of such appointments to the inspecting authorities both at District and State Level.

12. Allocation of 1/3rd Budget for Women Activities

This budget allocation should be done by all Departments for women activities. Proper monitoring of 1/3rd budget from the respective Departments may be done by constituting a high level committee.

13. Legal Measures and Awareness Programmes

1. Create awareness on the prevailing laws relating to women and children.
2. Provide counselling service to those material maladjustments and family disputes.
3. Provide preventive and rehabilitative services to

women and children who are victims of atrocities and exploitation

4. Provide referral services like free legal aid, short stay, treatment, vocational training etc.,
5. Conduct mobile camps in rural and urban slum areas where women are facing problems due to lack of awareness.
6. Conduct home´visits at villages/interior levels as part of counselling services.
7. Conduct monthly meetings with mother committees and women groups regularly.
8. Participate in issues including gender sensitization with subordinate police officers in their monthly crime meeting conducted by the Superintendent of Police.
9. Constitution of Dispute Resolution Group at district level with a sub-judge MRO, MPDO, Project Director, DW & CD Agency. A representative of District Collector and lawyers representing Family Court.
10. Adopting community convergence approach through NGO's and CBO's campaign will be done for.

    (a) Prevention of Child Marriages

    (b) Implementation of Dowry Prohibition Act, 1961

    (c) Strict implementation of Immoral Traffic Act, Equal Remuneration Act, Indecent Representation of Women (Prohibition) Act, Prenatal Diagnostic Techniques (Regulation of Prevention Act, 1994) i.e., Infanticide and probation of Sale of Girl Child.

14. Awareness Programme

1. Creating awareness on women rights, family planning, aids & drugs, health and common women diseases.
2. Ensuring immediate legal step to curb all social crimes

against women like rape, kidnapping, molesting, ragging etc.,

3. Strengthening of Self-Help Groups (DWCRA Mother Committees)

ACTION PLAN

Year	*No. of Centers*	*Amount (Rs. In lakhs)*
2000-2001	33	26.520
2001-2002	43	37.388
2002-2003	53	50.179
2003-2004	66	68.635
2004-2005	79	89.776
Total		272.498

15. Strengthening of Women Groups and Mother Committees

1. Selection of core groups to activate DWCRA group & Mother Committees.
2. Train the Core Group teams at Mandal Level in Programmes.
3. Using them as change agents.
4. Networking of Self-Help Groups.

16. District Women's Development Agency

1. The District Women Development Agency will be the focal point for interacting with all local bodies, NGOs and others or various women related programmes irrespective of the Department, which Finance such programmes.
2. The District Women Development Agency will prioritize programmes, which are required at the field level and channelise funds of the various Government Departments appropriately to those

activities, which are absolutely necessary to improve the condition of women.

3. The DWD Agency will also monitor and supervise the implementation of Various Programmes including if necessary government funded NGO projects and developmental programmes.
4. The DWD Agency will also prepare training module and access funds as deemed necessary for implementing such training programmes at the District level.
5. The DWD Agency will also set-up monitoring mechanism to have an effective development strategy towards women's empowerment at the District level.
6. The DWD Agency will act as catalyst for all the women related programmes. It will also be a bridge between Government, NGOs and local bodies.
7. The DWD Agency will be the nodal point for women for redressal of grievances for building a sustained development for the term benefit of women.

Following is the composition of District Women Development Agency.

1.	District Collector	Chairperson
2.	Superintendent of Police	Member
3.	District Educational Officer	Member
4.	District medical & Health Officer/ Senior Lady Medical Officer	Member
5.	Project director, DRDA	Member
6.	Project Director, ITDA	Member
7.	Municipal Commissioner	Member
8.	Asst. Director, Industries	Member
9.	Asst. Director, Agriculture	Member
10.	Asst. Director, Horticulture	Member

11.	Project Director, Women & Child Development Agency	Member
12.	Two women representatives of local banks	Member
13.	Two reputed non Government Organizations (Local)	Member
14.	District Manager, Mahila Pranganam	Convenor

17. Works on Women's Empowerment through Convergence

- To train on teamwork for economic sustainability.
- Co-ordination of Government Departments and NGOs.

Convergence of All Activities Relating to Women

- While the appeal of economic Programme will be to attract women's groups for an economic and remunerative activity, the main objective is to organize women in-groups to monitor the social development indicators intensively.

Our thrust areas for these women's group will be:

- Basic education for all women in the self-help groups.
- Launching a literacy mission for giving them basic reading ability initially.
- Launching health related programmes, which will cover family planning, counseling, Aids counselling and other health related problems specific to women, children and their families.
- Special programmes for nutrition with emphasis on iron deficiency, mal-nourishment, iodine deficiency etc.
- Concentration on adolescent girl child and improving dietary habits of mothers and children.
- Launching an insurance scheme for adolescent girls and mothers in productive and reproductive age groups.

- Launching an awareness campaign for women issues including legal aspects.
- An environment related programmes for conversation including water, energy, bio-diversity and ecological issues.

Marketing Support

Major areas for intervention for the long term and sustainable economic support programmes are:

Identifying markets which will provide a long term and sustained income for the women's groups - specially for every woman so that she does not have to depend on agricultural labour.

- Work on design development to meet the market requirements.
- Quality improvement and sustained high quality performance to sustain the market access.
- Promotion of the product, exhibitions, etc.
- Improved/appropriate packaging for long shelf life, prevention, transportation, exportability, etc.
- Publish material, pamphlets, etc to popularize products made by women's groups.

INSURANCE PROGRAMME

For adolescent girls and mothers in productive and reproductive age groups are suggested.

- The objective is to encourage families to contribute towards an Insurance Fund, which could be administered by the Government.
- Get women coverage for health care, supplementary nutrition, family Planning Programme, immunization

FIGURE 1

Implementation Arrangement

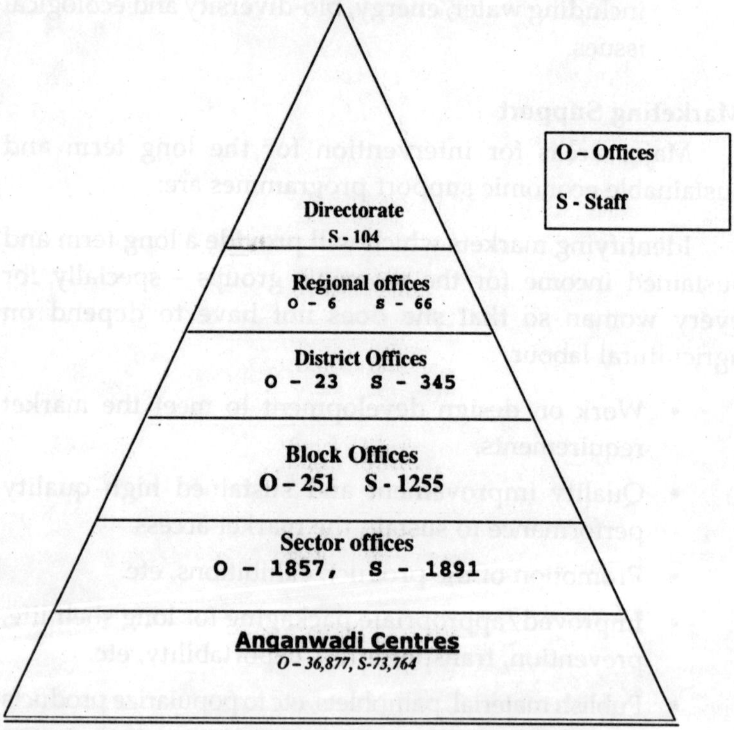

as well as legal aid in the event of family disputes, criminal and other offences against women.

SANITATION AND DRINKING WATER

To have awareness Programme for improved sanitary facilities and safe drinking water as well as target specific groups, using funds available locally and internationally in launching basic facilities, which are required for improving the quality of living conditions for women.

PMES - CORE, FUNCTIONAL & DEPARTMENTAL INDICATORS

S.No	*Core Indicator*	*Functional Indicator*	*Unit*
1.	Nutrition	Low Birth Weight	Percent
		Children (0-3 Months) exclusive breast-fed.	Percent
		Children (6-9 months) breast-fed with supplementary food.	Percent
		Children (20-23 months) breast-fed with supplementary food	Percent
		Children underweight	Percent
		Children Wasting	Percent
		Children Stunting	Percent
		Vitamin "A" doses	Percent
2.	Nutritional anemia	Registration at Anganwadi	Percent
		Hemoglobin level tested	Percent
		Severe cases	Percent
	Adolescent girls	Reported/referred/ treated	Percent
	Pregnant Mothers	Moderate cases reported / treated	Percent
	Lactating Mothers	Consumption of IFA tablets and deworming	Percent
3.	Welfare of Children	Admission	Percent
		In-country adoption	Percent
		Inter- country adoption	Percent
		Results class wise	Percent
4.	Child abuse	Infanticide cases reported	Percent
		Foeticide cases reported	Percent
		Bonded child labour	Percent

		Child maid servant	Percent
		Street children	Percent
		Child prostitutes	Percent
		Child trafficking	Percent
5.	Care & support to disabled children	Children with disability	Percent
		Children in institutions	Percent
		Children in Schools	Percent
6.	Juvenile Children Welfare	Restoration to parents	Percent
	• Delinquent	Admission in institutions	Percent
	• Neglected	Rehabilitation	Percent
7.	Welfare of Women	Skill Upgradation	Percent
		Settlement in life	Percent
8.	33 1/3 % reservation	Roster points	Nos
		Filled up	
		Carry forward	
9.	1/3 budget allocation	Department wise monitoring	Nos
10	Atrocities on women		
	• Rape	Reported/ booked/ convicted	Nos
		Rehabilitated	Nos
	• Dowry	Reported/booked/convicted	Nos
	• Violence	Reported/booked/convicted	Nos
	• Family disputes	No. of cases counseling done	Nos
		Amicable settlement	Nos
		Booked/convicted	Nos

PMES - CORE, FUNCTIONAL & DEPARTMENTAL INDICATORS

S. No.	*Departmental indicator*	*Unit*	*Achievements (2000-2001)*	*Target (2001-2002)*
1.	Children covered under SNP	Nos	14,45,385	16,62,192
2.	Children covered under Pre-School	Nos	7,99,136	9,19,006
3.	Children covered under Immunization	Nos	10,71,950	12,32,742
4.	Children covered under growth monitoring	Nos	21,43,901	24,65,486
5.	Children receiving deworming	Nos	6,93,900	7,97,985
6.	Children under normal grade	Nos	6,65,355	7,65,158

7.	Children under grade I	Nos	7.50,365	8,62,919
8.	Children under grade II	Nos	5,78,853	6,65,680
9.	Children under grade III	Nos	1,28,634	1,47,929
10.	Children under grade IV	Nos	20,692	23,795
11.	Children admitted in primary schools	Nos	2,91,488	3,35,211
12.	Children covered under Health check-up	Nos	4,40,407	5,06,468
13.	Child death recorded			
	Under 1 Year	Nos	26,800	
	Under 5 Years	Nos	NA	
14.	Women covered under health check-ups	Nos	1,70,059	1,95,567
15.	Mother's referred to hospitals	Nos	11,013	
16.	Adolescent girls enrolled in ICDS	Nos	6,93,900	7,97,985
17.	Adolescent girls received deworming & IFA tablets	Nos	6,93,900	7,97,985
18.	Adolescent girls attended maternal school	Nos	36,308	41,754
19.	Abandoned children admitted in the Shishuvihars	Nos	46	
	Children found normal	Nos	41	
	Children Found mentally retarded	Nos	5	
20.	Children given for adoption	Nos	3	
21.	Girls children sent to children's homes	Nos	5	
22.	Boys admitted in social welfare hostels	Nos	3	
23.	Children enrolled in GCPS	Nos	21,000	
24.	Children admitted in children homes	Nos	4,277	
25.	Girls appeared for 7th class	Nos	454	
	Girls passed		454	
26.	Girls appeared for X th class	Nos	218	
	Girls passed	Nos	109	
27.	Girls admitted in collegiate homes	Nos	156	
28.	Girls completed college studies	Nos	32	
29.	Working women admitted in WWH	Nos	580	
30.	Women admitted in service/ state homes	Nos	418	
	Women trained	Nos	336	
	Women rehabilitated	Nos	62	
	Girls got married and settled	Nos	14	
31.	Cases registered by legal and family	Nos	690	

	counselling centers			
	Cases settled	Nos	560	
32.	Anganwadi helpers trained			
	Orientation training	Nos	1,415	2,830
	Refresher training	Nos	Nil	1,000
33.	A W Ws trained			
	Job course	Nos	1,920	3,840
	Refresher course	Nos	126	252
34.	Supervisors trained			
	Job course	Nos	204	408
	Refresher course	Nos	Nil	100
35.	CDPOs trained			
	Job course	Nos	77	154
	Refresher course	Nos	14	28
36.	Training to senior officers of the Department	Nos	42	84
37.	Computer Training	Nos	15	115
38.	Training to members of the mothers committees	Nos	1,140	2,280
39.	Other kinds of trainings	Nos	122	244

THE ACTION TAKEN BY THE DEPARTMENT - ANALYSIS STRENGTH

- Introduction of participation of stakeholders group called Mothers Committees in the management of Anganwadi centers. Mothers Committees are catalysts, participants & recipients. For every Anganwadi, 8 mothers representing 4 categories of beneficiaries (0 - 3 Yrs, 3 - 6 Yrs, adolescent girls & pregnant/ lactating women) are constituting Mothers Committee. There are 36,877 Mothers Committees with a membership of 2,95,016 women.
- Formation of Resource Groups (TOTs).
- A training module for capacity building of Mothers Committees prepared.

- An Annual Activity Calendar cum self-appraisal for Mother Committees prepared.
- 3 day Residential Training to Mothers Committees along with Anganwadi workers conducted.
- 'Taruni Tarangalu' a monthly magazine launched for establishing communication with Mothers Committees.
- The construction of 8,816 Anganwadi buildings entrusted to Mothers Committees, 8151 buildings have been completed.
- Recruitment of Anganwadi workers & helpers delegated to Mothers Committee.
- 5,847 Anganwadis developed on a play school model.
- 23,905 nutrition melas organized during the 15th round of Janmabhoomi (Mahila & Sishu Janmabhoomi, June 2001).
- Introduction & implementation of weekly Mathrugoshti at Anganwadi centers.
- Women Empowerment Policy approved.
- Employees training policy in place.
- Starting State Women Administrative Training Institute (SWATI) in order to complete the backlog of training.
- Formulation of adolescent girls integrated development policy.
- Household survey on adolescent girls in 251 projects completed. Data is under computerization.
- Kishori Shakti Yojana (KSS) launched in 23 blocks with further expansion to 63 blocks.
- Preparation of IEC policy and strategy.
- In order to bring behavioural changes for improving

the nutritional level of Women & Children, Nutrition Health Education (NHED) strategy developed.

- Development of Mother & Child Growth Monitoring Card for 63 projects on a pilot basis.
- Conduction of workshops to prepare action plan for strengthening of Anganwadi centers as village resource centers for women & children.
- Development of requisite softwares on monitoring the scheme.
- Preparation of master plan for the computerization of the department
- Launching of the web-site "anganwadi.com"
- Establishing Local Area Network (LAN) in the Directorate.
- Development of GIS monitoring package (Rangareddy & Krishna districts)
- Launching of PMGY in 93 projects with current year expansion to 129 projects.
- Procurement of goods worth 21.50 crore as per the approved action plan.
- The administrative & management training to Assistant Directors & Deputy Directors at ASCI.
- 4,664 Anganwadi centers got inspected from 6-11th August 2001 in order to assess functioning of Anganwadi centers, Mothers Committees coverage of beneficiaries, to identify & analyze the reasons for ineffective functioning, for developing strategies and to develop strategies for strengthening & streamlining the delivery mechanism at Anganwadi centers.
- Performance indicators of the Department finalized (10 Core Indicators & 39 Departmental Indicators).
- Performance Monitoring & Evaluation System (PMES)

introduced in the department with backup support of software.

- -- Standardization of all reporting formats.
- -- A training module on PMES for field functionaries developed.
- -- Half-yearly performance of the department assessed.
- -- Time schedule for reviews prescribed for all functionaries.

- In order to know the functioning of ICDS in tribal blocks of 8 agency areas of the State 3,933 Anganwadi centers and 923 Mini Anganwadi centers were inspected from 10-16th December 2001.
- For improving the facilities of 118 homes serving orphan children & destitute women, yoga, meditation, library, sports & other facilities like solar water heating system, improvised cooking facilities, specially designated beds & almirahs are being provided.
- In all, 81-girl children homes "Bul-Bul & Guide Unit" introduced in order to inculcate discipline.
- External evaluation of Girl Child Protection Scheme taken up.
- Workshops for improving the functioning of all 118 institutions and bringing quality improvement in monitoring of atrocities on women conducted.
- The adoption system streamlined.
- 10 defunct schemes of 597 institutions with 1134 staff are being redeployed.
- In order to improve the functioning & coverage of the department and sustain the initiatives taken, a re-organization plan of directorate submitted to the Government.

WEAKNESS

- Universalization of ICDS could not be achieved.
- Supplementary Nutrition could not be provided in all new projects.
- No budget was released under Women Empowerment Policy.

Budget 2002-2003

S. No.	*Name of the Scheme*	*Rs. in Lakh* *Department Plan Outlay 2002-2003*
1.	Service for children in need of care and protection	36.00
2.	Children Home (SCP)	8.99
3.	Children Home (General)	17.98
4.	H. Qrs. Grant in aid	3.37
5.	Assistance to APWCFC	143.00
6.	GCP General	2,607.00
7.	GCP SCP	508.00
8.	GCP TSP	234.00
9.	State Commission for Women	33.00
10.	Nutrition - General	11,410.00
11.	Nutrition - SCP	742.00
12.	Nutrition - TSP	297.00
13.	Rescue & Rehabilitation of victims of trafficking	100.00
14.	IEC (Campaign)	23.00
	Total (A)	**16,163.34**
15.	PMGY - SCP	3,036.00
16.	PMGY - TSP	1650.00
	Total (B)	**4,686.00**

Centrally Sponsored Schemes		
17.	ICDS	9,020.80
18.	World Bank ICDs	5,935.19
19.	PMU (ICDU - WB)	193.69
20.	ICDS - Tribal	1,088.17
21.	Balika Samruddi Yojana	99.00
	Total (C)	**16,336.85**
Grand Total (A+B+C)		**37,186.19**

Source: Strategy Paper on Women Empowerment, Women Development, Child Welfare & Disable Welfare Department, Govt. of Andhra Pradesh.

4

Women, Empowerment and Economic Development

Abstract: Development policies and programs tend not to view women as integral to the economic development process. This is reflected in the higher investments in women's reproductive rather than their productive roles, mainly in population programs. Yet women throughout the developing world engage in economically productive work and earn incomes. They work primarily in agriculture and in the informal sector and, increasingly, in formal wage employment. Their earnings, however, are generally low. Since the 1950s, development agencies have responded to the need for poor women to earn incomes by making relatively small investments in income-generating projects. Often such projects fail because they are motivated by welfare and not development concerns, offering women temporary and part-time employment in traditionally feminine skills such as knitting and sewing that have limited markets. By contrast, over the past twenty years, some non-governmental organizations, such as the Self-Employed Women's Association in India, have been effective in improving women's economic status because they have started with the premise that women are fundamental to the process of economic development.

Over the past two decades, development policy has become increasingly poverty centered. Although poverty concerns

* *Source:* ANNALS, AAPSS, 554, November 1997, pp. 136-149.

have long been on the development agenda, the implementation of development policies has not always directly addressed poverty alleviation. More recently, along with macroeconomic reform and growth, there has been growing recognition of the need to address basic human needs and to adopt more participatory approaches to achieve development goals. These changes have been both the stimulus for and the result of the growth and development of non-governmental organizations (NGOs) that work directly at the grassroots level with low-income people like small-scale farmers and micro-entrepreneurs. Governments and donors have begun to rely increasingly on NGOs in developed and developing countries as partners in the development process. Many NGOs have demonstrated an interest not only in improving people's economic status and well-being but also in empowering the people themselves to obtain improvements in their lives.

Promoting empowerment is of particular interest to some NGOs working with poor women. Although four decades of development (1950-90) have yielded important benefits to women, significant gender gaps still remain. Improvements in women's well-being are reflected in the behaviour of four key indicators between 1970 and 1990, as shown in Table 1: (1) life expectancy among women increased significantly in all regions; (2) girls enrollment in primary school increased in most regions; (3) total fertility rates declined; and (4) women's access to contraception increased. On the other hand, world wide, twice as many women as men are still illiterate; girls represent the majority of the 130 million children without access to primary school; and almost twice as many women as men suffer from iron-deficiency anemia.[1]

The most telling statistic reflecting gender bias is the low ratios of females to males (94 females for every 100 males) in China and South and West Asia due to non-preference. This contradicts the biological pattern, where the ratios favour females. The preference for sons manifests itself through the neglect of female children, selective abortion, and female infanticide and has prompted researchers to attempt to estimate the number of "missing girls." Amartya K. Sen. estimates that 4 million girls are missing in India alone, while globally the estimate is more than 100 million women. [2] Further, recent estimates show that male preference is not, as one would expect, tapering with economic development. Instead, in the 1980s, 1 million more girls were lost in India due to development and infanticide.[3]

TABLE - 1

Four Key Indicators of Women's Social Status

	Life Expectancy at Birth		*Fertility Percentage of*		*Females as Women (ages 15-49) in Primary School*		*Percentage of Total Enrollment Using Modern Contraception*	
Region	1970	1990	1970	1990	1970	1990	1980	1990
East Asia	64.5	75.2	4.65	2.48	48	48	65.8	81.2
Southeast Asia and Oceania	57.2	66.4	5.35	3.86	47	48	44.2	53.5
South Asia	48.3	58	6.29	5.29	36	41	21.5	35.9
Latin America & the Caribbean	64.0	71.5	5.00	3.27	49	49	39.3	44.9
Sub-Saharan Africa	46.7	53.1	6.52	6.17	39	44	15.3	24.7
Organization for Economic Cooperation and Development	75.4	79.8	2.25	1.75	49	49	70.0	74.3
Arab States	58.0	68.8	6.83	5.02	36	44	24.2	44.7

 # *Source:* WISTAT Database (Version 3) (United Nations). The regional average is based on countries averages.

Empowerment, Capabilities and Opportunities

These data demonstrate the need for development policies and programs that can enable girls and women to challenge current norms and change conditions - a process that can be termed "empowerment." Definitions of empowerment vary greatly. Therefore, empowerment must be qualified and measured depending on the particular context. In the context of women and development, the definition of empowerment should include the expansion of choices for women and an increase in women's ability to exercise choice. For example, improvements in women's access to economic opportunities such as credit and employment expand choices, while health services and education improve women's capabilities to take advantage of those choices.

The two elements of this definition of empowerment are interrelated, but the correspondence between them may not be, and often is not, exact. Interventions that expand women's choices, for instance, by increasing women's access to employment should raise women's ability to exercise choices (for example, to decide when to marry or to have children). Actions that attempt to strength women's capacity to choose can amplify their choices. For example, schooling for girls should both increase their voice in the family and the range of job options underlying social, cultural, and institutional reasons, there are often carrying degrees of choices for women and varying degrees of ability to exercise those choices. Also, the ability of policy makers and of women themselves to influence and change the factors underlying their disempowerment varies.

Empirical data show that it has been relatively easier to expand women's capabilities than their opportunities. Table 1 shows that considerable progress has been made in improving women's capabilities - in building their human capital through improvements in access to primary education and better health care. There has been much slower progress in enhancing women's choices, however, particularly access to economic opportunities. Just over one-third of women are economically active worldwide. As Figure 1 shows, even participation rates such as those in East Asia and sub-Saharan Africa, less than half of the women are economically active. In South Asia and sub-Saharan Africa, moreover, economic activity rates among women have actually declined. In India, women as a proportion to the economically active population fell from almost 25 percent in 1970 to nearly 20 percent in 1990 [4]. The gender gap in economic activity rates is also large and, globally among women who are employed, wages are about two-thirds those of men. There are similar lags in women's political participation. Women hold just 10 percent of the seats in legislative bodies in developing countries, and only 5 percent of cabinet seats are held by women[5].

Development Policies and the Welfare Model

The uneven progress in women's well-being reflects the emphasis of development policies that, historically, focused on women's reproductive roles, mainly on fertility reduction. Policies and investments also emphasized improvements in women's health and education. Interestingly, investments in women's health and education were often rationalized in terms of their impact on lowering birth rates and on improving the well-being of children. Seldom were they justified in terms of their intrinsic importance to women's well-being of children. Seldom were they justified in terms of improving women's human capital so women might expand their ability to exercise choices. Also, women's economic roles were simply not acknowledged.

In general, the welfare model of development, employed by governments, donors, and NGOs, regards women as recipients of benefits such as health care, literacy, social services, and family planning rather than as independent economic actors in their own right. Because women's roles as mothers and wives have dominated development thinking, development planners and policymakers have missed important opportunities for having a significant impact on the lives of poor women. Valuable resources have been misallocated and misspent. Very little has been invested in women's productive lives, where the opportunities truly lie for reducing poverty and improving women's lives.

Why Women Need Development

Women are disproportionately represented among the poor, and the number of women in poverty in the rural areas of developing countries is growing faster than the number of men. In 1988, an estimated 564 million rural women lived below the poverty line, representing an increase of 47 percent since 1965-70. In comparison, the number of men living below the poverty line increased 30 percent over the same period. Factors contributing to the increase in rural poverty are economic recession, civil strife, and natural disasters. In addition, the rise in the number of households supported solely by women is an important variable explaining the increase in poverty among women. The households tend to be over represented among the poor.

In Africa, for example, it is estimated that 96 percent of rural women engage in farm work and 40 percent of small-farms are managed by women[6]. As a result of this work, women contribute both cash and subsistence income to household, the more women work for income, and the larger the proportion of household in India, for instance, women are often the main or even the sole income earners in their households[7].

Some studies show that women's earnings contribute more directly in family welfare than do men's earnings contribute more directly to family welfare than do men's earnings because they go toward food and children's education[8].

Much of the work women do goes unrecorded because it takes place in the informal sector. Estimating women's participation in the informal sector, however, is difficult. Data are hard to obtain because they are not generally collected by census bureaus and other official statisticians. Nevertheless, estimates have been made for some countries, as shown in Table 2. The higher percentage of women to men employed in the informal sector reflects women's difficulty in obtaining access to employment because their higher rates of illiteracy, lower levels of education, lack of job skills and the social and cultural barriers to formal employment that women face.

Thus much of the development support women need is outside the formal economy, where they engage in activities such as petty trade, household help, food processing, garment manufacturing, and agriculture. Some of this employment, as in household services and agriculture, is wage employment but much of it is non-wage or self-employment, where the scale of operation is small or very small (micro-enterprise), undercapitalized, and concentrated in the low-growth sub-sectors, where returns are low, working conditions difficult, and benefits virtually non-existent.[9]

TABLE - 2

Proportion of Men and Women in Nonwage Employment

Country	*Year*	*Men*	*Women*	*Income Level*
Bolivia	1991	42	70	Middle
Cape Vendee	1990	42	54	Middle
Egypt	1989	46	74	Low
B Salvador	1991	28	48	Middle
Ghana	1989	69	92	Low
Indonesia	1989	70	79	Middle
Korea	1991	38	43	Middle
Republic of Pakistan	1992	66	77	Low
Peru	1991	39	55	Middle
Tanzania	1988	84	95	Low

Thailand	1989	71	76	Middle
Turnisia	1989	36	51	Middle
Turkey	1991	55	80	Middle

Source: World Bank, World Development Report (Washington DC: World Bank, 1995).

Women's enterprises face numerous other constraints. At the household level, for example, micro-entrepreneurs need to adjust to seasonal fluctuations, to balance multiple economic activities in order to spread risk and to balance short-term cash flow requirements against longer-term investment requirements. In addition, due to sickly defined gender roles and relationships, women face particular constraints that men do not. They may not be able to own resources and property and may have limited access to credit, skills training, or extension services. Women also face institutional barriers that may, for example, subject them to police harassment. They, as opposed to men, are often unable, for instance, to obtain licenses to sell their goods in regulated market places. At the macro-economic level, women are affected by financing or regulatory policies that can restrict their access to credit from institutional sources such as banks and thrift and savings associations. Successful interventions to strengthen women's economic activities, therefore, require addressing these constraints.

Fortunately, there are a number of examples of efforts that have been successful in strengthening women's enterprises, raising women's incomes, and empowering women politically. NGOs have often led the way. A leading example is the Self-Employed Women's Association (SEWA) in India.

The Self-Employed Women's Association

Inspired by Gandhian teachings, SEWA drew upon strategies employed by three different movements: the labour movement, co-operatives, and the women's movement.[10] Its membership consists mainly of self-employed workers and low-paid labourers. They include hawkers and vendors who sell their products from baskets, carts, and small shops; home-based workers such as weavers, potters, garment workers, and food processors; and manual labourers and service providers like head loaders (women who transparent goods on their heads), domestic help, and construction workers. The difficulties confronting these workers include very low earnings, police harassment and extortion, and lack of organization and representation. SEWA set itself the mission of organizing its members and helping them enter the economic mainstream through a dual strategy that helps women (1) to strengthen their economic enterprises and (2) to advocate for their economic and political rights.

In order to support women's enterprises and activities, SEWA facilitated the provision of financial and non-financial, or business development, services to its members. A key component of the economic strategy was the creation of the SEWA Cooperative Bank founded in 1974. The bank developed out of members need for working capital. At first, SEWA functioned as an intermediary institution linking its members to formal-sector banks. Difficulties in working with the commercial system prompted the creation of the SEWA bank. Commercial banks are generally unwilling to provide financial services to the poor, women among them, partly because they find it too costly to meet the needs of this specialized clientele. These needs include small loans, flexibility in repayment terms, simplified administrative procedures for obtaining loans (for example, filling out forms), and loan guarantee alternatives that do not include fixed assets, which poor people cannot generally provide [11].

The SEWA bank has proved to be one of the pioneers in developing and implementing creative and cost effective strategies to meet the specialized demand of its members.

The bank has simplified loan procedures and forms, helped clients fill out applications, accepted group guarantees in lieu of other forms of collateral, made small loans (averaging $230), and allowed for frequent repayment possibilities matched to client earnings schedules. The SEWA bank provides both savings and credit facilities for its members. As a cooperative, the bank obtains loan capital from a combination of savings deposits, share capital, and plowed back profits. Borrowers are required to buy 5 percent of the loan amount in bank shares when receiving a loan and to open a savings account. Like similar institutions, the SEWA bank attempts to cover its operating costs by charging market or above-market rates of interest and fees for other services. It is important to note that market rates of interest do not pose a disincentive to SEWA's clients because the available alternative is borrowing in the informal sector at much higher rates.[12]

In addition to banking, SEWA provided its members with a variety of other business development services, including organizing them into more than fifty cooperatives. For women employed in dairy production, SEWA helps set up linkages to enable them to register inquiry cooperatives and to participation and benefit from the services offered through the government's National Dairy Development Board. SEWA also helps women dairy producers obtain government loans, provides training in animal care and other aspects of dairy development and supports women's leadership within the cooperatives.[13] SEWA has also helped women in a variety of industries, improve marketing skills and linkages. Members have been taught the essentials of market differentiation, quality control, and timing.[14]

The organization has helped its members organize, define, and understand their problems, identify solution and demand action from the appropriate authority. This is reflected in its work with vegetable vendors. In addition to lack of access to capital, SEWA's research showed that vegetable vendors were subjected to constant harassment by police because vending was not a licensed activity and had no designated space on city-street. SEWA organized its members to demand an end to police harassment and to apply for licenses. When police resisted the women's demands, public protests were organized and the case was taken to India's Supreme Court. The vegetable vendors succeeded in obtaining licenses, official vending sites, and SEWA membership cards to show police the legitimacy of their trade. Later, when the city offered resistance to complying with the Supreme Court ruling, SEWA helped the vendors pressure city officials to comply.[15]

Home-based workers represented, in 1994, 40 percent of SEWA's membership of 220,000 women. SEWA organized these workers to demand higher wages and better working conditions. Most home-based work in India is not protected by legislation. SEWA, however, engaged in a successful five-year struggle to obtain legal recognition for garment workers so that they might receive the minimum wage. The organization also worked for a decade to enable workers in the bidi industry in Ahmedabad to earn the equivalent of the minimum wage, effectively doubling their wages. Support for obtaining maternity and social security benefits for some of its members have also been provided.[16]

SEWA's services now also include assistance with literacy, education, job skills and leadership training, health care, and research and communications through publications, journals and videos. SEWA in Ahmedabad serves as a model for other SEWA organizations around India that have independently set up banks and business development services for women and have organized producer cooperatives.

SEWA's success has been due in large measure to its recognition of the fundamental importance of poor women's economic roles. In contrast to the welfare model of development, SEWA's work is grounded in the premise that women, like men, need incomes to support themselves and their families. Therefore SEWA works with women to improve and increase the returns from their ongoing enterprises, rather than introducing them to new and unfamiliar income-generating activities. It provides assistance that makes good economic sense; capital, support for organizing cooperatives to increase women's bargaining power, marketing assistance, and specialized skills training. SEWA also supports women in advocacy, leadership and training. It serves as an intermediary on behalf of women at a policy level, providing access to legal and other resources to address the broader policy issues that affect women's economic and social advancement and their well-being.

Initially, SEWA's leaders were not grassroots women but well-educated middle-class and upper-class women who played a critical role in interacting with the government and private institutions, filling in the gaps for which its members did not have the skills and education. As the organization has grown and developed, however, women who started out as illiterate rag-pickers and head loaders were trained to take over stall and leadership positions in the organization.

SEWA has succeeded in both enhancing women's choices and enabling them to implement those choices economically and politically. In short, it has empowered its members.

Future Prospects

Recent trends show a movement away from welfare approaches among NGOs working with women. A review of eight South Asian NGOs working with women is instructive in highlighting successful strategies for the future. The review documents the successful employment of the advocacy and economic growth strategies similar to those pursued by

SEWA.[17] The emphasis of these NGOs is on organizing women and using comprehensive approaches that address the multiple sources of women's disempowerment. Economic and political strategies are linked.

Key elements of success include responding to women's priorities to obtain employment and income; recognizing that economic empowerment of women is an important entry point in working with women; mobilizing savings and assets and putting them under women's control; and advocacy. Also, their approach is both responsive and participatory.

Finally, the NGOs reach a sizable number of women and therefore can have a significant impact. Membership in some of the larger, older organizations ranges from half a million to 1 million women and is still growing. Even the membership of smaller organizations reaches hundreds of thousands of women.[18]

These NGOs, SEWA among them, have demonstrated that it is both necessary and possible to bring women into the mainstream of economic development. The strategies they employ are replicable and sustainable and can have large-scale impact that is needed to improve the lives of poor women and their families. They offer lessons that could be employed by a variety of other organizations involved in development: governments, donors, and other NGOs.

REFERENCES

1. United Nations Development Programme, Human Development Report 1955 (New York: United Nations, 1985)
2. Amartya Sen, "Women's Survival as a Development Problem" (Talk given at the 1700th stated meeting of the American Academy of Arts and Sciences, Harvard University, Cambridge, MA, 8 Mar. 1989).
3. Rick Weiss, "Anti-Girl Bias Rises in Asia, Studies Show. "Washington Post. 11 May 1999.

4. WISTAT Database (Version 1) (United Nations)
5. United Nations Development.
6. Rekha Mehra, Women land, and Sustainable Development (Washington, DC: International Center for Research on Women, 1995), p. 16
7. Bina Agarwal, "Who Sows? Who Reaps?
8. Marya Buvinic et al., "The Fortunes of Adolescent Mothers and Their Children: The Transmission of Poverty in Santiago, Chile," Population and Development Review, 18(2): 269-97(1991); Patrice Engle, "Influences of Mother's and Father's Income on Children's Nutritional Status in Guaternala, "Social Science and Medicine, 37 (11) : 1303-12(1993); Eileen Kennedy, "Effects of Gender of Head of Household on Women's and Children's Nutritional Status" (Paper delivered at the Workshop on the Effects of Policies and programs on Women, Washington, DC, 1992); Duncan Themas. "Intra Household Resources Allocation.
9. Martha Alter Chen, Beyond Credit: A sub-sector Approach to Promoting Women's Engagement.
10. Renana Jhabvala and Jane Tate, Out of the Shadows: home based Workers Organize for International Recognition (New York: Seeds, 1996)
11. Women's World Banking, "Best Practices in Financial Services to Micro-entrepreneurs", what works:

    A Women's World banking Newsletter (1994): Rekha Mehra, Annelies Drost-Maasry, and Ruba Rahman, Credit for Women (Washington DC: International Center for Research on Women, 1995).
12. Mehra, Drost Manary, and Rahman, Credit for Women
13. Chen, Beyond Credit
14. Jhabvala and Tate, Out of the Shadows.
15. Chen, Beyond Credit
16. Jhabvala and Tate, Out of the Shadows.
17. Marilyn Carr, Martha Chen, and Renana Jhabvala, Speaking Out: Women's Economic Empowerment in South Asia (London: Intermediate Technology, 1996). The NGOs are as follows: the Bangladesh Rural Advancement Committee, Proshika, the Aga Khan Rural Support Programme, the Women's Development

Federation, Informal Sector Unions in Tamil Nadu, the Co-operative Development Foundation, the Self-Employed Women's Association/Kheda and the Self-Employed Women's Association/Banaskantha.

18. Ibid.

5

Elements of Empowerment

One of the most important things that a woman needs in order to be successful as an entrepreneur or for that matter in any activity is to become empowered. Women face many social barriers in their attempts to become entrepreneurs. Hence, it takes a great deal of courage & desire for her to actually try to become an entrepreneur. She also needs persistence & determination to succeed in her effort.

EMPOWERMENT FOR A WOMAN MEANS BEING ABLE

- To over come shyness
- To talk & act confidently
- To look at herself honestly
- To know & accept her capabilities & limitations
- To break through barriers.
- To know her desires & turn them into objectives
- To develop a strong will to achieve her objectives

Why is empowerment important, or is it necessary at all? Can a woman become successful as an entrepreneur without such empowerment?

These are questions that will naturally confront the facilitator in his/her efforts to help women to become empowered. Social roles have cast women in a secondary role for such a long time that women themselves often perceive their own role as secondary and as such, may not be comfortable with the idea of empowern.ent.

It is precisely because of this taken for granted secondary role that women need empowerment. Women have been treated so long as ones lacking in ability and fit only for certain traditional tasks, that their confidence in themselves and in their abilities has shrunk greatly which further reinforced the prevalent attitudes. In order to help women to come out of this vicious cycle, it becomes essential that they are supported and guided in the path of empowerment.

Due to the social cultural and economic conditions, women generally have low self-confidence, poor exposure to the outside world in general and much less to the business environment in particular and therefore, need support in developing the confidence and the abilities required to run an enterprise successfully. Women must be helped to forge what they want to be and do, develop their abilities and forge them together to become truly empowered. Women need support, counseling and training in order to become empowered.

THE PROCESS OF EMPOWERMENT

Empowerment helps the entrepreneur not only to take charge of her business or enterprise, but also to take charge of her life. Empowerment will increase the effectiveness of her relationships with others both within the sphere of her near surroundings and outside. Empowerment is a process -

- Which will make the entrepreneur understand her unique potential and enable her to break barrier and make her realize that she has the capacity to utilize her full potential.
- By which the entrepreneur will be willing to think

independently, to live in her own way, and to have the courage to make her own perceptions and judgment.

- By which the entrepreneur will be willing to know not only what she thinks, but also what she feels, what she wants, needs, desires, suffer or gets frightened or angered by and to accept her right to experience such feelings.
- By which the entrepreneur lives authentically, to speak and act from her innermost convictions and feelings.
- By which the entrepreneur is committed to her right to exist. As a result, she will realize that her life does not belong to others and that she is not here on earth to live up to someone else's expectation.
- By which the entrepreneur starts respecting herself and understands the possibility of growth and experiences joy in the process of exploring her distinct potential.

Elements of Empowerment

This process of the woman understanding what she wants to do and developing her will and courage as well as the competence needed is called empowerment. This can be expressed, as I WANT TO DO + I CAN DO = I WILL DO

(Motivation) (Enabling) (Empowerment)

As can be seen, we are calling the State of "I want to do" as motivation, the state of "I can do" as enabling and the two add up together to a positive statement of intent. "I will do" which is what we call empowerment. It can be seen that this statement implies that the woman wants to do something; it can also be seen that the woman develops her ability to act, and more important, knows clearly that she will achieve what she wants to do. This combination of desire and ability is empowerment. Note that if the statement is "I will try to do" it does not signify empowerment.

Facilitating and Inhibiting factors for empowerment

Facilitating	*Inhibiting*
• Positive self-esteem	• Negative and low self-esteem
• Strong will	• Weak will
• Awareness of one's potential	• Not aware
• Self reliant	• Dependent
• Reaching out	• Withdrawn
• Highly motivated	• Low motivation
• Awareness and understanding of one's own feelings/emotions	• Unaware

Motivation

Every action of a living being is carried out in order to satisfy some need or want. These needs can be elementary, such as food, clothing and shelter, or may be more complex, such as the need to earn a living, the need to be recognized, or the need to be one's own boss. Any need or want, as we can see all around us, induces a desire in people to satisfy such a need, and in turn, this desire makes people carry out certain actions, which actually fulfill the need. Such a desire, or urge to act, is therefore the cause for the action and is called a motive.

When any person carries out an action as a result of a motive, the person is more likely to act and is said to have a high motivation. On the other hand, if the desire or motive is not strong or if the person feels that he/she cannot perform the action, then he/she is less likely to act, and is said to have low motivation, or, in extreme cases, no motivation.

As mentioned earlier, motives may be of different types. Some actions arise from a biological or physiological need, which people do not have much control. Such motives are common to the entire animal kingdom. But there are certain crucial and higher order needs, which are common to human beings. These human motives are unrelated to biological and physiological needs, but are related to feelings competence, social acceptance etc.

Motives for Entrepreneurship

There are many motives for anyone wanting to put up a business. The reasons or motives, and how strong they are, have a great effect on the business itself. Some of the motives are shown below (note that there may be more other motives as well and it is for the facilitator to help the woman understand what her motives are).

Monetary

- To earn a living
- To become rich
- To attain financial stability

Social

- To gain prestige/status
- To be recognized in society
- To be a model to others

Service

- To employ people
- To help the economy of the community

Familiar

- For future welfare of the family
- To please parents
- To please husband/wife

Self Fulfillment

- To be independent

- To achieve something through business
- To use personal capacities to the maximum

Entrepreneurship and Motivation

As said in the previous paragraph, setting up and running a business needs strong motives or the entrepreneur should have a high degree of motivation. Setting up and running a business is not an easy task and success does not come in a short time. Therefore, if the entrepreneur has motives, which need immediate fulfillment, it is quite possible that she may feel disheartened. This would result in a loss of motivation, causing further difficulties for the business.

The type of motivation and the degree of motivation is, therefore, very important for an entrepreneur. She must realize that there will be many difficulties in business and should still be prepared to continue with the business in spite of them. This is where the facilitator has a great deal of responsibility in helping the women develop motivation that is long lasting and is very strong.

Of the different types of motives that have been listed earlier, it has been seen by psychologists that motives relating to self fulfillment or self-actualization are the longest lasting and exert maximum influence on the human being. This is because the actions motivated by such needs are long lasting themselves and self-actualization is a life long process. Also satisfying these motives leads to the person feeling happy and confident of her abilities and to the realization that she is capable of even more. This, in turn, leads to further actions to realize those capabilities giving rise to a benevolent outward spiral of confidence, ability and happiness.

How Do We Help Women to Motivate?

As seen earlier, there are different kinds of motives leading to entrepreneurship. One of the first steps in motivation is to help women understand what their motives are and which urge them to start an enterprise. Understanding one's own motives goes a long way in making her conscious of it, and this itself starts the woman on a path of motivation. The more conscious she is of her basic motives, and the more she thinks about them the greater is the intensity of the motive. In turn, this leads to high motivation.

In conclusion we can say that motivation in general is an important determinant for entrepreneurial growth and development in society. However, under the broad spectrum of motivation certain motives have been found to be significantly related to entrepreneurial behaviour such as.

- The need for achievement
- The need for power.
- The need for affiliation.

Entrepreneurial motivation should be viewed in terms of set of motives of varying strengths such as a high need for achievement, moderate need for power and low affiliation motive.

For an entrepreneur, to have the right kind of motivation is more important than technical and/or management skills for success in starting a new business. An entrepreneur who is motivated would go in for the right technical and managerial expertise required for her business.

Enabling

If motivation brings in a strong sense of "I want to do" then enabling can be said to bring in a sense of "I can do" we, therefore, call enabling the process by which the woman not only gains certain abilities, but also gains the confidence that she is indeed capable and can learn all the other abilities needed for entrepreneurship, which she has not yet acquired.

The important fact is that she knows something and she knows that she can learn the rest.

This confidence in oneself and in one's abilities provides the woman with the energy to focus her motivation and transform it into action.

For a Woman, Enabling Means

- A strong sense of "can do"
- A feeling of control over her life
- Being aware of her strengths & weakness
- Being aware of her values and attitudes
- Being confident of her ability to achieve these goals
- Most of all, leading an active and fulfilled life.

For women enabling is a crucial factor. Given the social milieu and the secondary role most of them play, women often do not see themselves as strong individuals, but as extension is of others in society-somebody's daughter, wife or mother. The process of confidence building in women involves their looking at themselves as individuals in their own right and realizing their potential.

This does not mean spurning of the earlier relationships. In fact, with the increased confidence, the same relationship takes on a new with deeper fulfillment. It is true that the process may lead to some anger in some women, but this is to be treated as a passing phase and the facilitator must work with the women and build up their confidence even further, where the anger is no longer necessary.

Self Awareness (Discovering One's Own Potential)

The potential in any woman is surrounded by the instincts and drives, positive and negative reinforcement experienced in her life and the mask, i.e. the nature presented the society covering all these aspects. In order to understand the potential within the woman, you have to unmask and look at the reinforcements, analyse the potential objectively and relate it to her instincts and drives. Only then she would be able to look at her and understand and realize her potential.

In order to start this unmasking process and explore this potential, the entrepreneur is asked the question "who are you". She will probably respond by giving her name, while it is her identifying tag. If asked the question again she may give a deeper answer, which refers to her nationality, social position, work or achievements.

All these refer to external sources of identity. Asking the question yet again may even make her focus on her inner sources of identity such as her beliefs, values, interest, worries or ambition in life. The questions can be asked again and again until all the answers have been exhausted and she is left with a wordless experience of her own being.

That is probably the nearest she can get to the answer. The encounter with who, she really is, her real identity, is often a powerful experience though it is difficult to articulate or communicate.

Different people express this identity in different ways. Most women seem to gain their identity through reference points themselves. Fewer women seem to gain their identity from internal source within themselves. However, every woman definitely has some internal sources for her real identify. It is the knowledge of these internal sources of her identify that relates to self awareness for a woman. Some internal sources are those relating to her self-image, her beliefs, values, desires, hopes and needs.

It is the knowledge that she has an independent identity, rooted in her own perception of herself that provides the start to the confidence building process. At his point it is very essential to continue counseling the woman. The process of looking inward tends to break down earlier notions of herself that the woman had and it is necessary for her to "rebuild herself, mentally and emotionally, so that her conscious image of herself is positive and is based on her own internal source.

Positive Self-esteem and Self Image

Positive self-esteem = self confidence + self respect

In the process of entrepreneurship, all too often the entrepreneur has to contend with setbacks and problems, such experiences, in turn, can lead to loss of confidence, or some disheartening and loss of motivation. Such experiences, which lead to a lessening of motivation are usually, called "negative, reinforcements" in behavioural terms. Conversely, a good experience leads to higher motivation and is called "positive reinforcement". Dealing with positive reinforcements is very easy as well as comforting. In the case of negative reinforcements, the effect, they have on the woman depends a great deal on her self-esteem. A woman, who is "enabled" with a clear understanding of her capabilities and limitations, has confidence in herself and therefore, has a good amount of self respect.

Self respect is some thing that a woman develops as she acquires a sense of being a capable person and progressively becomes aware of her own power to choose her actions she experiences that she is right as a person, right in her characteristic manner of action and feels that she is good.

Self confidence It is a woman's confidence in the reliability of her mind. It is not the conviction that one can never make an error. It is the conviction that one is able to think, judge, know and correct errors.

The integrated self-confidence and self-respect is called a

positive "self esteem." Positive self esteem is an important factor in determining how a woman reacts or responds to reinforcements that she receives from the environment especially the negative reinforcements. Since the environment in entrepreneurship continuously requires her to choose among alternatives, she is constantly obliged to make decision concerning her interaction with the environment.

Threshold Crossing and Breaking Barriers

Once the entrepreneur identifies where she is in her journey of life and acquires or cultivates a positive self-esteem, then she needs to clarify where she is going. Many people set off in several directions simultaneously and feel that their energies are split in so many definite ways, that progress becomes difficult. Only by finding a direction, that honors and resolves the conflicts both internal and external, can a person create a sense of well being and progress.

A tortoise, its head is in its shell, does not show any sign of life. A tortoise moves only when it puts its head out of the shell. Similarly unless a woman makes a decision to act and sticks her head out, she will not be able to move forward. In the process of moving towards her goals, a woman has to make individual choices, which necessitate running into obstacles and having to work within various constraints. The choices she makes are invariably influenced by her past experiences and mental and emotional blocks that such experiences may have caused. These blocks may be clear and conscious in her mind, or as is most common, vague or unconscious.

Unless and until these blocks are confronted and resolved a woman finds it difficult to break out of the barriers that she faces

This means that the blocks need to be raised from the

subconscious to the conscious level of woman's mind and she has to be helped in looking at them free from past colouring.

By raising these blocks to conscious awareness, a woman can choose a way of dealing with them. Blocks faced by women are of different kinds. Some of the blocks or barriers which stop a person from progressing are:

- Lack of motivation
- poor self image
- Certain beliefs
- guilt
- Fear
- resistance to change
- Poor skills or lack of skills (communication, managerial etc.)

Identifying and understanding the blocks are important elements in breaking barriers. After identifying the blocks, defining them as problems and outlining the efforts of these problems, a woman needs to identify the cause of the problem Brainstorm solutions to the problem, analysis each solution, select a solution and implement it. After implementation, one needs to monitor and adapt so that it facilitates one's progress.

Experience sharing by women entrepreneurships have helped many women in understanding their blocks which hinder their progress and also in understanding their potential. These blocks act as barriers, forming a threshold which the woman does not form a known area to an unknown area. Most women think that they are comfortable where they are, not because they are really content, but, as they fear the unknown that lies beyond, with all its consequences.

Identifying and understanding the blocks is essential, but not enough for a woman to over come them. Paradoxically, it is only when she actually performs some action that symbolically cross the threshold that she is able to experience the fact that blocks can overcome.

In order to help the woman perform such an action, the counselor asks her to do something small may be even trivial, which she had always wanted to do but never did. This is done only after the unmasking and the subsequent confidence building process are complete and the woman has faith and confidence in the counselor.

This activity is called "crossing the threshold" and can be done only with the counselor present. Such an activity usually brings about a tremendous sense of freedom, of breaking of bonds and leads to self-confidence in the woman.

CONCLUSION

Empowerment is a process of transcending from a lower level of development to higher level of self-realization. It is to raise above a limited context or perspective to a wider field of vision. The process of empowerment enables the entrepreneur to be highly enthusiastic and energized to accomplish whatever she has set for herself. It enables her to manage and come out of any difficult situation and makes her look at obstacles as a part of life and positive challenge. It is empowerment that ultimately produces the energy to overcome the most difficult blocks or barriers in her life.

Points to Ponder

Often it is hard for people to recognize their feelings, particularly, negative feelings. Ability to discriminate feeling needs to be acquired. A woman needs to have her feelings accepted and value before she can learn such discrimination.

A woman has a choice of different types of behaviour, when she expresses her feelings, she can

- Express them verbally;
- control them by no longer identifying with them;
- release them, in a non-destructive manner and in an appropriate place; and transmute or transform them into constructive actions, artistic creation or self realization.

These become important for the facilitator or the counselor, when he/she tries to understand the blocks that a woman may face. Remember when a woman feels a sense of well being it can help her to

- find out what she wants and what is right for her
- Communicate her priorities and needs to others;
- emphasize with others and with herself;
- motivate her to grow.

Sources: Entrepreneurship Development for Rural Woman, Vol.1, Facilitator Hand Book, Editor Dr. S. Siva Kamagun Devi. Asia & Pacific Centre for Transfer of Technology.

6

Women and Society

Introduction

In the historical evolution of mankind, woman has been an economic partner to man, besides her biological and social roles. It is said that it was the woman who discovered the possibility of domesticating plants for food and beginning the rudiments of hoe-culture. It was so when man was in the hunting and gathering stage. Since then, through agricultural and industrial revolutions, she has been an economic partner in the family of man. She started the enterprise of food cultivation and later adopted bartering the food articles for other necessities of life.

Over a period of time, certain patterns of life and the division of labour changed. She worked on the farm, kept the house and reared the children. Further, in the Indian (Hindu) context, when social stratification (caste-system) and occupations became institutionalized, the womenfolk confined themselves to the chores assigned to them and assumed by themselves in their respective occupations or professions. Again over a period of time, class distinctions emerged, accompanied with restrictions, norms of time or social sanctions and certain freedom enjoyed by women. In the general society, high- and middle -class women tended to confine themselves to the biological and social roles of rearing children and keeping the house. But in the case of economically lower-class women, besides their bio-social roles, they had equal or more than equal share in the economic activities of the family.

In the recent past, as a result of increase in women's education, industrialization, urbanization, social and occupational mobility, the emergence of nuclear families, westernization, politico-social movements and changes in the value system, some educated women have taken to certain careers. Some, compelled by economic necessity, have taken to small business and trade.

Woman has been the economic partner of man in several fields, but when it comes to entrepreneurship, man seems, outwardly, at any rate, to dominate the entrepreneurial world. Entrepreneurship is not simply a masculine job as army or navy. She, too, is equally endowed with the psychological qualities and managerial abilities that matter in successful entrepreneurship. Sometimes, the environment and opportunities are the same both for man and woman. But interestingly, the entrepreneurial activity in the traditional developing societies has been restricted to man. Time has come when one starts thinking, exploring and working towards the woman entrepreneurship.

Women clientele could be categorized into several groups, based on residence, education, family occupation or profession, socio-economic level and employment. Based on the above criteria, we can think of the women in terms of: (a) rural, (b) urban, (c) educated employed, (d) educated unemployed, (e) land owning, (f) landless, (g) tenant farmer, (h) artisan groups, (i) supporting the family economically, (j) just keeping the house, (k) enjoying considerable leisure, and (l) just thinking of doing some small business or activity to supplement the family's income.

Two Objectives

The entrepreneur maybe either an individual or a group;

both are equally significant in less developed countries. Though choosing an enterprise is an individual's free-choice activity, in most cases, it is the decision of the family, the kin-group or the community. There is need to stimulate and influence the group so that the potential entrepreneur gets the kind of encouragement and support to start and run the chosen enterprise. Women constitute a significant lot in the group.

Women are to be reached and motivated, so that they extend a helping hand to men in their entrepreneurial venture and the women too, take to some enterprises.

The Clientele

Though the focus here is on entrepreneurship among women, the men folk are not ignored in the approach; they are also to be influenced and worked with, so that the women secure the freedom and support to venture into some entrepreneurial activity with social and cultural sanctions and not hampering their familial roles. The development of entrepreneurship could be simultaneous among men and women, as the latter constitute fifty per cent of the population.

Now the question is: Who are the prospective woman entrepreneurs? We can think of three general groups of women, amongst whom we can attempt entrepreneurial activity. They are: (a) the rural, (b) urban, and (c) the tribal women with variables such as, education, skill, aptitude, abilities, economic level, employment and entrepreneurial opportunities distributed among the three groups in varying degrees.

A word here about the tribal women. Women in the tribal societies contribute as much as or more than men to the family income. In a relative sense, they enjoy greater social and economic freedom than the women in the caste society in India. For instance, the tribal women in Manipur, Mizoram, Meghalaya and Nagaland are in the forefront in running small business and trade. In Imphal, a market complex is exclusively run by women. A similar practice obtains in Aizwal (Mizoram), where one can see a large number of women carrying on business and trade in garments, textiles, cosmetics, electronic goods, etc. There is much scope to develop entrepreneurship among tribal women.

Potential Entrepreneur

In general, the potential woman entrepreneur may be a teacher, a nurse, a secretary, or any woman stuck in a job that does not fulfill her or which does not bring sufficient income. The entrepreneurial woman is simply the woman who wants to start her own business.

The personnel in the various agencies engaged in socio-economic developmental programmes, more especially, the extension functionaries of the entrepreneurial development agencies come into contact with and address mostly the tasks of the menfolk in the client community. Seldom are women contacted. The decision-making is not done by man alone though he is in the forefront in all business and commercial activities. The woman is there behind many decisions that concern social and economic issues of a family. It is a paradoxical situation that though woman is in the background, her understanding and choices influence the kind of decision a man takes and the course of action he pursues.

It may be said that women are the missing link in the chain of entrepreneurial development programmes. We may briefly look into the problems, and prospects of entrepreneurship and the approach towards entrepreneurship development among them. This situation leads us to a brief understanding of women and their socio-cultural milieu.[1]

Women entering the field of entrepreneurship is not altogether new and depending upon the family occupations, the services rendered by the family traditionally, women have been there as part contributors to the income of the family. This contribution may be in terms of their knowledge and skills and support to the enterprise of the family. However, statistically speaking their involvement especially in case of some ethnic groups and classes is rather very marginal. This marginality of their involvement or their association with the enterprises varies from community to community and from culture to culture.

There are several contributing factors and hurdles or barriers to promotion of entrepreneurship especially among the women in the rural areas. We may just mention the barriers or impediments in generating entrepreneurial activity among the women folk. First, it is the individual, then the family of the individual and the third dimension is the community wherein the individual lives. Within the community you have the kind of leadership, which may either facilitate or block the movement of women taking up entrepreneurial activity. One may approach the question of EDP among women either from the macro level or from the micro level. Both these approaches are essential to build a conducive entrepreneurial climate in the community. To begin with one has to identify the potential entrepreneurs and try to motivate them and at the same time prepare the family and the community for extending their support and encouraging the individual woman to move into some entrepreneurial activity. As mentioned above, the promotor of entrepreneurship amongst women may begin with the individual, identify the individual, find out the educational level, knowledge and skills and the level of motivation on the part of the individual woman, whether she has any idea, any inclination go get employed or shoulder some responsibility in initiating some entrepreneurial activity. Sometimes, the individual may not be ready to venture into action for it is something new that she is asked to enter, but at the same time she may have some interest and may be ready to take some risk in starting some enterprise. So long there is no objection from the family members and that she is prepared to venture into some enterprise then there will be no problem. In such a situation, it is up to the industrial development agency, or entrepreneurship promoters to provide her the support so that she can make a beginning. Sometimes, in rural tribal settings based on their tradition and value system especially in the case of women venturing into a new kind of economic activity they may not get the support or approval from the family and the community. Here comes the task of educating and mobilizing support to all the individual women, families and the communities, so that as mentioned above, over a period of time you build a climate which will facilitate the individuals and the families moving into activities which would generate employment and income for them.

One has to take into account the kind of leadership that obtains in the community, the influence of leaders on individuals. We may note that in several instances, though the individuals are ready to take to some entrepreneurial activity they look for a nominal formal approval from the opinion leaders in the community. In any community the leaders play a dual role support or obstruct. Some are positively oriented towards individual development. Some of them try to have a grip on the community, exercise their authority and command over them. They entertain some fear that once the individuals especially some entrepreneurs earn money, generate employment, become economically sound, the leaders may find that kind of a change in development threatening to them. The idea here is, that all the leaders are not positively disposed towards development among the members in the community. Therefore, whether the leaders are positive or negative, the industrial promotion agent has to prepare the leaders so that they do not discourage women taking to entrepreneurial activity. We speak of this kind of situation in traditional type of communities.

When it comes to educated woman members coming from liberal type of families who are looking for opportunities to better their economic status, one may not find social-cultural barriers preventing them taking up enterprises. One may think of several levels of potential entrepreneurs in the population. In some cases, one has to prepare assiduously in respect to the lowest layer of the potential entrepreneurs. In some cases, one has to start right from the beginning which will be mostly of motivational nature and in other cases it will be helping them in respect to location of a site, financial and technical assistance and in most of the cases in marketing of the products. Especially, in traditional type of communities, this is the way to motivate women and prepare the ground for their venture into entrepreneurial activity. It is empowering women through entrepreneurial activity. The employment they generate, the income they contribute strengthen their status in the family and in the society.

We may also think of the existing traditional occupations and services rendered by different communities that pave the way for entrepreneurial activity with improved technology, diversification of products and finding new markets. And at the same time going in for new kind of economic activities.

In the context of promoting entrepreneurship, one may think of the Hindu Jajmani System which has emerged and survived as an institution for centuries in India.

The Hindu Jajmani system which has gradually evolved and functioned as an institution for centuries in India has systematized distinctive occupations and activities among various groups of people. It has assured occupations to different groups which prevailed as a mechanism of interdependency amongst various communities in terms of goods and services. It has provided knowledge and skills for each occupational and servicing groups and each community was assured of occupation and service. These occupational and servicing groups for centuries never or seldom thought of moving out of their traditional prescribed occupations. But over a period of time, with the advent of industrialization and literacy and educational level on the part of the younger generation, some of the members in the family slowly moved out of the traditional occupations taking to other jobs and entering other services. Sometimes, inadequate means of survival within the traditional occupations or professions made people gradually go in for other kinds of livelihood pursuits. Here lies the encouraging climate among the traditional occupational and servicing castes for developing entrepreneurship.

Women's economic contribution more often has not been reckoned with. Their contribution in the family occupation or service has been rather invisible in many of the communities in agriculture, or in non-agricultural fields. But once they go in for some enterprises managed by them it brings some change in their status and behaviour. It is likely to bring a change in the attitude of male members towards women and change in their behaviour towards them. It builds confidence among women and their self-esteem is likely to increase. In a larger sense, it is utilization of human resources for productive purposes creating wealth in order to better the living standards of people. It is to generate entrepreneurship among the poor since most of them being landless. It will help them self-employed and also the enterprises they may take to would sustain them and better their living. Some of the enterprises may be based on the knowledge and skills they have at the moment. They are to be trained providing them knowledge and technical and managerial skills required in respect to the enterprises they have started.

As mentioned above, efforts are to be made modernizing or improving local community based enterprises wherein the new woman entrepreneurs may make use of their traditional knowledge and skills. To start with sometimes, one may think of enterprises based on the locally available resources to meet the local demands of certain articles or services.

We may have to sometimes assume that there is zero entrepreneurial activity in a particular community. With that kind of presumption we have to go in for educating and motivating the individual, the family and the community. Things were started only in this manner earlier also. One may have to think of all possible ways of earning or increasing income and creating wealth.

The suggestion here is clinical approach to EDP among women: Here it is a question of slowly bringing about change in the value system, attitude or disposition on the part of the prospective woman entrepreneurs and the members in the family concerned. It should also extend to the community from wherein the women are expected to emerge as small entrepreneurs.

Approach

Entrepreneurship is a function of certain socio-cultural setting. Though the focus in the book is on developing entrepreneurship among women, we cannot exclusively approach women and motivate them to take to some entrepreneurial activity. We can expect emergence of women entrepreneurship when conditibns are created by the state in terms of policy measures and diverse type of assistance i.e., to b extended to the neo-woman entrepreneurs. Keeping this in mind, we have included a detailed picture of entrepreneurship development, rural industrialization pertaining to Asia and in particular in respect of India. These chapters could be taken as a kind of a general background or socio-economic environment which, it is believed, would facilitate emergence of women entrepreneurship.

In developing entrepreneurship, we need to take women

into account, understand and motivate them gradually bringing about changes in the culture of the group.

The natural resources in a given area and the associated economic and industrial activities and the skills thereof provide a base, a starter for some enterprises that may be taken up by the potential woman entrepreneurs. Further, based on the resources, skills and needs, some new enterprises and services can be listed and canvassed among the prospective woman entrepreneurs. While surveying, identifying and recommending enterprises, the location, qualifications, skill and market for the products and services may be borne in mind. There can be enterprises that suit rural, tribal and urban conditions. Some maybe rural-specific and some urban-specific and still some may be common to both rural and urban conditions. For instance, dairying, poultry, food products, hotel industry, vegetable-vending kitchen-gardening (on commercial lines), weaving and making incense sticks, may suit the rural clientele. Similarly, enterprises such as radio-repairing, dry-washing, watch repairing, running libraries on commercial lines, preparing ready-made garments, tailoring, toy making, hand-printing and running salons, can be the enterprises that the towns-folk can take up. Some activities, whether they are connected with manufacturing, processing, producing and servicing goods can be taken up both in the rural and urban areas.

It may be relevant here to mention that Small Industries Service Institute (SISI), Indore, Madhya Pradesh, India has been for some years now, organizing training programme for prospective woman entrepreneurs and helping them to start their enterprises. In the Silver Jubilee Commemorations publication *Small Industries for Woman Entrepreneurs*, 1979, the SISI has listed 114 enterprises that may be taken up by woman entrepreneurs. The suggested enterprises fall under: (a) chemical industries, (b) food industries, (c) paper-conversion industries, (d) hosiery and textile industries, (e) ceramic and glass industries, (f) leather industries, (g) engineering industries and (h) electrical/electronic industries. Most of the above industries are urban-oriented.

Institutional Support

The promotion of entrepreneurship among women depends very much upon organization, education, stimulation and motivation of the clientele through concerted and systematic approach, focusing on the individuals and groups. This objective can be accomplished gradually through working with people and demonstrating the possibilities of women venturing into entrepreneurial activities, accompanied with adequate rewards-economic development and social growth.

The existing official machinery can carry out this task of EDP among women. These agencies may lay emphasis on the clientele under discussion and also fix up some targets in their case and there can be sub-plans for EDP in the case of women.

With respect to EDP among women, the women development or welfare organizations can work towards creating an entrepreneurial climate among women and also can help the industrial personnel in stimulating, identifying, motivating and selecting prospective woman entrepreneurs.

At the district and sub-district levels, the women welfare workers who are supposed to be in the know of, and in close touch with the womenfolk, can play a significant role in creating awareness and can guide the potential woman entrepreneurs. The question that matters here is how best the existing development agencies work, mobilize, communicate and coordinate their activities in reaching the potential woman entrepreneurs and create a climate for entrepreneurial movement among them.

Women's Clubs

The women's clubs that have been organized in rural and urban areas during the past decades are under the purview of the district women welfare agencies. They are feeder institutions and are voluntary. However fragile or strong and enduring they may be, they serve as sources and internal agencies for entrepreneurial development among women. Some of the clubs organize and perform some economic activities, such as sewing, knitting, leaf-plate-making and food processing, besides their social, educational and cultural activities. The woman workers are in touch with these bodies. At the moment, the women's club can be a potential and a promising institution that can be utilized under the EDP among women.

Self-employment

One potential source for woman entrepreneurs is the educated women who plan and prepare themselves for some career. Till now, we have not made any significant effort in creating awareness of self-employment or entrepreneurial possibilities while the women are still on the campuses of educational institutions or universities. The entrepreneurial development agencies, along with the management of educational institutions, may organize training programmes for the senior students during summer holidays, exposing them to the feasible enterprises they can take up after completing their education. They should be acquainted with the scope available in the areas of their specialization and the kind of support they can expect from governmental agencies in starting and running their enterprises.

Role of Educational Institutions

It is not only the self-generated motivation on the part of the individual and encouraged by understanding the need and demand for a particular service and good and influenced by a conducive environment, the individual takes initiative towards some entrepreneurial activity. Besides this self-motivated initiative and action on the part of the individual, the educational institutions right from the high school and up to the university level could play a very positive and significant role in motivating the students of both the sexes to venture into self-employment, or go in for some enterprise. Today, entrepreneurship development as a regular course is being offered in some of the institutions both at the graduate and undergraduate level. One may even think of introducing a course on entrepreneurship development in schools of management, and in polytechnics. Even if it were not to be a regular course with some credits, the institutions may invite personnel from District Industries Centre, Directorate of Industries and Khadi and Village Industries Commission and several other organizations who deal with promoting entrepreneurship and arrange guest lectures to the students. When you look at the other developed countries in the world, the percentage of people going in for employment in government is far less and on the other hand, they take to self-employment or get into industrial and service sector. Therefore, there is a need to sow the seed of EDP right at the high school and college level, so that, the students prior to their graduation may plan to go in for some kind of entrepreneurship. In a systematic way this kind of awakening and motivating the individuals prior to their leaving the school or college to think of various potential alternatives for entering into some profitable kind of enterprises. Such an approach would bring in substantive change in the economic development generating young entrepreneurs.

Of several educational institutions, the women polytechnics are a rich and promising area where the development programme of entrepreneurial motivation can be organized as a regular extra-curricular activity. Further, the institutions which offer courses in agriculture and home sciences, horticulture, sericulture, sylviculture do offer innumerable possibilities of self-employment in the fields the students study and specialize.

Further, organizations such as Lions Club, Rotary and Jaycee can take up entrepreneurial development programme among women.

Social Infrastructure

The multiplicity of agencies that function in the field of entrepreneurial development can with comparative ease provide the physical and economic infrastructural facilities for starting enterprises. But the formidable problem that we face in promoting entrepreneurship among women is resistance, apathy, shyness, inhibition, conservatism, poor response, all governed by cultural traditions, value system and social sanctions. Interestingly, women, in general, share several traits. There is no denying the fact that it is an uphill task to develop entrepreneurship among women. But one encouraging feature is that there is no zero level of entrepreneurship and we are not operating in an entrepreneurial vacuum in the case of women.

What is required is a congenial entrepreneurial climate which motivates, encourages and facilitates individual and group movement conducive to entrepreneurial activities. Today, the entrepreneurial climate is rather lacking both among men and women. But there exists the potential and the prospect.

The entrepreneurial climate consists in creating positive attitudes among the people, developing new needs, increasing the level of aspiration, helping people to see the possibilities of alternative and remunerative avocations, preparing people to accept changes in the economic and social spheres and working through important persons, leaders and local institutions, all converging on entrepreneurial movement and activity. This aspect of building up the social infrastructure can be accomplished only through educating and organizing the community and ED Promotional agencies providing the requisite physical and economic infrastructural facilities.

Training

The training of personnel for promoting entrepreneurship among women is an essential part of the programme. The emphasis in the training programme is on understanding the culture and the styles of life and the kind of approach, skills and strategy required in promoting entrepreneurship among women, besides the other inputs that go into the general entrepreneurial development programme. *(Please see Appendix-I for further details)*

Conclusion

The primary or the principal factor in developing entrepreneurship among women is not in terms of infrastructure or financial assistance or identifying an enterprise but it is a question of clearing the ground for their movement into entrepreneurship. For ages together they have been confined to a secondary role and confined to the homes and you have to bring them out so that they become self-reliant, self-respecting enterprising people. Though there are several factors contributing to the emergence of women as entrepreneurs, the sustained and coordinated effort from all dimensions would pave the way for the woman moving into entrepreneurial activity thus contributing to the social and economic development of the members of the family and thereby gaining equality and equal importance for themselves. In a word, one cannot think of empowerment of women minus the economic component. The main economic component should be in terms of women entering diverse fields of entrepreneurship.

In sum, we may say that the women constitute a significant segment in the population. Till now, they have not been the focus of entrepreneurial development. The need today to develop entrepreneurship among them is imperative, the development of entrepreneurship among men and women being simultaneous. The question of EDP among women is a question of choice, priority and organization.

REFERENCE

1. E. Desingu Setty, 'Developing Entrepreneurship Among Women' in *Man and Development*, Vol.II, No.3 (Chandigarh: Centre for Research in Rural and Industrial Development, 1980).

7

A Model for Developing Agro-Enterprises Among Farm Women in Asia

In the preceding chapters, we have briefly looked into the ways to go about establishing small-scale and cottage industries and development of entrepreneurship, here is a model which focuses on development of agro-enterprises among farmwomen..

Woman has been the economic partner of man in several fields, but when it comes to entrepreneurship man seems, outwardly, at any rate, to dominate the entrepreneurial world. Entrepreneurship is not simply a masculine job such as the army or navy. Woman too, is equally endowed with the psychological qualities and managerial abilities that matter in successful entrepreneurship. Sometimes, the environment and opportunities are the same both for men and women. But interestingly, the entrepreneurial activity in the traditional developing societies has been restricted to man (Setty, 1980).

Although women "hold up half the sky", as the Chinese saying goes, until recently they have remained invisible in most development plans. Where programmes have addressed women's productive capacity at all, they have tended to incorporate a welfare bias rather than promoting genuine opportunities for economic independence. As a consequence, rural women in many developing countries find themselves bypassed by the social and economic advantages accruing to men. Dixon (1978) attributes this neglect of women by the development planners mainly to the following four factors:

(1) Male dominance in decision making in international and national planning agencies, as well as the under-representation or non-representation of women of these bodies.

(2) The "invisibility" of rural women's productive activities because of their concentration in the informal sectors of the economy, in subsistence agriculture, and in the home.

(3) The primitive kind of technology used by women in domestic work and agriculture which requires solution in small-scale intermediate technology rather than the grand scheme so favoured by planners and

(4) The powerlessness of the women themselves, resulting both from their lack of economic leverage and from cultural restrictions that severely limit their ability to press for policy changes on their own behalf.

However, the picture has gradually changed. Increasingly, international agencies are turning their attention to the integration of women in development as a strategy for improving economic conditions and promoting the adoption of family planning. Attesting to this concern are numerous resolutions from the 1974 International Women's Year Conference in Mexico City, and from the voluminous background papers and UN agency reports preceding and following these conferences. Individual donor governments, too, are expressing interest in policies linking development with the status of women and population questions.

The Percy Amendment to the U.S. Foreign Assistance

Act, for example, requires that the provisions of the Act "shall be administered so as to give attention to those programmes, projects, and activities which tend to integrate women into the national economies of foreign countries, thus, improving their status and assisting the total development effort". Thus it could be noted that the leverage of good intentions already exists at the international level and in many cases at the national level, and what is needed are concrete proposals for action and research.

With increasing attention recently being paid to rural women, the major bilateral and multilateral aid agencies are apparently looking for fundable projects that would promote the integration of women in development while simultaneously leading to a reduction of births. The World Bank in India for example, has funded smaller projects that employed rural women in the production of goods with export potential. The IRDP in Bangladesh has received a large World Bank loan to build a family planning component into the rural women's cooperative scheme.

The "Credit Scheme for a Training-cum-Production Centre: Income Generating Activities for Women", funded by FAO in India, in collaboration with non-governmental organizations, aims to develop centers accessible to rural women for promoting various types of small-scale cottage industries and agro-based industries. It hopes gradually to diversify the training to include other appropriate and profitable income generating activities e.g., machine embroidery, quilt making, woolen and cotton handloom weaving, processing of marketable food products and others. The immediate objectives were to provide employment for a specific group of 500 village women and to establish the main training-production centre so that the village women could be trained to produce goods of improved design with a traditional embroidery called "kasooh".

The findings of a comprehensive study on "Rural Women's Participation in Development" published by the UNDP (1980) propose that for rural women new initiatives are particularly urgent in matters of agricultural production, cottage and small-scale industry, credit, marketing, energy, technology, education and training.

Asian Women at Work

Throughout Asia women have been making an important contribution to family income. The lower the socio-economic level of the family, the greater the proportion of total income contributed by women. More and more women are bringing cash to the family budget, either from the sale of grain received as payment for labour on large landholding, as cash pay, or small sums derived from a multiplicity of secondary pursuits such as weaving, sewing, mat making, and the preparation and sale of snacks.

Markets in Southeast Asia, from Myanmar to the Chinese border, are dominated by women selling small quantities of fruits and vegetables, grown by themselves or bought from others. In the Philippines, women are self-employed in low income, low prestige, traditionally feminine types of work which permit them to look after home and family. Filipino women also care for chicken and pigs, fetch water, perform household tasks and fish by traps. Petty trade is carried on mainly by women.

In Laos, petty trading in village shops is mostly in the hands of women: they purchase fruits and vegetables from middleman and sell in markets.

In Nepal, during the slack agricultural season, men may leave home on trading ventures or go to India for seasonal work; many men serve abroad in Gurkha regiments. Women brew beer, distill liquor and sell the products.

The Sri Lankan women are more important in economic activities in the dry zone than in the wet zone. As family income rises, women and girls are withdrawn from labour, working only on the family farm during seasonal peak times. The head of the family decides who will do what work.

Women in the tribal societies of India contribute as much as or more than men to the family income. In a relative sense, they enjoy greater social and economic freedom than the women in the caste society in India. For instance, the tribal women in Manipur, Mizoram, Meghalaya and Nagaland are in the forefront in running small business and trade. In Imphal, a market complex is run exclusively by women. A similar practice obtains in Aizwal, Mizoram, where one can see a large number of women carrying on business and trade in garments, textiles, cosmetics, electronic goods etc. (Setty, 1980).

Thus it may be observed that most Asian women prefer work that can be carried out in or near the home, to avoid conflict between their roles as homemaker and wage-earner. A widespread source of income is the care of domestic livestock and the sale of their products. Women invariably look after scavenging chicken, milk and feed cattle in the Indian subcontinent, attend to poultry and often cattle in Indonesia and Thailand.

A recent study of six Asian countries by Campbell (1990) attempts to provide some insights into the complexities of rural economy and society in a comparative framework of Asia and highlights some of the social changes that may have occurred in rural communities that have transferred from traditional cultivation practices to mechanized farming. The case studies of India, Indonesia, Korea, Nepal, Philippines and Thailand find that finance and record keeping are largely in the hands of the senior women of rural households. Women have become less dependent upon agriculture and are used less in the cultivation of land. This has freed them for other occupations and allowed a greater diversification of the economic base.

Need for Developing Entrepreneurship among Farm Women

Most rural women's work remains outside the cash sector, which so far has debarred their economic activities from being quantified and included in national income statistics. Urban-based planners, according to Epstein and Watts (1981), should take the blame. These planners lack familiarity with village life, therefore, they hardly take into account women's economic importance not only in their indirectly productive activities as household managers and reproducers of labour, but also in their income-earning roles as farm workers, traders, etc. Female labour is thus still excluded from any concerns for increased rural productivity.

In the developing countries it is observed that unemployment and underemployment are greater for women than for men. Moreover, increasing the efficiency of agriculture has been widely shown to have adverse effects on the employment of women, due to the realignment of tasks in the sexual division of labour. Only now it is beginning to be realized that plans for development must have components aimed specifically at women, if women are to benefit from them. In this context, it has been suggested that the upgrading of women's productive activities by the provision of income-generating employment outside the home may break the cycle of rural poverty and high fertility characteristic of economically stagnant rural economies. The employment of women is expected to function as significant prong in strategies to increase productivity and alleviate poverty. Women's earnings raise total household income. Their earnings are of particular importance if they constitute one unit of an income-generating partnership.

To meet their survival requirements, households have practised division of labour, based on sex and age, long before Adam Smith ever propounded the advantages of specialization. Improved domestic technology is an aspect of rural development which has so far received far too little attention. It must precede any attempt to enable women to get more involved in direct productive activities. It is also an essential part of the improvement of the quality of rural life, and moreover it is likely to facilitate the formation of more active female pressure groups in rural Asia.

Efforts to promote small enterprise development in rural areas have, until now, been directed towards men only. Women are equally endowed with motivation and managerial capabilities in starting and running small enterprises located in their own homes or communities. Promoting and developing such entrepreneurship among rural women will require initiative, encouragement and support from the development agencies.

Experience has it that the new farm technologies often result in displacement of farm labor, increase in leisure time and surplus agricultural production. This opens up opportunities and incentives for developing alternative income-generating activities within the community. Potential areas are utilization of agro-products in small processing enterprises and the allocation of redundant female agricultural labour to off-farm employment. It must be recognized that as long as total income in most of the rural communities of Asia is inadequate to maintain acceptable standards of living for the family as a whole, attempts to improve the position specifically of women are not likely to proceed far beyond the realm of good intentions. This calls our attention to the urgent need for developing entrepreneurship among farmwomen.

Agro-enterprise for Women

There are several issues involved when one thinks of the entrepreneurship development among women. One is widespread ignorance about the kind of work farm women do. It is intended that the collection, in one place, of this much detail about the work they do should help planners and programme implementers at all levels, as well as donors, to learn about the aspects of household and rural economy that women are in charge of. Such information not only establishes the fact of women's integration in the household and rural economy, but it indicates why they must be included in rural development efforts to increase production and provide equitable distribution. At a very practical level, it indicates which rural extension services must be directed to women in order to be effective in increasing food production.

Though choosing an enterprise is an individual's free-choice activity, in most cases, it is the decision of the family, the kin-group or the community. There is need to stimulate and influence the group so that the potential entrepreneur gets the kind of encouragement and support to start and run his enterprise. Women constitute a significant lot in the group (Setty, 1980).

The agro-enterprises to be promoted for such a client group constitute a special entity. The philosophy behind the modern concept of agro-enterprises is integrating industry with agriculture for planned, harmonious and balanced growth and development of the two, encompassing all the operations from primary production through processing to the marketing of ultimate products, including by-products.

Such agro-industrial development implies the growth of industries in rural areas through interdependence on agriculture under a system of mutual and complementary output. It is a process of simultaneous growth of industry and agriculture, in which the output of one serves as the input of the other and vice-versa. It signifies the proximity and affinity between agriculture and industry (Setty, 1991). In view of this, some important resources and their industrial uses where women could be self-employed are recommended (*For further details, please see Appendix-III (A)*)

The principal agricultural resources found commonly in Asian countries are paddy, sugarcane, barley, corn and maize, cotton, coconut, cashew nut, tea, coffee, jute and other fibre crops. Such resources and their by-products permit many known and some less known industrial uses. The list of items appended here though not exhaustive, may form the basis for agro-industrial promotion (*For further details please see Appendix - III(B)*).

The Model

The primary purpose of the proposed model is to aid in the development of the strategies for creating employment and generating income for the rural people in general and the womenfolk in particular.

The majority of population in developing countries lives in the rural areas with employment provided by the agriculture sector. About two-thirds of the employment for a total of three-fourths of the rural population in the developing countries is provided by agriculture alone. The present model could form an important component of employment generating as well as small-scale industrial development programmes (SSID). More specifically, it is expected to provide the necessary prong to the entrepreneurship development programme (EDP) efforts in respective countries.

As an approach, the proposed model could stand by itself that is without being integrated as a component of an EDP or SSID programme, it could be taken up as an approach by a development agency in its efforts to identify, train and promote potential entrepreneurs. Figure-1 presents the basic structure of this model.

It is misconception that planning economic activities for women requires any special expertise and different techniques. With some training, women from the villages are able to perform almost all primary sector activities with ease and confidence and, therefore, it is wrong to assume that they can do only special types of activity. Expertise is, however, necessary for identifying characteristics of different groups of poor women in mobilizing them, in assisting them in organization building, in identifying sources or fund, training and other inputs. The model proposed for developing agro-enterprises for farmwomen in Asia aims to serve as an aide to the change agents. It presents a pragmatic approach to trainers, implementers, as well as planners.

Objective of the model: The model is expected to help the users in reaching and motivating women, so that they extend a helping hand to men in their entrepreneurial venture and the women too, take to some enterprises. Although, the model focuses on entrepreneurship among women, the menfolk are not ignored in the approach; they are also to be influenced and worked with, so that the women secure the freedom and support to venture into some entrepreneurial activity with social and cultural sanctions and not hampering their familial roles. The development of entrepreneurship could be simultaneous among men and women.

The specific objectives of the model could be stated as:

1. To assess the industrial/entrepreneurial potential of the agro-products in the study area, including the availability of human and material resources and consumer demand in the local communities.
2. To provide training and resources for economically

FIGURE 1

A Model for Developing Agro-enterprises among Farm Women in Asia

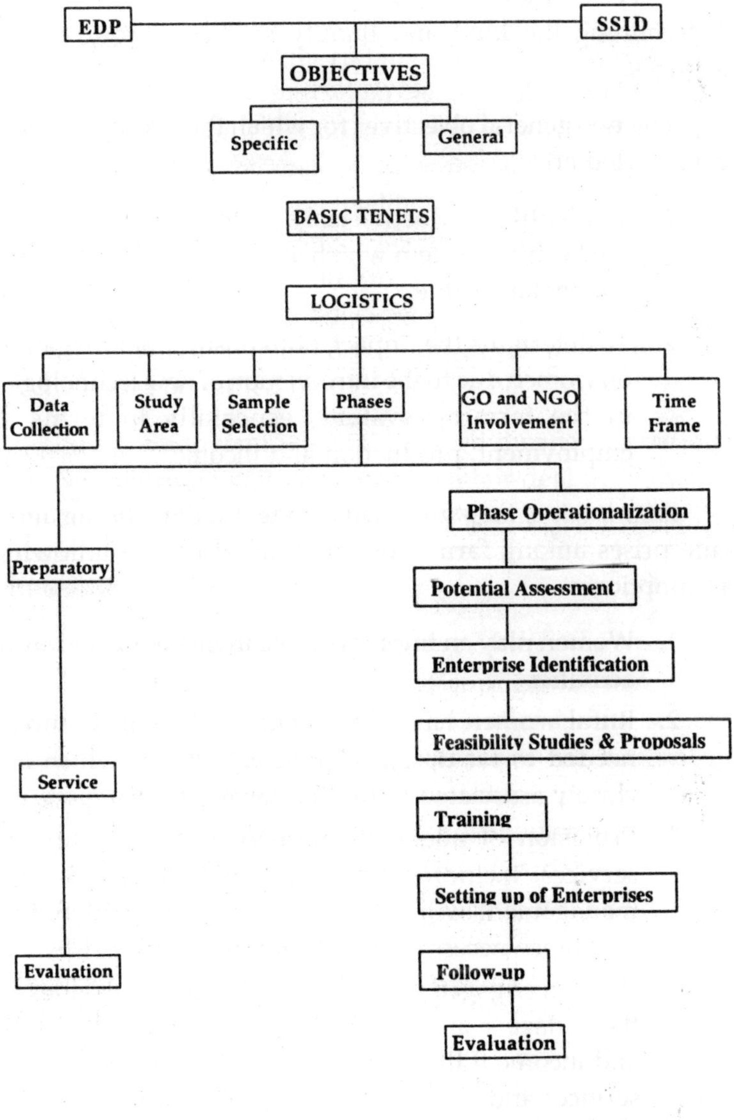

gainful activities and to create an atmosphere in which women can pursue them.

To enable women to have direct access to the resources and services they need as women and a direct voice in determining the kind and quality of these resources and services.

The two general objectives for which this model has been constructed are:

1. To identify productive tasks performed by women in the farming system which are not generally ascribed a monetary value.
2. To determine the impact, both positive and negative, on women due to the introduction of new technologies in the farming systems especially in terms of employment, production and income.

Basic tenets of the model:- This model for developing agro-enterprises among farm women is based on the following assumptions:

1. Women play an important role in income-generating activities.
2. Rural women have the labour, skills and resources needed to set up agro-based enterprises which are closely associated with their farm activities.
3. Provision of adequate infrastructure and support services, including training in technical skills and management will give women the motivation and assistance necessary to develop new enterprises.
4. Women engaged in farming and related activities in the village communities can increase productivity and income if they are given required resources and services and institutional and policy support within the existing socio-cultural and economic system.

5. Demonstration of economic benefits will motivate rural women to develop entrepreneurial activities.

MODEL LOGISTICS

I. The Method of Data Collection

Data are to be collected through an industrial potential survey. Individual and group interviews could also be held. Secondary data are to be obtained from development agencies on natural resources and the field crops, animal husbandry, forestry, and fisheries enterprises in the study area. Primary data are to be collected on the most promising resources and their potential used for developing agro-based enterprises for women should be assessed.

It is proposed that the project based on this model could be carried out in the following three phases:

1. *Preparatory Phase.* In the preparatory phase, field workers would be engaged in general information and orientation work, which would consist of sensitizing the men to the importance of women having access to improved technologies and of informing the women about the types of income-generating activities available and how these can help them. The women would also be taught how to organize themselves into groups or cooperatives so that they can collectively purchase needed technologies when credit becomes available. During this phase, the technologists and field workers would also identify priority needs and collect cultural and socio-economic data for consideration while promoting income-generating activities.
2. *Service Phase.* In this phase, credit would be provided to women's groups and cooperatives to help them take up an activity. They would be taught how to

operate and maintain the equipment. They would be given training (for instance, in soap making, vegetable gardening, or some other money earning activity) so that any released time can be used productively and savings are generated to pay back loans and maintain equipment properly. When necessary, credit is to be provided to enable the women to purchase any tools or equipment related to the money-earning activity. Progress should be monitored on a regular basis and advice given on how to overcome any technical, financial, marketing or social problems that arise.

3. *Evaluation Phase.* Finally, the scheme or programme would be evaluated in terms of impact of the entrepreneurial activity on each member of the household and the community as a whole. This would clarify what, if any, further policy changes are needed.

In order to follow the phase-wise programme based on the model, the following steps are proposed:

Step 1: Potential Assessment. First, a study and assessment of the potential for agro-based enterprises in the target area need to be made. The questions to be raised and answered at this level are: (a) What do the rural women do in the rural economy? (b) What are the bases for cooperation and conflict among rural women? (c) To what extent are women engaged in moneymaking activities? (d) What is the balance of power between men and women? (e) Are there women leaders? Or are there any potential women leaders?

Step-2: Enterprise Identification. Second, identification of specific new enterprises for recommendation to rural women is to be made. At this level, attention will be focused on identifying agro-based rural industries with consideration to (i) the resource based rural industries which involve low capital and simple technologies and (ii). the rural products which enjoy a considerable demand.

Step 3: Feasibility studies and proposals. Third, feasibility studies based on the resources available in the target area, including market, financial and technical analyses are to be prepared. Preparation of small project proposals along with the feasibility in terms of (i) practicability and (ii) profitability should be looked into.

The important questions raised would be:

On practicability. (a) Can such an activity be taken up and operated by the woman herself? (b) Is it convenient for the woman to take up? (c) Can it be easily sustained?

On profitability. (a) Does it provide more income? (b) Are there no marketing problems?

Step 4: Training. The fourth step comprises the identification and training of potential women entrepreneurs. From the sample mentioned below the potential women entrepreneurs are to be selected for training.

Step 5: Follow-up. The fifth step includes guidance and assistance given to the trained women entrepreneurs in establishing and running their small enterprises.

Step 6: Evaluation. Evaluation of the action programme.

II. Selection of the Sample

Women from the following two different socio-economic classes in the rural agricultural sector of the selected area could be the centre for focus in the project based on the proposed model:

(i). Women belonging to landless households or households with insufficient land to fulfill, on its basis alone, the family's subsistence needs and who, in addition to their roles as child bearers and as family domestic workers, need to hire themselves out as wage labourers to help provide an adequate income for themselves and their families.

(ii). Women belonging to small cultivator households, which have adequate land for subsistence but which have to depend essentially on family labour for cultivation and who, in addition to their reproductive roles and domestic chores, need to do some manual work on the family farm, although they do not have to hire themselves out as wage labourers.

Women of agricultural labour households constitute a major focus of concern since, economically they are amongst the worst off and in many Asian countries they constitute the largest percentage of rural woman workers.

III. Study Area

A cluster of villages could be selected from the developing countries. The project using this model could be taken up simultaneously in the selected countries involving the local Department of Small-Scale Enterprise Development (Ministry of Industry, Department of Small-Scale Industries). The local Department of Small-Scale Industries could be involved in the identification of potential woman entrepreneurs and suitable small-scale enterprises and organizing the training programmes and the follow-up support systems to help the identified potential woman entrepreneurs in establishing and running their enterprises.

IV. NGOs Involvement

Experience has it that besides the government, few NGOs are actively involved in promoting small enterprise development among rural and urban women. When it comes to urban areas, we have, what are called livelihood projects, especially promoted among the slum dwellers in metropolitan centers. Some of the NGOs operate in limited jurisdictions covering especially the underprivileged and weaker sections in the community. If partnership of such NGOs could be secured in the project as partners or, sole agencies in terms of identifying the entrepreneurs and candidate enterprises for different types of individuals and groups, it would be more effective and it would also serve as a demonstration of successful entrepreneurial development among women which may have a spread effect in the neighbouring areas. The project could also be extended, wherever it is feasible, to involve both the Government Department of Small-Scale Industries and one or two NGOs.

The project could be spread over a period of two years for one cycle of operation.

Prospective Outcome

The model is expected to yield the following results upon successful operationalization:

(1) Enable women in need, of whatever class, to work for monetary gain.

(2) Women will become able to act in meeting their own needs and that of their families and will have alternatives to dependency on males.

(3) Women who contribute income to the family will have increased authority to make decisions, and increased access to resources enabling them to act on those decisions in the aspects of life and work which are already their sphere of responsibility.

(4) The economy will benefit through an increase in needed production from shifting rural women's work from domestic to commercial production, increasing family income and savings, thus, enhancing the fungibility of the womenfolk in the household.

(5) It is likely to empower women and alleviate their poverty.

When used as an approach, the proposed model is also expected to help indirectly the development agency to:

(1) Study the development and dissemination of labour-saving technology for household activities, particularly in rural areas.

(2) Examine the role of women in the unorganized sector, for instance the contribution to family income, measurement of productivity in various activities etc,;

(3) Examine the appropriateness of census data for analysis of the position of women and monitoring of their position over time;

(4) Calculate cash contributions by rural women to the family income.

Conclusion

The concern for gender development is unquestionable and imperative. The only meaningful approach to enhance the economic and social status of women is through enabling and facilitating them through self-employment and income-generating activities.

One can think of several approaches to remedy the gender imbalances in development, but one substantive approach which is close to the available natural, material and human resources is the one that the present model purports. The usefulness of this approach depends on how seriously and faithfully it is translated into action. Unless there is something exclusive, answering the cause and ameliorating the economic conditions of women, any grand designs and diluted approaches in the name of women development will hardly succeed.

REFERENCES

1. Campbell, M.J., (ed.), 1990, New Technology and Rural Development - The social Impact, Routledge, Chapman and Hall Inc., New York.
2. Dixon Ruth, B., 1978, Rural Women at Work: Strategies for Development in South Asia, Johns Hopkins University Press, London.
3. Epstein, T.S., and Watts. R.A., (ed.), 1981, The Endless Day - Some Case Material on Asian Rural Women, Pergamon Press, Oxford.
4. Setty, E.D., 1980, Developing Entrepreneurship Among Women, Man and Development, Vol. II, No.3, pp.92-96.
5. Setty, E.D., 1991, Rural Industrialization, Small Scale and Cottage Industries in Asia, UNCRD Working Paper No.91-2, United Nations Centre for Regional Development, Nagoya, Japan.

Note:- Please See Appendices-III (A), III (B) & III (C)

"It may be noted that in Appendix-III (C), some of the items mentioned under Appendix-III (A) & III(B) are repeated. However, since the list of items is issued by the Small Scale Industries and Tiny Sector, Ministry of SSI, Govt. of India, 2000, and it may be mentioned that the list may be relevant to the prospective or ongoing entrepreneurs."

8

Collective Approach to Development of Enterprises by Women in Bangladesh

Introduction

Empowerment is both a means and an end in itself. Empowerment through legislative, political, economic and social means will facilitate development among women. Similarly any development measures encouraging women creating and providing opportunities to them in the field of especially entrepreneurship development would empower them. Empowerment and development are related to each other. One serves as means and the other as the end and vis-à-vis. While we speak of empowerment and development we have a dual approach simultaneously providing opportunities effecting changes, so that we can achieve twin objectives in respect to the women folk in any society. In this context, it would be interesting to look at a case what BRAC (Bangladesh Rural Advancement Committee) has done dealing with the poor and their development. As one could see, it was a collective and sustained approach where the poor were brought together wherein they gain the strength. As Mohd. Younis, the Father of Grameen Bank, has pointed out, "When the Poor stand alone they are poor, but when they are brought together they gain strength."

While discussing the dual objective of empowerment of women and developing entrepreneurship among them, the case study in respect of what BRAC has been doing in Bangladesh is quite relevant.

If we are looking for an organization generating a genuine, authentic, systematic, meaningful, enlightened and highly motivated popular participation of the poor in their poverty alleviation and social empowerment programmes, we can cite Bangladesh Rural Advancement Committee, popularly and widely known by its acronym *BRAC*. It is a non-governmental organization, perhaps the largest in Asia. A giant private organization working for the poor. It does not simply dole out relief to the poor and the disadvantaged but it works with them at the grassroots and steadily helps them help themselves. We may call it a process of development with dignity for the poor.

BRAC is a multi-faceted organization with diverse activities all converging in terms of its philosophy and strategies on two major goals: alleviation of poverty and empowerment of the poor.[1]

Formed in 1972, BRAC began its activities with the objectives of relief and rehabilitation of thousands of displaced people during the war of liberation. The rehabilitation task was carried out successfully and the normalcy has come back to the people. But this was largely a relief measure and so BRAC moved on to multi-sectoral village development programme focusing on the poor. Over the past twenty seven years since its birth, BRAC has emerged as a parallel agency to the national government in the field of development especially in reaching the poor.

Management of BRAC

A Governing Body is vested with the management of BRAC. The Executive Director and Founder of BRAC, Mr.

F.H. Abed is the Chief Executive Officer. Mr. Abed is the creative, imaginative and guiding force behind this massive programme of developing the poor. At the top, mid and field levels, BRAC is managed by development managers with years of professional experience. BRAC pursues a system of participatory and decentralized management. BRAC programmes are planned through participation of all levels of workers. Within the framework of programme plans, each level of management is encouraged to exercise appropriate authority, to embrace creative solutions and to generate innovations. BRAC provides its managers freedom to take initiatives which stimulate participation and a continuous search for excellence.

Since BRAC demands a high level of work ethics and performance standard not commonly found in Bangladesh, it decided to develop its management cadre from within the organization. Consequently, a policy of recruiting young people with high educational qualifications for placement at the lowest level of programme operation has been pursued over the past two and a half decades. This policy exposes potential managers to the dynamics of grassroot mobilization and problem solving. As a result, large numbers of qualified and experienced development practitioners stand ready to manage future expansion.

Over the years BRAC has pursued a vigorous policy of management development through training at home and abroad including post-graduate and doctoral level degree courses. It has set up its own Management development Programme to take responsibility for management training and value creation.

Bringing women at the top management is a valued policy of BRAC. This is done not only to promote gender equity but also for balanced development of the society. In pursuance of this policy BRAC has started grooming the potential woman workers for managerial positions.

Collaboration with Public Sector

BRAC considers it important to develop a system of effective collaboration with the public sector. It feels that such cooperation can enhance the capacity of people's organization and support of the process of development of the poor. Thus BRAC has established linkages with various Ministries such as Health, Relief and Rehabilitation, Fisheries and Livestock, Education etc. This cooperation has also been useful for the government to strengthen its existing programmes and increase their effectiveness. A few cases may illustrate the kinds of collaboration and their results.

BRAC assisted the Ministry of Health and Family Welfare in achieving the goals of its Expanded Programme on Immunization (EPI) in 124 up-zillas of Bangladesh. BRAC provided training to the government staff on programme management and created a demand for immunization at the community level through social mobilization. The results have been highly satisfactory both for the government and BRAC. Evaluation studies conducted by BRAC as well as by some external agencies have shown that the highest coverage of EPI in Bangladesh was in those areas where BRAC worked.

BRAC's poultry development programme is another illustration of collaboration with the public system. BRAC has trained several thousand destitute women on poultry rearing and vaccination of birds. These women, trained as vaccinators, have been linked to the government's department of livestock which supplies free vaccine. These women now provide vaccination services to the villagers for a small fee. By cutting the poultry mortality rate, the programme ensured increased production of eggs and birds.

Education, sericulture and family planning are some of

the other areas of collaboration. BRAC feels that such partnership with the public system can strengthen the process of sustainable development of the rural poor.

People's participation is accomplished through the social mechanism of forming Village Organizations both for men and women and their periodic meetings to deliberate over issues that various development programmes that are carried on by BRAC.

Over the years, BRAC has grown into a multi-faceted organization with more than 8600 men and women workers and a variety of development programmes in various parts of the country. Its basic rural development activities have until now been organized over 11,842 landless groups in some 5,414 villages. A separate Rural Credit Project was initiated in 1990 to institutionalize the credit component. The wide-scale Oral Therapy Extension Programme (OTEP) teaching a home-based oral solution for the prevention of diarrhea has reached all the households in the country expanding into a more extensive primary health care programme. The Women's Health and Development Programme, embarked in early 1991, aims to pursue a dual purpose of decreasing maternal and infant mortality. BRAC's non-formal primary education programme has so far opened more than 6,000 schools for poor rural children, especially girls.

BRAC activities include: Rural Development Programme (RDP), Rural Credit Project (RCP), Women's Health and Development Programme (WHDP), Training, Management Development Programme (MDP), Income Generation for Vulnerable Group Development (IGVGD), Rural Enterprises Project (REP), Non-Formal Primary Education Programme (NFPE), Research and Evaluation Division(RED), Craft Development and Marketing Services through Aarong and several other commercial projects.

Empowering the Poor Facilitating their Participation

Empowering is a social, psychic and to a limited extent a material (in the initial stages) process. It has to grow over a period of time in the once socially and economically poor and disadvantaged groups at the individual, family and the community levels and between both the sexes and amongst all the age groups. Empowerment in the psychic and social sense does not come about to the target population by receiving money and other material things alone.

The poor or for that matter any marginalized group can feel a sense of power when they are recognized, when their voices are heard, when they can choose and have their choice, when they are partners in decisions and deeds that concern them and the larger emphasize here that BRAC's approach to its twin objective of poverty alleviation and empowerment is through identification and organizing landless poor into viable, functional social groups. Here the dynamics or call it chemistry of development is interesting. Empowerment secures social strength, negotiating power, accessibility to resources and thus contributing to alleviation of poverty and the decrease in the poverty level is likely to increase empowerment, one supporting and strengthening the other.

BRAC has made a pragmatic approach in organizing the poor into groups with specific functions and responsibilities to be carried out by the general membership, office bearers and the small group leaders. With one strategic social stroke, it has facilitated and encouraged people's participation in their development. There is a fusion of the clientele group and BRAC as a development agency. The bridge between the development agency and the people is narrowed. This has come about what may be called as institution building that BRAC has successfully accomplished. As mentioned earlier, this organizational mechanism of institution building contributed a great deal to real people's participation. In this context we may briefly look into BRAC's objectives of development and the methodology of its organizing the clientele groups and the functions and some highlights of the Village Organizations.

Institution Building

Before we look into the institution building process in BRAC, a word on what is an institution is in order. The terms institution and organization are commonly used interchangeably and this contributes to ambiguity and confusion. Three categories are commonly recognized: (a) organizations that are not institutions (*e.g.*, a firm of lawyers); (b) institutions that are not organizations (*e.g.*, law); and (c) organizations that are institutions (*e.g.*, courts) or *vice-versa* institutions, that are organizations.[2]

To the extent that an organization has acquired special status and legitimacy for having satisfied people's needs and for having met their normative expectations over time, one can say that an organization such as BRAC, VO, has become institutionalized. In general, institutions, whether, organizations or not are complexes of norms and behaviours that persist overtime by servicing collectively valued purposes. Institutions are stable, valued, recurring patterns of behaviour. Institutions change over time, decay and some institutions are born. It is a continuous social process.

We find that BRAC has spelled out activities as underlying its approach to institution building *vis-à-vis* village organizations. They are[3]:

(a) Resource mobilization,

(b) Organizational discipline,

(c) Social corruption, vices, superstition,

(d) Financial discipline,

(e) Economic activities,

(f) Local body participation/influence, and
(g) Social justice.

BRAC tries to translate the above activities which may be taken as its objectives in empowering the landless poor and alleviating their poverty as follows:

(i) Remind people where they are, why they are, what they are,
(ii) Functional and consciousness raising education,
(iii) Leadership training and developing leadership,
(iv) Monthly issue-based meetings,
(v) Stimulating economic activities,
(vi) Secure for the poor the khas land, water bodies for fishing (ox bow lakes) and markets,
(vii) Secure for the poor the facilities meant for them,
(viii) Raising their political consciousness and social awareness,
(ix) Savings,
(x) Credit, and
(xi) Non-formal primary education.

BRAC's Institution Building

BRAC's institution building may be viewed as three pronged: within BRAC, in the client groups it served and with the development departments of the government. Within BRAC as an organization, the noteworthy and laudable procedures, norms, regulations, work ethics relate to personnel selection, training, job rotation, target fixing, monitoring, reporting and development communication within the staff and between the staff and the clientele system.

The whole process of setting up an Area Office, selection of villages in the service area, conducting of pre-survey, followed by detailed socio-economic surveys, identification of the landless poor, meeting them individually and in small groups and making them reflect on the deplorable conditions they live in, the scope and potential for their modest growth and development once they organize themselves into groups, forming them into what are called Village Organizations (VOs), for male and female members, followed by a series of training programmes, functional education, consciousness raising education, leadership, management and enterprise related education and training and the introduction of savings and credit system and the weekly and monthly meetings constitute the institutional building in the client system.

The functional relationship BRAC has established with the government development departments in respect to poultry development, livestock, fishery, apiary, sericulture and irrigation through Deep Tube Wells may be construed as mentioned earlier, institution building. In other words, the whole gamut of institution building revolves around new structure and functional mechanisms developed by BRAC in formulating, implementing and evaluating its programmes to empower and enrich the landless poor.

The Village Organizations (VOs)

The VOs as organized, monitored, supported, educated, motivated and developed by BRAC constitute the bedrock of its promotional operations in respect of the landless poor. The VOs provide a forum for interaction, mutual help, individual and collective initiative and social action. The secret of BRAC's success and popularity in serving the poor, owes a great deal to the VOs. One may imagine as to what would have happened to RDP and RCP and other programmes in the absence of VOs. BRAC's socio-economic programmes have filled in a vacuum which should have been filled in by the government and other agencies like Grameen Bank and NGOs. The landless poor in a helpless state with feeble hopes for a minimal meaningful life, found an anchor and hope in the VO which may become their own self-managed organization.

Structure of VOs

An Area Office covers approximately 100 village organizations (VOs)-50 for landless women and 50 for landless men, with a combined membership of 6,000 to 7,000. It is not in fixed ratio. We find that two-thirds of the VOs are female VOs. The minimum size of a VO is 45 and the maximum 55. Each VO comprises small groups of 5-7 members. BRAC has introduced an interesting principle that in the small groups of VO, there will be no close affinal or consanguineous kin. The small group is headed by a Secretary. The larger group is managed by a Management Committee (MC) consisting of 7 members, which includes a Chairman, a Secretary and a Treasurer. Members of the MC are either elected or selected for a period of one year and no member can be on MC for more than two terms, thus giving an opportunity for all members of group to serve on the MC over a period of time. The group meets once in a week on a fixed day and hour to organize their financial activities, viz., small savings and weekly loan installment payments coordinated by the *Gram Sevak* (GS) and once in a month to discuss the issues that interest the group, facilitated by a BRAC official - a programme organizer.

Growth of VOs

The VOs have been increasing in number as new areas are added under BRAC's constantly increasing volume of activity, with the same pattern of surveys, identification of the landless poor and forming them into VOs. The progress of the VOs up till the end of December, 1991 is shown in Table 8.1.

TABLE 8.1

Village Organization Status by the End of December 1991

Programme	*No. of branches*	*Villages covered*	*Village organi-zations (Total)*	*VOs Male*	*VOs Female*	*Membership (total)*	*Male*	*Female*
All Total	125	5,414	11,842	4,061	7,781	617,136	197,923	419,213
Total RCP+RDP	120	5,198	11,376	3,911	7,465	598,123	192,149	405,974
RCP	30	1,682	3,687	1,284	2,403	201,118	62,714	138,404
Year 6	10	568	1,232	424	808	69,222	22,539	46,683
Year 5	20	1,114	2,455	860	1,595	131,896	40,175	91,721
RDP	90	3,516	7,689	2,627	5,062	387,005	129,435	267,570
Year 4	20	982	2,468	259	1,509	126,760	44,190	82,570
Year 3	20	889	2,108	886	1,222	144,955	47,037	67,918
Year 2	20	924	1,917	577	1,340	96,966	28,001	68,965
Year 1	30	721	1,196	205	991	58,324	10,207	48,117
HSD	4	166	363	144	249	15,760	4,85	10,907
SP	1	50	103	36	67	3,253	921	2,332

Source: BRAC Report, No.1, December, 1991.

Emphasis on Female VOs

In the cultural context of Bangladesh, the idea of separate organization for women is prudent and pragmatic. BRAC's policy of emphasis on women's progress is reflected in the significantly large number of female VOs as of December 1991 (7,781) as compared to male VOs (4,061) and female membership (419,213) as compared to male membership (197,923).

Elements that Strengthen and Keep Going the VOs

We may discern two sets of elements or activities that strengthen and keep going the VOs. The first set of elements constitute the whole process of contact with the group members, motivating and mobilizing them and organizing them into larger and smaller groups followed by Functional, Consciousness Raising Education for all members and training in leadership and management for the selected members of the group. The second set of elements are the recurring, regulatory weekly and monthly meetings wherein the substantive activities of the group such as savings, loan repayment and life issues are transacted.

It is found that Functional Education is a key element in the process of institution building. An FE course is obligatory for all group members under RDP. It is also a pre-requisite for credit entitlement. FE plays a crucial role in conscientising the target population and emboldening them to confront the problems they face.

The process of preparing and educating the members of the VOs may be described as going through three phases: in the first year, it is mainly preaching the dos and don'ts. In the second phase which lasts for three years (RDP), it is preaching and regulating the members' behaviour in credit operations and other social programmes. The third phase (RCP) may be described as commercial relationship. It is a gradual movement and the whole process is institutionalization aiming at taking people to a state of self-reliance and sustainability. This is evident to a large measure in the field situation.

Effect of VOs on their Members

Based on the empirical evidence collected through interviews, meetings and discussions with the female and male members of VOs in several villages in the districts of Narsingdi, Pabna and Natore (several areas of RDP and branches of RCP) recently and corroborated by the non-members, the better off people in some of the villages, feel positive about the whole process of VO formation and its functioning.

The members of the VOs are especially, the female feel that BRAC through its VOs has kindled new hopes for them for a better life. It facilitated accessibility to credit and means to go in for self-employment in small enterprises and trade. The members expressed a sense of achievement that they have learnt to sign their names and are becoming aware of what they are, why they are, what they are, what they can do by themselves, the resources they have and what they can expect from external sources.

The members of the VOs who were interviewed were unanimous that the VOs have brought them into a forum for individual and collective growth. It brought in a new value system, group work ethics, group identity, group solidarity, group commitment, identity of a common cause, discipline, order, a habit of savings and a certain degree of social cohesiveness. The members have learnt that so long they live up to the functional norms of the VO, their interests would be served. Further, the female members of the VOs feel that they have gained some respectability at home and in the community by virtue of their supplementing their family's income through their earnings (some of them through self-employment in chicken raising, sericulture, deep tube well etc.) and by virtue of the new knowledge they have gained through education and training. The very fact of women sitting together exclusively and deliberating over polygyny, divorce, dowry, child marriage and ill-treatment meted out to them by the male members in their families is an unprecedented and an uncommon phenomenon in the local culture. In a sense, it is a revolutionary change, especially among the poorest-segments in Bangladesh society.

The members of the VOs indicated in the interviews that the credit programmes channeled through VOs foster and build discipline among them. It is a question of weekly payment of loan installment due, and a small amount of savings. This element of compulsory weekly payment and answerability to the peer group in the VO, is said to keep the members alert, sensitive and responsible in repayment. They say it is a question of individual prestige and honour, to pay on time, however poor a person is. Credit programmes through VOs not only contribute to economic betterment but also bring in a social behavioural transformation. What is to be reckoned here is the VO which serves as an organization comprising members and at the same time as an institution with a set of newly established norms, procedures, regulation, obligations, rights and duties, all of them ensuring the interests of the individual and the group.

The process of building rural organizations has already initiated considerable social changes, both individual and collective, in the rural disadvantaged people, especially women. Both men and women say that they are more aware of their rights as citizens and how they have been exploited by the rich. One-woman member of a VO (Putia, Natore Region) has put it, "To be together is strength".

In material terms, in six years time from 1981 to 1987, per

capita real income of the programme households has increased by 116 per cent while the real income of the non-programme households has declined by 15.6 per cent. Zafar Ahmed reports in the same paper that in the year 1981, 89.7 per cent of the non-programme households were below the poverty line and 10.3 per cent above the poverty line. But overtime, the poverty situation amongst the non-programme households has deteriorated. In the year 1987, the percentage of below poverty line households has increased to 97.4 from 89.7, while the households above the poverty line has declined from 2.6 per cent in 1981 to 0.3 percent in 1987.

But the situation in the programme households is almost the opposite. In the year 1987, the below poverty line households has declined from 91.2 per cent in 1981 to 25.9 per cent in 1987, and above the poverty line households has increased from 8.8 per cent in 1981 to 74.1 per cent in 1987. This shows an appreciable effect of VOs and the poverty alleviation programmes carried through them on the households who have been members of the VOs.[4]

Besides the weekly savings and loan repayment meetings, the monthly so-called issue-based meetings, however unspontaneous they are, they provide a continuous education to the members. Whether the issues related to khas land (government land), women's exploitation, dowry, child marriages, health issues, wages and village touts are resolved or not, they are deliberated upon in a group sitting. The group sitting normally encourages the individual to voice his/her feelings and opinions. The discussions are not casual but deliberate and purposeful. The individual in such group sittings leans on the group and the group sometimes shares the individual's views and supports the individual's stand. Public opinion sometimes for or against an issue gets crystallized and gains momentum in such group meetings.

Despite the positive and facilitating factors in respect of the monthly meetings of the VOs, there are a few limitations pertaining to them. Sometimes, the issues discussed in the monthly meetings are not the keenly-felt-needs of the members, that they have no resources and strength to resolve them, that the issues are not spontaneous, that the issues have deep roots in the value system and the tradition of the larger society.

Maturity Level of VOs

The VOs as chief instruments and vehicles of institution building are deliberately built-groups with certain values, norms, procedures, objectives, expectations, rights and obligations, and naturally each VO is to be treated as an unique social entity. It is a growing organization. The VOs are at different levels of maturity in terms of regular attendance to weekly and monthly meetings, payment of savings and loan installments and managing their individual and collective enterprises. It is gathered that some of the VOs in the RCP areas are managing the credit operations in the absence of BRAC personnel. The maturity of the VOs is manifest in the level of awareness, self-confidence and in articulation of ideas for development among the members of VOs. The case in point is the female VO in Baichitola village in Maheshpur Area Office, Pabna District. The women interviewed at Baichitola were quite clear as to the usefulness of the VO and that they would work towards advancement, strengthening their organization. They feel that the VO as a new forum has given them a social shelter for development. It is gratifying to note that the survival rate of the VOs is extremely high. The dropout cases of members of VOs and what is called disintegration of VOs has been negligible.

It may be relevant here to briefly describe the forming or dissolving of village organization. As mentioned earlier, the minimum number of members to form a VO is 45. Sometimes, it takes a couple of months to reach this minimum number. When members in the target population, say some 20 or 30 come forward for a VO, it is tantamount on their part to mobilize the strength in order to reach the minimum required and once the minimum is reached, the VO is formed formally. Similarly, when the members leave the VO on their own accord or asked to leave, when found that they did not satisfy the conditions to be members of the VO, the VO is dissolved. The reasons for the members voluntarily leaving the organization are their not being satisfied with the VO and inconvenient timing of the weekly meetings. The weekly meetings are held in the mornings before 7.30. It is fixed. An instance was reported by the BRAC monitoring Division that a Vo of fishermen had to be dissolved because, the fishermen found it to be impracticable to attend the weekly meetings in the morning at which hour they are to do fishing. The fixed hour of the weekly meeting inconvenienced the fishermen.

Future of VOs

The VOs as deliberately built vehicles of development of the landless poor, as the media at the village level for BRAC for its development operations are slowly taking roots in the social and livelihood pursuits of their members. It may be observed that the VOs in the context of prevailing socio-economic conditions of the landless poor, are the only foothold and anchor for the poor. The VOs are to be described primarily as associations or organizations of people and are in the process of establishing themselves as institutions. The VOs have a specific function to fulfill, to serve as an institutional, social-collective force to reach the poor to the basic minimum level of life. They may continue to be useful organizations, even after BRAC withdraws from them. However, it may be pointed out, that the VOs in a sense are transitory *ad hoc* organizations, unlike other social, economic and political institutions. Their survival is a question of their function in respect of the clientele for whom they were created. Even though, the VOs may not continue with the present structure and functions, they may continue in a modified form. The form it would take and the strength it would gain and the needs it would serve largely depend on the local clientele group.

The whole process and operation associated with VOs has brought in a great degree of self-regulation and maturity on the part of the VOs. In one sense, the VOs are project related and time-bound organizations meeting the economic and social interests of the group, but at the same time, they are not as pointed out above as enduring and strong as religious and social institutions such as a mosque, church, marriage or caste. It appears as though that the VOs require the paternal support of BRAC for some more years, so that the VOs become part of the social institutional fabric of the poor.

It is reported that many VOs have been developed into well-managed democratic institutions which have been able to resolve local conflicts, undertake joint economic schemes and lobby for government services. By being strong in number and unified in purpose, many VOs, it has been reported, have been able to decrease their dependence on local elite for guidance and advice in resolving conflicts and exploitation in money lending.

Conclusion

It will not be far from truth to say that BRAC has been exceedingly successful in applied social sciences in understanding the landless poor, their socio-economic milieu, in establishing rapport with them, in motivating them, organizing them and forming them into larger and small groups, imparting them with functional knowledge and skills, infusing confidence and hope in them inducing initiative in them for social and economic movement forward.

In building and in facilitating the VOs as live and active social organizations, the secret of the approach lies in BRAC meeting the psychological, social and economic needs of the landless poor at the individual, family and community level.

The structure of small groups within the VO, the constitution of a Management Committee (MC), the system of electing or selecting small group leaders and MC members, and the periodic rotation of leadership and the functions assigned to the group leaders and MC, reflect a system of built-in checks and balances, and also contributing equal opportunity to the members to participate in the activities for their betterment.

The VOs are growing people's institutions and they are at varied states of maturity and BRAC may have to continue nurturing them for some more years. The VO concept is a significant and innovating idea in BRAC's development strategy, the nucleus ingredients being credit, weekly savings and loan installment payment meetings and the monthly meetings.

The effects and impact of VOs on their members have been impressive. They have kindled hope in the members, unity, individual and group action for social and economic betterment.

While speaking of the sustained success of BRAC, we have to give extra weightage to the factor that BRAC's clientele are the disadvantaged and distressed poor. Organizing them and working with them is a laudable achievement. The poor and their participatory planning and development is a unique lesson that others may emulate.

Activities of Village Organization

Resource Mobilization	*Organizational Discipline*	*Social Corruption*	*Financial Discipline*	*Economic Activities*	*Local Body Participation*	*Social Justice*
Govt. Khas	Regular Meeting	Bribe Divorce	Budgeting Procedure	Income and employment generation activities	Participation in all local committees/ bodies expert pressure and influence for administration	Participation & influence on local issues
Food for work	Participation & collective development	Nepotism Dowry	Accounts	Conformity with social values appropriate to the local situation		Assurance of social fair services
General Wages	Human & Material control	Theft Polygamy	Proper recording of financial transactions			
Govt. Support Services	Intra & Inter organizational cooperation	Women status Usury rate of interest	Periodical reports/ statement			
Govt. Subsidized resources	Collective responsibility Documentation and record keeping	Unfair wages	Fund generation proper utilization of fund			

NOTES AND REFERENCES

1. The material in this case study is based on: (i) BRAC Report, 1990; (ii) BRAC 1992 Diary and (iii) the author's own observations in the field. The author would like to express his sincere thanks to BRAC and to the Donor Liaison Office, Dhaka.
2. Uphoff, Norman, (1989). *Local Institutional Development*, Kumarian Press; p.8.
3. BRAC documents (please refer to Appendix I for details).
4. Zafar Ahmad, (1991). *Group Approach to Empowering Women: An Emerging Development Paradigm from South Asia;* BRAC (1991).

9

Role of Banks in Entrepreneurship Development

In many instances whether it is men or women motivated to take to some entrepreneurial activity by themselves may not be in a position to finance their enterprises. Financial institutions especially the banks by their assistance to the neo or ongoing entrepreneurs really create a positive impetus for accelerating and successfully running the enterprises small or large. When we say banks, the concept stands for all kinds of financial institutions helping the entrepreneurs in their ventures. Here, we may briefly look into the role of banks in entrepreneurship development.

Entrepreneurship development as a socio-cultural concomitant to small-scale industrial development in the country envisages a multi-institutional approach. Of several institutions engaged in the promotion of entrepreneurship, banks constitute a significant factor. The paper attempts a brief discussion on the role of those banks could play as vital partners in the task and the approach to inducing entrepreneurial ventures on the part of a large number of people in the country.

Most of the Asian countries have of late adopted a deliberate policy of promoting and encouraging small enterprises as a strategy for the overall development of their countries. During the past five decades, India has been engaged in the task of promoting and developing entrepreneurship. Priority has been accorded to small-scale industries and stimulating and finding entrepreneurs. The agencies promoting entrepreneurial development try to cater to the needs of two types of clientele: the spontaneously emerging entrepreneurs, and those who have been induced to take up entrepreneurial activity by the promotional agencies.

Banks as Major partners in EDP

Though organizations such as the District-Industries Centres, Small Industry Service Institutes and other state corporations are engaged in the primary task of stimulating and supporting entrepreneurial activity, it is the banks and other financial institutions that have a major role in developing entrepreneurship. Until recently, the activity of EDP has been rather confined to the promotional agencies but today the banks are more involved not only in the financing the enterprises of the entrepreneurs, but they do associate themselves in stimulating, and motivating entrepreneurial activity.

The volume of activity on the part of the banks in entrepreneurial development is not only quantitative but also qualitative. There is a change in the orientation of the banks' role in this field. Today, the need and the emphasis is to go beyond the financing of the enterprise. It is to motivate and develop entrepreneurial climate in the community. In the context of developing entrepreneurship, we are dealing with induced entrepreneurs, and the banks have to take into account the limitations on the part of the new entrepreneurs, and appreciate their problems and their unfamiliarity with banking institutions.

The banks are not alone in the field; several agencies as mentioned earlier are engaged in the task of EDP and unless there is an inter-institutional coordination, the effectiveness of the whole activity will be lost. There is a need for teamwork in the case of agencies engaged in the task. The banker as a major promoter of EDP has to work in unison with other promotional agencies.

In the interaction between the banker and the customer, the communication on the part of the banker may be emphasized. Whether this interpersonal communication is oral or written the banker has to see that he speaks and writes to the customer in the wave length of the latter, so that the customer understands and appreciates the role of the bank, and the bank in turn, builds up confidence in the customer and contributes to the credibility of the bank. The personnel of the bank who meet and interact with the customer need a special kind of orientation especially in the case of rural-tribal entrepreneurs.

As we have mentioned earlier, the banks are to be participants in the journey of EDP right from the start of the process. Instead of indulging in mutual accusations (DICs blaming the financial institutions and the financial institutions blaming the DICs etc.), it is desirable that they join hands right from the beginning as a team and help the entrepreneur. Their association may have to start right from the point of identification of entrepreneurs and training them till the enterprise becomes viable.

It is presumed that banking institutions are facing some institutional problems. Since the banks are playing and need to play a significant role in EDP, the banking system has to attend to these problems and streamline the entire working system-internal as well as inter-institutional to help and facilitate rapid and sustained growth in the field of entrepreneurial development.

Role of Banks

With the nationalization of major commercial banks in 1969, banks have been playing a pivotal role in development financing - the small sector in particular, as also contributing to the development of backward regions of the country with the abetment of other developmental institutions.

In the context of the continuing paucity of entrepreneurial talent and scarcity of investable resources, commercial banks in India are playing a dynamic and positive role in igniting the forces of innovation and helping to foster and broad-base new entrepreneurship.

The functions of development banking include providing loans and working capital, formulation of project ideas, identification of specific projects suitable to local conditions, location and induction of new entrepreneurs into entrepreneurial activity and offering of technical and managerial guidance.

The public sector banks have been experimenting with wide range of special schemes to finance engineers, doctors, technically qualified entrepreneurs apart from promoting several schemes for funding self-employment endeavours among the weaker sections of society and the educated unemployed. Wherever possible, banks are collaborating with other developmental institutions representing industry, trade or commerce. Various schemes have been in the preparation of area potential studies, bankable projects and collection of information useful to potential entrepreneurs. For enterprises that are export-oriented, apart from financing, banks offer a wide range of services.

Specific to entrepreneurial activity, nationalized banks are guided in their endeavour to provide the following services:

- Assisting entrepreneurs in selection of industry, preparation and evaluation of project reports and conducting market survey.
- Providing short-term and long-term finance.
- Assisting in obtaining clearance, machinery and equipment.
- Assisting in setting up production and control processes, offer management and technical guidance.

EDP in Backward Areas

In order to accelerate industrial development in backward areas, banks are now involved in identifying industrial potential and motivating entrepreneurs to take up activities to exploit it. Banks are identifying and training entrepreneurs by conducting EDPs for them. Each of these programmes is followed by a support phase which provides counseling and consultancy services on a continuing basis. Banks are nominating project leaders to assist entrepreneurs in product selection and see them through various phases of the project until the unit is established.

Equity Fund Scheme

The State Bank of India introduced an Equity Fund Scheme in 1978 to help small but credit-worthy units to expand their equity base. First of its kind to be implemented in the country, the scheme extends assistance to small units in the form of loans ranging from Rs.5,000/- to Rs.50,000/-. The loans are repayable in a period of seven years, after a moratorium of five to seven years.

Secondment of Bank Personnel

Another contribution that banks are making towards EDP is by deputing their officers for posting to District Industries Centres as Credit Managers. These officers facilitate entrepreneurial activity by speeding up completion of formalities relating to sanctions, approvals, quotas, etc. These personnel are also actively involved in designing and organizing training programmes and coordinating such programmes in various parts of the country by preparing training manuals.

Conflicting Situations

While the policies and priorities of the Govt. are directed towards development banking and while the focus is on weaker sections and inducing entrepreneurship or industrial activity among the people who are new to these, and who have never approached the banks for any developmental purpose, the managers of branches who are the ultimate people in assessing, appraising and advancing loans to new entrepreneurs, meet with certain dilemmas; on one hand the directives from above are to lend money to a variety of customers, who may not, in terms of security meet the requirements, but at the same time, such customers are to be helped. And in such a context, the branch manager meets with a conflicting situation; whether he should discharge his functions as per the policies and directives of the government or not and at the same time ensure security of the money he lends and save his position. Many of the branch managers of banks today may be experiencing this kind of difficulty.

As it is, it is the promotional agencies like the DICs who make promises to the entrepreneur that he could/would secure bank loan for his enterprise. Sometimes, the promotional agency might not have looked into it in detail, the technical and economic feasibility of the enterprise and also studied the background and competence on the part of the entrepreneur; and when the entrepreneur meets the banker with all expectations, he fails to meet the requirements as per the banker. Since a number of institutions are engaged in the task of EDP, the banker as a promotional agent whose stake is around 80% in the venture of the entrepreneur, there is a dire need for the banker to be a major promoter and more involved in the process of EDP.

The banks could play a significant and substantive role in all the phases of entrepreneurship development. This could be on their own initiative and more often in collaboration with the DICs and other agencies in the field of ED.

Role of Banks: A Vision

The banks and other financial institutions as instruments of economic development and welfare of people have basically two things to work with: the material resources and the human resources. Wherever finance is a factor to harness and boost these two basic resources, it will be the banks that would play a prime and sustaining role. The banks as they are doing today, will extend their support and guidance technical and managerial, to the ongoing and potential entrepreneurs and establish themselves as pervasive and enduring institutions.

It may be the individual who meets the banker and who establishes an enterprise, but as the individual is placed in the social-cultural network, there is a need on the part of the bank to go beyond the individual, developing rapport with the group and the community of the individual. The banks are to motivate the individual, and to do so, they have a role to educate the community in which they operate, to make the bank a partner in the development of community resources and in raising the standards of living in the community. The banks through their activities and involvement over a period of time, should become an integral system of the individual and community development.

Statistically speaking, the banks today may be touching

only a small segment of the economic community in the country. The vision that one envisages is that banks extend their supportive limbs to all potential individuals and families in developing them so that they develop the resources towards attaining a meaningful quality of life.

10

Extension Education in Aid of Agricultural Marketing

Extension which may be called as an applied social science though began with agriculture, the very concept and the methods are applicable to several fields and especially to the field of small scale industrial development. One of the major problems that governs small-scale and cottage industries is marketing of goods and services. The chapter though here deals with agricultural marketing, the principles and the methodology are equally relevant and applicable to industrial extension.

It is paradoxical that agricultural extension tries to help the farmers with a package of improved farm practices to improve and increase farm production and productivity, but unfortunately, it stops with the production function only. Negligible attention is paid by the extension agency in helping the farmer in the marketing of the produce. There is a need for a new kind of extension education especially in helping the farmers in securing remunerative prices for their hard earned produce.

Before we look into extension education in aid of agricultural marketing let us briefly look into the concept and other dimensions of extension education.

(1) The Concept

(i) Helping people by means of education to put useful knowledge to work for them, is the essence of extension education.

(ii) The process of selling across new ideas and new techniques based on the knowledge of recent advances in science and technology to people who need to use it most is generally called "Extension" and the method is "Education".

(iii) It is working with people for their betterment.

(iv) It is a two-way communication.

(v) It is an applied education.

(vi) It aims at change in the ways of life of people through education.

(2) Activity-wise it Consists of

(i) Imparting of new knowledge

(ii) Imparting of new skills

(iii) Change of outlook/attitude

(iv) Supplies

(v) Services

(3) It is Based on the Triple Tenets of Faith

(i) Faith in the individual

(ii) Faith in democracy

(iii) Faith in science and technology

(4) As an Applied Education it Comprises

(i) Research findings

(ii) Accumulated field experiences

(iii) A judicious dose of appropriate technology

(iv) A body of philosophy, principles and methods based on behavioural sciences.

(5) Philosophy of Extension

(i) Extension has a philosophy of democracy.

(ii) Extension has a philosophy of co-operating with agencies that are interested in the common welfare of the people.

(iii) The basic philosophy of extension is centred around the welfare of the individuals and their families.

(iv) The great principles underlying the philosophy and extension are:

-- The individual is supreme in democracy.

-- The home is a fundamental unit in civilization.

-- The family is the first training ground of the human race.

(v) Extension has a philosophy of working out problems by group action, based upon the needs of the people and developed by the people.

(vi) Extension has a philosophy of education for all.

(vii) Extension has a philosophy covering teaching.

In the words of Seaman A Knapp *"What we hear we may doubt. What we see we may possibly doubt but what we do we cannot doubt"*.

(viii) Extension has a philosophy of truth and seeking for truth.

(ix) Extension has a philosophy of culture, it recognizes the customs, manners, conventions, norms, habits and behavior of the people.

(x) Extension has a philosophy of leadership (working with local leaders - developing new leadership)

(xi. Extension has a philosophy of the dignity of the individual.

(xii. Extension has a philosophy of local responsibility (people's participation)

(6). Principles of Extension

(i) Extension work must be educational.

(ii) Extension must work through understanding the traditions, customs, manners, and cultural values of the people so that it is in harmony with the culture of the people.

(iii) Extension work must be started where the people are, at their economic, educational, social, physical and cultural level. The technical knowledge, education, intelligence, capacity of understanding and group and physical standard should be considered.

(iv) Extension programmes should be based on the interests and needs of the people, which are determined by general acceptance and full support of those for whom they are chalked out. They should not have undue support from the government, except that of technical guidance and essential finances, the government acting as a catalyst.

(v) Extension should use democratic methods.

(vi) The implementation of an extension programme must be done by the people through their local leaders, the govt. agency giving proper guidance at the appropriate time.

(vii) As extension is a two-way channel, the extension worker should not hesitate to learn from the people while he helps them solve their problems.

(viii) The extension programme should be started first with those problems which appear simple yet, are very important and urgent in nature.

(ix) Extension programme must be flexible. It should permit adjustments to local needs.

(x) Extension work must always be educational. It should be persuasive and convincing but never coercive.

(xi) Extension must be a continuous and an on-going process.

(xii) It should evaluate and re-adjust or modify according to need.

(xiii) Extension programme must suit young and old, men and women. Extension work should be challenging and satisfying.

(xiv) Extension should work with all classes of people irrespective of race, creed, caste or community.

(xv) Extension work must not be combined with regulatory functions.

(xvi) Extension work must develop programmes gradually.

(xvii) Extension must promote the fuller utilization of local resources, both physical and human.

(xviii) Extension must keep in view the national policies and programmes.

(xix) Extension must use the community approach.

(xx) Extension work should be supported by technical expertise, services and supplies.

The proper recognition of the philosophy underlying extension work and applying the principles are bound to bring in the desirable changes among people to reach the ultimate objective of:

- Developing finer families
- Living in better homes
- On more productive farms
- In more progressive communities

(7) Main Components of Extension

(a) Programme planning

(b) Programme implementation

(c) Programme evaluation

-- The entire process of planning for agricultural marketing development implies a need for change.

-- The question then arises; change from what, to what, by whom, where, by what methods?

-- "If we could but know where we are now, and where ought to go, we could better judge what to do, and how to do it" - Abraham Lincoln.

(a) Programme Planning Focuses on

- Needs
- Resources
- Obstacles
- Processes - Steps
- Methods
- Evaluation

(b) Programme Implementation implies

(i) Organizing wide publicity to the programme

(ii) Drawing up a plan of action

(iii) Evaluating the programme during and after its execution

(iv) Four pillars of implementation

-- Research

-- Service

-- Supplies

-- Credit

(c) Programme Evaluation

Evaluation is an integral part of extension cycle. The following steps illustrate the place and importance of extension evaluation in the entire extension cycle.

1. Analyse situation
2. Identify objectives
3. Determine objectives
4. Plan programme
5. Decide on subject - matter or methods
6. Make changes as needed
7. Plan evaluation
8. Collect information
9. Summarize and report findings
10. Interpret and use findings

(8) Extension Methods in Aid of Agricultural Marketing:

(i) Farm and home visits

(ii) General meetings

(iii) Group contacts

(iv) Campaigns

(v) Working with voluntary and local leaders

(vi) Exhibits and models

(vii) Tours and excursions

(viii) Literature-leaflets, folders, circular letters and newspapers on prices and prospects of remunerative marketing agri-products.

(ix) Farmers' calls.

(x) Radio/TV programmes

Prior to helping the farmer in marketing his produce there is a greater need to help him produce more at an economical cost. This leads us to a closer view of the farmers' culture and psychology. Farmers share a village agricultural point of view. It is characterized by:

- *A holistic outlook*: Agriculture is a central activity, but it is only part of a whole, a connected way of life. For example, things which can be contributed to farm work like money and labour are constantly required to meet other family needs as well. The village family allocates these resources by looking at the whole.
- *Environmental Sensitivity*: All farmers have to be extremely sensitive to their environments in order to survive. They sense from collective and individual observation what elements of the environment are critical to their success as farmers. They are particularly sensitive to cyclical things like rainfall and storm patterns. More than any one else, they know the mini-environments of their individual farms intimately.
- *Local Focus*: Small-scale farmers especially know a lot about local things and much less about regional, national or global things. Most of these farmers' *interests* are local as well.
- *Self - Interest*: Each small-scale farmer has a list of priorities that helps him make decisions. This list defines a farmer's self-interest, which is a central part of his worldview.
- *Farmer's bias*: A farmer's view of things is colored by the physical and economic realities of farm work. These practical preoccupations are uppermost in a farmer's mind.
- *Tradition, fatalism and adaptability to change:* Carrying

out the tradition of farming is a normal and reliable habit of mind. This unchanging habit of mind is negatively reinforced by adverse outside opinions about village people like small-scale farmers. It has also been reinforced by the inability of tradition to contend with the new problems brought on by accelerated change. As a result, one of the extremes of a small-scale farmers' point of view is a kind of fatalism and feeling of impotence amid rapid change. The other end of the spectrum is a real, though often talent openness and adaptability to change, for farming is a constant process of successful adaptation. Like other people, small-scale farmers are ambivalent towards change.

For small-scale farmers with all the above characteristics, change is not worthwhile unless it is:

- Culturally appropriate
- In agreement with self-interest
- Respectful of tradition
- Clearly beneficial
- Not economically risky

Elaborating on economic risk, John Guy Smith offered this description in 1970: "Farming is subject to numerous risks from weather, pests, diseases, price fluctuations and other uncertainties. For the small-scale farmer, these risks are accentuated by his precarious economic condition. Much of a small-scale farmer's supposed conservatism is really a very shrewd attempt to avoid or minimize risk".

For example, Yigi Kamara grows rice in Sierra Leone. Every year, he grows his crop during May to September, the rainy season. In August and September, while waiting for the harvest, the stores from the previous year dwindle, and there is a "hungry season". Yigi plants millet and cassava on a hillside in March and April to deal with this. In order to grow rice year round and perhaps even grow a surplus, Yigi is thinking of building gravity-fed ditches and dikes in a swamp near his hill farm. The work will take four months, from January to May. Is it worth the effort? If he doesn't plant millet or cassava, will there be enough food this "hungry season"? Can he afford a shovel? Will his family be able to harvest, thresh, store and grind all the expected new rice? Can he sell some to make it worthwhile? What will his neighbours say? What about the old stores about the dangers of working in the swamp?

Small-scale farmers like Yigi change as individual cultural beings, as practical farmers, and as economic producers. They have considerable resources which they bring to bear on the problems of agricultural production and livelihood in developing countries:

- Expertise in local technologies and a variety of practical skills (eg. - masonry, carpentry, etc.)
- Expertise regarding local conditions affecting farming
- Status as independent economic unit
- Experience as farmers (traditions)
- A practical, critical viewpoint
- Adaptability
- Openness to producing a usable surplus
- Their limitations include:
- Lack of capital beyond family supply
- Habit of not investing in or using credit or outside inputs
- Interests and roles which compete with agriculture

- Little access to outside agricultural support services
- Reluctance to take risks

Along with these, however, there are factors from beyond the village which also limit the small-scale farmer's ability to deal with change. Most directed technological change, like the promoting of new practices, is based on the priorities and interests of development planners and leaders. This may exclude small-scale farmers or be irrelevant to their needs. Governments, development agencies and private business promote change this way. Example may be mechanization or mono-cropping which benefit large-scale farmers and foreign markets more than small-scale farmers.

Understanding People

Self-interest is the basis for all that a farmer does. The source of a farmer's motivation, whatever it may be in a given case, can be quite obscure to the extension worker. A farmer who seems to be strong, intelligent, financially secure, and aware enough to be successful, may still cling to his timeworn practices rather than opt for something new that he perceives to be against his interest. Neither repeated contact with an extension agent nor weighty scientific evidence will change his mind. The farmer's personal concerns - his religion, his desire for material possessions that he feels can be more quickly had by other means - are foremost in his mind. As such they are of primary concern to extension workers.

An extension agent needs to learn what the people he lives with value and consider important. This understanding is at the heart of the two-way communication process. Without it, the extensionist can gain no perspective on the appropriateness of the change he promotes. Nor can he determine what training methods are most suitable to local people's needs. Finally, and perhaps most importantly, the agent will be unable to emphasize or even communicate effectively with his friends and neighbours.

To learn anything about a person's self-interest requires time and shared experience. It takes hours sweating over plow blades, eating from the same bowl and walking together in sadness in a funeral procession. The "methods" used are informal, but the information gleaned is of crucial importance. The farming aspect of a villager's life, is connected with all other aspects. Labour resources for farm work are also labour resources required by virtue of kinship and money for improved livestock strains can just as easily become money for a niece's school fees. As an extension worker enters a community, and begins to make initial social contacts, he should take note of the various special interests people display in order to better understand how to go about his work.

Administering Credit

Farmers can exercise certain options only when they have the financial resources to do so. Accumulating these resources (*sometimes called "capital"*) is a necessary first step toward innovation and change. Farmers can accumulate resource by saving surplus income or borrowing resources from other sources. To the small-scale farmer saving presents a major problem because even the diligent application of customary farm practices does not often yield much surplus beyond home needs. One of the major catalysts of potential farmer innovation in developing countries is therefore the provision of credit.

There are many kinds of credit: informal sharing of a plough and family communal labour, village-level borrowing at the money lender's bank loans or input-credit schemes. Beyond the village level, credit is both a powerful tool and a potential cause of dependence. Cooperative ventures and capital-sharing are better ways to help small scale-farmers gain access to the resources for change.

Farmers themselves have various motives for using credit:

Consumer Credit

- *Survival* - when a crop failure or family illness causes the normal balance of home needs and harvest to go out of balance
- *Family and Social Obligations* - when a wedding, funeral or other family obligation requires money or resources not at hand
- *Consumption* - when something the farm family wants is beyond normal means
- *Investment in the Home or Cottage Industry* - when the farm family wants to buy a labour-saving device *(corn grinder)*, set up cottage industry *(sewing machine and cloth)* or repair/expand a house.

Agricultural Credit

- *Survival of Farm Enterprise - (e.g. securing seed or using a cultivator)* securing resources necessary to keep the farm going
- *Paying for Seasonal Labour* - Extra labour beyond the family may be needed to plant, weed or harvest when there is no surplus to provide wages
- *Acquiring inputs* - purchasing new tools, fertilizer or equipment to carry out a new package of practices
- *Increasing Efficiency* - sometimes farmers wish to substitute animal or machine power for human power for land preparation, for example, but need to borrow to employ it before realizing profits.
- *Marketing* - while waiting for a good price for their produce farmers may need to borrow to survive

- *Expanding the Scale of Farm Business* - to acquire additional land, to finance farm improvements *(clearing land, building storage facilities, constructing irrigation works, etc.)* to increase herd size.

It is important for the extension worker and farmers to understand why and how credit is extended to farmers. Credit being a form of dependence on resources beyond the farmer's control, it should be carefully and cautiously used. When the motivation of the lender is different than the farmer's motivation, there is much less opportunity for informality, for leeway with regard to the repayment of loan, and generally for sympathy for the farmer's precarious position. It is of prime importance that the extension worker and farmer seeking credit be aware of the motives of lenders.

Locally, credit can be extended as a social obligation or an aspect of friendship or family responsibility. However, credit is most often proffered in order to earn interest on the loan. This is the basis of commercial lending in and out of the village. Beyond earning interest, credit is loaned to facilitate sales, to assure the delivery of farm products or as public service through development projects. These motives are important to consider in seeking credit with farmers.

Most of the cost of a commercial loan is interest. Interest is calculated in a variety of ways, each resulting in a different amount of credit and a different costs. A common form of interest for small-scale farmers is the advance sale of crops, in which the lender is promised crops at current prices even though the price will be higher at harvest time. The different in price constitutes a loss to the farmer which is a form of interest, or credit cost.

"Credit terms" are all the conditions, including credit costs that are part of an agreement between lender and borrower. The usefulness of credit is a measure of the costs and terms versus the returns or results or credit use. Cost/benefit is calculated in monetary terms for most commercial credit, although timeliness, social appropriateness and other considerations also must be weighed. Most especially, the extension worker must help a farmer weigh the value of credit against the danger of dependency on factors beyond the farmer's control. This must always be part of the calculation of credit cost/benefit.

Because most commercial credit is extended for profit, it is rarely extended to the small-scale farmer. What with the uncertainties of weather, pests and diseases, the limited money-making ability of the small-scale farm, and the inconvenience of the administering credit to a far-flung clientele in rural areas, the small-scale farmer is often not considered a good "risk".

Other forms of institutional credit (through development project or agro product distributors), where these exist, are more readily available to small-scale farmers, but do not allow freedom to use the loan for any purpose. The loan must go to producing a certain crop or buying certain inputs. Thus, it is not easy to help small-scale farmers gain access to credit.

The process of acquiring credit involves, first, surveying a farmers' needs and clarifying with him the specific need to borrow capital. Secondly, the farmer and extensionist must inventory local credit sources. Next, extensionist and farmer must calculate the costs of credit and estimate the returns to the credit to determine the cost/benefit of employing the credit opportunities identified. This would include clarifying the terms of credit. Finally, the extensionist must help the farmer honor the terms of the loan and re-pay it when due.

One facilitating means for the farmer to secure credit is the village cooperative society. It can not only serve his credit needs but it can also be used effectively in marketing his farm produce at a reasonably better price at the appropriate time to the benefit of the farmer.

Providing Storage

Storage facilities constitute a significant factor in agricultural marketing.

Approximately thirty per cent of grain in storage all over the world is lost because of insects, rodents and moulds. For the small-scale farmers with whom extensionists work, this is a major problem of every day life. In villages, protection from such pests and moulds is lacking. Since this is a vital area in which to help the farmer, attention may be focused on the following topics:

- The Grain Storage Problems
- Grain Is a Living Thing
- Grain, Moisture and Air
- Preparing Grain for Storage
- Grain Dryer Models
- Enemies of Grain
- Storage Methods

Extension workers must focus some of their attention on issues beyond the production of agricultural products. By helping a farmer double his grain or vegetable yield, an extensionist may cause a major storage problem. Where does the new grain go? How does the farmer protect it from pests, moisture, thieves? The technical information necessary to solve storage problems is to be provided to the farmers. An extensionist can help by encouraging farmers to plan their storage strategies. Also, farmers can determine the most appropriate storage facilities and strategies with the extension worker's help. Finally, adequate storage is the most practical marketing tool a farmer has. He or she can hold onto a crop until prices become favourable if storage is adequate. The importance of storage facilities cannot be over emphasized.

Besides storage, pooling of grain by the farmers at the village level and also of grading of grain or agri-products are conducive to fetching better prices. These could be done through the local cooperative or Farmers' Association.

Marketing Agricultural Products

The extensionist is often in a good position to help farmers understand and participate more successfully in the marketing system. One of the largest and most uninviting areas the small-scale farmer enters by virtue of change is the market place. In it, he is subject to the forces of supply, demand, big business and government policies and regulations. Here, if anywhere, the farmer needs the direct assistance an extensionist can provide.

There are two main ways in which extensionists can help small-scale farmers successfully approach the market system: by organizing large-scale cooperative groups aimed at gaining local or regional price advantages, or by securing favourable prices through timely marketing, and or through cooperative marketing.

The process of helping farmers secure price advantages through timely marketing involves four steps:

I.Establish who controls the crop/animals at harvest and under what conditions

(a) Advance sales: farmers may receive payment in advance for a crop thereby obligating it to a buyer.

(b) Contracted sales: farmers may contact to sell a crop to buyer at a certain price for certain quality and quantity.

(c) Loan or credit restrictions on sale: farmers may have to sell a harvest when a loan payment is due.

(d) Tenancy or rent restrictions on sale: farmers may have to sell or give part of a harvest to a landowner or local leader due to tenancy terms, rent due or local customs.

II. Estimate the Costs of Holding Products Off the Market

(a) Estimate the average length of the "holding period" between the middle of the period of average high price and average low prices.

(b) Estimate roughly the cost of holding each product *(rice or any product)* off the market. *(eg.-storage facility cost or depreciation; storage losses; handling costs, etc.).*

(c) Estimate the profit or loss to the farmer by holding a crop out of the market. (This depends on the difference between the cost of holding out and the anticipated seasonal price rise).

Net Benefit:- Estimate Price rise - Estimated holding cost = Net Benefit (per unit of crop)

III. Decide to Hold Crop or Sell

Before a farmer can contemplate marketing strategies, his crop must be free at harvest of any restricting arrangements. If the crop is free at harvest, and if the net benefit of holding the crop out of the market place is significant (more than 25 per cent), then the extensionist can advise the farmer to hold his crop out until the price rises to the seasonal average high price.

There are other strategies for successfully participating in the market system. They are listed as one of the *TOOLS*, "interventions by Farmers in the Market System". This tool also serves to illustrate the points raised in this section.

ILLUSTRATION

THE FARMER HAS A VESTED INTEREST IN	BECAUSE IT DETERMINES	AND HE PROBABLY RELATED KNOWS IT'S TO	BUT HE PROBABLY DOES NOT KNOW IT IS RELATED TO
MARKET	Which commodities he can produce	Transport facilities, quotas, "monopoly" control	Effects of government policies
MARKETING STANDARDS (WEIGHTS, GRADES)	How he prepares his crop for market	Local customs. Buyers' preferences	Legislation. Processors' preferences.
THE AVAILABILITY AND QUALITY OF DIRECT MARKETING SERVICES (weighing, timeliness of payment credit, others	His choice of buyers for his crop	His personal relationship with buyers. The buyers' honesty. The buyer's resources.	Buyer's management ability How much it costs the buyer to perform marketing functions.
OVERALL MARKETING EFFICIENCY	Marketing margins and the price he receives.	How efficiently the transport and assembly functions are performed.	Management and technical skills. Productivity of labour. Many and varied costs. The less visible market functions.
COMPETITIVENESS OF THE SYSTEM	Marketing margins and the price he receives. His choice buyers.	Number of potential buyers, and alternative markets. The buyers' financial and political power.	Control of financing. National policies. The subtler forms of influence.
THE MARKET EQUATING SUPPLY AND DEMAND (price determination)	More than any other factor determines the prices he receives for his products, planting and harvesting schedules, and his farm enterprise mix.	Orderly marketing. Seasonal factors. The size of the total crop. Distant demand factors beyond his control.	National policies. How much of the consumer price is absorbed by the market process. Internal supply and demand. Costs of holding the crop.

TOOL

Checklist for Collecting Price Data

Source of Data (Current)

- Actual sales
  - -- reported by farmers

-- reported by local people

-- reported by handlers of products

- Reports by ministries, market publications, etc. (Historical)
- Recent memory

  -- as above
- Official reports and studies as above.

Analyzing Data

- Collect data from sources
- Convert all data to common units of value.
- Check prices to eliminate abnormally high or low prices.
- Make sure information on prices is relevant to the community in which farmers/clients live.
- Establish average prices by observing them over a regular period of time (2 or 3 weeks).

TOOL

Interventions Farmers Can Make in the Market System

Farmers can influence four factors which affect the prices of their products over a short period of time:

- Time of sale
- Choice of buyer
- Collective or individual marketing
- Condition of the product

Farmers can learn about their options concerning these four factors with extension workers. Often the price of a product is lower near normal harvest time, so holding the product in storage is often a way to gain a higher price.

Storage depends on perishability, facilities, farmer's ability to wait for income, etc. The choice of buyers is often limited for small-scale farmers, due to transportation costs. Collective marketing is advantageous when costly transportation is a means to a higher price. Collective marketing involves thorough planning of harvest, handling and storage as well as price and profit-sharing agreements. The extension worker can help point out the need for these considerations and can facilitate the process of dealing with them.

It may not be out of place here to briefly look into the marketing of rural industries products. In a larger sense they are allied to agri-products.

Marketing Rural Industries Products

Rural Industries Products

The problem of marketing rural industries products stems from the poor socio-economic background of the artisans, competition from the better-equipped factory sector, lack of sufficient infrastructural facilities in producing raw materials, products not changing rapidly enough with consumer tastes and preferences, labour-intensive technology, inadequate storage facilities and the non-availability of distribution channels.

S. Vanaja Rao (Economic Times, Jan.10, 1984) observes that few organizations serve as a link between village industry producers and the market and makes out a case for a district-level organization for procuring raw material and finding markets for the finished products.

To assist the marketing of rural industries products she suggests:

- The KVIC *(Khadi & Village Industries Commission)* open more bhandars and bhavans (emporia) at the block and district level.

- The KVIC renovate existing bhandars and bhavans and set up a big emporium at each state headquarters, supported by a number of bhandars.
- A separate marketing organization to be set up for each village industry for raw material supply and procuring finished products for sale to bhandars and bhavans.
- Action should be taken against government departments which do not purchase reserved items from the KVIC/Small Scale Sector.
- The KVIC and other organizations engaged in marketing V&CI products should take the assistance of the public distribution systems and the marketing outlets of corporate public sector organizations.
- Sale of some products can be made on a contractual basis while for others, intensive sales drives can be encouraged.
- Commercial banks should come in a big way to provide assistance to entrepreneurs who take up marketing and distribution of these products.
- The government controlled media should publicize these products on a preferential basis.
- The quality of products be improved.
- The KVIC should supply suitable machinery and spares that will enable production of improved products.
- The staff or managers of the KVIC and retail organizations should be better compensated to attract suitable persons to man sales depots *(incentives).*

Mass Media

Vehicles of information normally classed under the heading of "mass media" - television, radio, newspapers, magazines, and newsletters - can be used by extension agents. Usually, extensionists involved in mass communication efforts adopt other training methods to a larger audience size. Role-plays and dramas are shifted from verandah and village clearings to stages where a hundred or more people can view them simultaneously. Poster designs originally intended only for local use can prove successful enough at calling attention to some new aspect of agriculture to warrant mass production and distribution through Ministry channels over a much wider area.

Media within the realm of possibility for extension work include periodicals, fairs, and radio. Periodicals can be used as discussion starters in farmer meetings where at least a portion of those present are literate. Agricultural fairs are conducted in many developing countries to encourage agriculture development. Volunteers can make use of these fairs by encouraging some of the farmers in certain areas to compete for prizes in farm produce competitions. Such prizes can be valuable form of reward and recognition for a farmer's achievements. Radio provides the most exciting opportunity of any of the standard mass communication devices. This medium can be put to use as a simple information vehicle - to relay announcements of upcoming farmer meetings in an area, for example, or it can be employed in more creative ways. Extensionists with experience in radio broadcasting and production may be able to work within Ministry channels to produce simple and yet highly effective advertisements on the radio for new techniques. Serialized skits, songs and humorous stories are very popular in countries where national radio stations, receive widespread attention.

Radio and TV in local languages would be an effective media for disseminating marketing information.

Conclusion

At the field level there is a greater need to carry out marketing extension education by the village level extension functionaries, village panchayats, youth clubs, farmers' forums, mahila mandals. Though some of the above mentioned people's organizations have their own unique functions as people's institutions, they can be used as an effective means and media to disseminate market information to the farmers. There is a greater need to have a synergetic effect of personal field extension and mass media such as, Radio, TV and newspapers. The extension functionaries to be effective as agri-marketing specialists may have to acquaint themselves with the ongoing agri-marketing practices and the problems and bottlenecks in respect to transportation, communication, storage facility, staying capacity and credit requirements on the part of the farmers. The agricultural marketing extension agents are to be aware of the existing system of agri-marketing and the better prospects available outside the system and also create better prospects in respect to profitable marketing of agricultural produce.

There is a need for continuous concerted efforts on the part of the farmers themselves, farm leaders, local institutions, extension agents to really help the farmers not only produce more but also to have better price for their products.

11

Promotion of Small-Scale and Cottage Industries in Asia

Introduction

In the context of the majority of the population in the developing countries in Asia being ruralite, engaged predominantly in agricultural and allied activities with low income levels and in a relative sense with a poor quality of life - against a background of considerable to abundant natural and human resources and potentialities for economic development leading to fuller employment, increased incomes and better quality of life - the obvious and only alternative is to go in for a gradual, well-supported, and sustained rural industrialization, promoting small-scale and cottage industries in the rural areas. All countries in Asia, in principle, recognize the importance of small-scale industries and the role they should play in the socioeconomic development of the people, but in terms of political commitment, industrial policies, organizational structure and institutional support and incentives provided, there is considerable variation from country to country. Some countries (e.g., India, Indonesia, the Philippines), have accorded small-scale and cottage industries a primary position in their planned economic development. Some are concerned simply with industrial development and export markets and devote little attention to balanced regional development or even distribution of small-scale enterprises in the rural areas among various segments of the population. The programmes of rural industrialization are not supported by realistic and coordinated action at the field level, especially entrepreneurship development. It may be stated here that there is no shortage of potential entrepreneurial talent in the rural areas. What is required is the creation of conducive climate for entrepreneurial development which in turn would generate and foster small employment for both the sexes to lead a qualitative life.

With the exception of Brunei, Hong Kong, Singapore, and to some extent South Korea and Taiwan Province of China, the economies of other Asian countries from Afghanistan to Vietnam are basically rural and agricultural with a population ranging from 60 to 90 percent living in rural areas and pursuing predominantly agricultural activities. Consequently, a major part of the labour force in these countries is engaged in activities falling under primary sector with comparatively low per capita income and low standard of living. This is the state of affairs in respect to over fifty per cent of the world's population which lives in South and Southeast Asia. Improving the quality of life of millions of people in Asia is an enormous and a challenging problem and solutions or answers to this problem are to be found within these countries. In essence, it boils down to generating employment, increasing income, basically harnessing and utilizing the primary and secondary resources that the countries are endowed with.

During the past few years many Asian countries realized the importance of promoting and developing small industrial enterprises as a part of their overall strategy of national economic development. In many instances, this was based on evidence of the failure of the strategy of developing large-scale industries to solve problems of unemployment, poverty, regional imbalances and economic inequality. In spite of this realization on the part of the policy-makers, administrators, planners and industrial extension agents, the progress made in this direction has been far from satisfactory and at any rate, varied from country to country. Since many of the Asian countries have common economic, social, cultural and to a large measure political characteristics and face similar socio-economic problems, the approach and methods discussed in the following pages would, it is believed, ensure a meaningful, realistic and sustained growth and development of small-scale and cottage industries in rural areas and thus, realize the triple objective of generating local self-employment, increasing income and making use of local primary and secondary resources, both material and human.

It is in order here to briefly look into the sub-categories within rural industries that are in vogue in different countries in Asia.

Rural Small Industries

The term 'industry' covers any productive activity involving collection, processing, manufacturing, repairing, addition or alteration, servicing etc. Small industries as a category are distinguished from medium, large or heavy industries. Though the primary criterion for 'small' is the size of the unit, definitions of small industries vary a great deal. Across the countries in Asia, there is no uniformity of definition of small industries. Agencies involved in the development of small-scale industries provide different criteria in defining this category of enterprises. At times, the criteria chosen vary from agency to agency such as the Ministry of Industry in charge of small industry development and finance institutions within the same country. The usual bases used in 'defining the small-scale industries are the number of employees, the capital invested on plant and machinery and the volume or the value of the output. Even with these criteria, diversity in definition is in vogue in different countries.

Rural industries, for all practical purposes imply rural small-scale and cottage industries inclusive of handicrafts and artisan enterprises. It is, however, necessary to indicate clearly the distinction between 'handicrafts' and 'village industries'. The handicraft industry is cottage or small-scale industry, the products of which are artistic in nature and require individual skill and craftsmanship in their manufacture. The handicrafts are both rural and urban in nature. Although, it is a labour intensive industry, it produces higher value-added items or articles whereas, the village industries produce articles of daily use for the people.

Cottage industry is usually defined as one which is carried out wholly or primarily with the help of members of family either as a full-time or part-time occupation. These industries are traditional in character, i.e., son inheriting the skill from the father. It is an industrial enterprise carried out by individual households mainly with the household workers and sometimes or occasionally employing outside labour. The fundamental characteristic of this category of industries is that the work is or, can be done as and when the household members find it convenient and not on the basis of any regular working hours or working days. Crafts or handicrafts requiring personal skill of producers and having individualistic rather than mass character fall in this group. Sometimes, the terms 'cottage and village' as prefixes to category of industries are used interchangeably.

The criteria such as, number of employees, the amount of capital investment on plant and machinery, and use of electricity or otherwise, and sometimes the kind of products manufactured and the service rendered by in regard to small industries relate to policy measures and institutional support such as fiscal support, credit policy, labour legislation, research and development, state support in the form of reservation, purchase preference, allocation of scarce raw material, freight structure, electricity rates, price subsidies, import of machinery and equipment, excise duty, income tax and free or subsidized preparation of a bankable project. Further, the sub-categorization within small industry as traditional cottage or village industries, modern small-scale industries, handicrafts and artisan enterprises is for the purpose of institutional jurisdiction, promotion and development. India provides an interesting example of this kind of organizational, and development administrative setup. In India the village and small industries sector is divided into eight sub-sectors namely, Khadi (handspun and handwoven cloth), village industries, Handlooms, Sericulture, Handicrafts, Coir, Small-Scale Industries, and powerlooms. The Khadi and Village Industries are under the jurisdiction of the Khadi and Village Industries Commission, modern small-scale industries under Small-Scale Industry Board and Development Commissioner for Small-Scale Industries and the other sub-sectors, mentioned above, each come under a national board.

Small industry, by definition, may be considered to include all forms of small-scale enterprises with fewer than one hundred employees. Further, within the major sub-category of small-scale industries, we have what are called traditional sector and modern sector. The traditional sector by import implies the age-old ones which have been there as part of rural economy and the modern ones are of an organized nature dealing in manufacturing, engineering, processing and servicing, more usually with modern, sophisticated technology.

Traditional small industries are engaged in the type of manufacturing that is common and caters to the needs of a traditional economy, whether rural or urban. These types of small industries are characterized by products, techniques, markets and organizations and are in a position to change to modern small-scale industries, although they are not free from the problems of such industries that are commonly found in the developing countries. The traditional small industries still can cater to the needs of the emerging economy and use the advantages of modern science and technology.

Small industries, as mentioned earlier, can be rural or urban, located in the village, in a small market town, or a large city. Here, energy may or may not be used. The type of products produced, the value of the product, the physical resources available for production, the number of workers, the organization, the total capital investment, the type of business, the market arrangements and the efficiency of production are the features that distinguish one industry from another. It may be noted that the traditional small industries do not disappear as developing countries become industrialized.

Developing countries as of now are at various stages of transition from traditional modes of manufacturing to modern ones. In some Asian countries, traditional systems of manufacturing are still important particularly where cottage industries still predominate in rural and urban areas. In the developing countries the traditional artisan and cottage industrial workers coexist with the factory sector that utilizes highly developed production techniques and organizational methods. The spread of education, planned socio-economic development, a gradual increase in income levels, increase in purchasing power and change in taste and life-styles have a profound influence on change towards modern small-scale industries.

Even though, industries in general as secondary sector activities are spread both in rural and urban areas, their concentration predominantly has been in urban centers, while primary sector activities comprising agriculture and allied economic pursuits have been the main stay in rural areas. In view of the inherent limitations in respect to agriculture in sustaining the growing population, the time has come to gradually promote and develop small-scale enterprises in rural areas along with improvements in agricultural practices towards higher productivity. This process of generating industrial activities in rural areas may be called "Rural Industrialization".

The theme "Rural Industrialization" has recently emerged in the context of improving living conditions of the rural people in developing countries. These countries in their attempts to develop rural areas have placed greater emphasis on agricultural development. Most of the developing countries are characterized by high rates of population growth and predominantly depend on agriculture as means of livelihood. Agriculture as a means has limitations in terms of inadequacy of arable land, irrigation facilities and natural calamities as flood, drought and the system of land tenure. Even where agriculture can be developed, it is clear that it cannot absorb the additional labour force caused by rapid population growth without decreasing labour productivity. Although the agricultural sector is of prime importance in the improvement of the living conditions of the rural people, sustainable rural development cannot be achieved by developing the agricultural sector alone and unquestionably the other sectors must be included in a meaningful integrated approach.

Manufacturing activities in rural areas are usually on a small-scale. In view of this, small-scale industries in rural areas may help to diversify the rural economy and stimulate income-generating opportunities for rural people. There are a number of positive factors that facilitate promotion and development of small enterprises in the rural areas. Large-scale industries usually absorb a large share of the investment but generate only a small number of employment opportunities, whereas, the small-scale industries employ a large proportion of the labourers employed in manufacturing in developing countries. Moreover, in the rural areas there are people who are able to accumulate small amounts of capital and are willing to venture into some entrepreneurial activity. Small-scale industry then provides a good starting point for the mobilization and utilization of both their talents and their capital. Employment opportunities available in urban centers in the developing countries are not sufficient to absorb the influx of rural labour in search of employment, and the problems that this creates are well known. A possible and in a way, the only solution would be for rural industries to create employment opportunities for local labour and thus reduce rural-urban migration. Large-scale industries very often depend on technology from industrialized countries and therefore show a high degree of dependence. Most small-scale industries in the rural areas, on the other hand, can be developed with indigenous technology that is familiar to the people. It does not mean the modern technology could not be introduced to rural areas. In course of time, any useful, efficacious, cost effective and high productive technology will spread all over urban and rural areas.

Despite low productivity, lack of quality control and inefficient management of resources in many instances, the rural industries may have to stay and some of them will adapt to changing demands and technology and some may disappear. Even if they are less efficient in comparison with the large and medium industries, they serve a purpose and the question is not to ignore and overlook them, but to revive and revamp them.

National policies can in certain circumstances affect industries located in rural areas and their survival may be at stake. Most of the small-scale industries sell their products in their own locality and competition arising due to national policy decisions can sometimes disrupt them. They can be particularly vulnerable to competition arising from foreign products and domestic products from large-scale industries mostly located in metropolitan centres. If a country wants to pursue a free market policy, the types of industries which can survive in rural areas may be limited because in many respects the entrepreneurs from rural areas are at a disadvantage compared with their counterparts in urban areas. Manufactures in urban areas usually have added advantage of economies of scale, access to credit, modern technology, information, management skills and marketing strategies. Efforts centred around promoting small-scale industries in rural areas may have to recognize the above constraints and take adequate measures.

Financing of small-scale industries appears to be an important problem. One of the first things that Japan did at its early stages of industrial development was to build an extensive network of financial institutions. In most of the Asian countries such a network, especially in the case of small enterprises in rural areas, is lacking. This lacuna should be filled through institutional credit reaching the very small-to-small enterprise in the rural areas.

Changes in formal financing institutions for the promotion of small-scale industries are desirable, but liberalizing credit facilities alone would not suffice. Changes have to be combined with other institutional support. Production is rather straightforward but selling the product is a challenging task for the small-scale entrepreneur. In some rural industrial development programmes, the state has assumed the responsibility of marketing. Although such a help in the initial stage is desirable, taking the entire responsibility of marketing by the state leaves the entrepreneurs unaware of the difficulty of marketing and they may assume that it is the duty of the state to market whatever they produce. In other words, if the marketing responsibility is carried on by the state for a prolonged period, it is likely to deprive the entrepreneurs, the opportunity of developing their marketing skills. It may be for sometime, but not all through. If small-scale industries in the rural areas are to be successful, the rural entrepreneurs should share the responsibility of marketing. Then the producers will be more responsive to the conditions prevailing in the marketplace. This is one of the areas where small-scale entrepreneurs do not have sufficient knowledge and where industrial marketing extension services can play a helpful role.

Against the preceding brief discussion of rural industrialization as a theme, we may at length look at the prevailing economic situation in most of the countries in Asia and how industrialization could be the answer.

Prevailing Economic Situation

The economic situation as of today in most of the developing countries may be summarized as under:

- Heavy population
- Unemployment
- Under-employment
- Majority of the population living in rural areas
- Predominance of agriculture
- Low levels of production
- Low productivity
- Low per capita income
- Low economic growth rate
- High population growth rate
- Agriculture having reached a saturation point in some developing countries.

Industrialization: The Answer

Under the conditions summarized above, against abundant human resources and under-utilized material resources that the developing countries are endowed with, the answer is industrialization. There seems to be no other way out. As the late Sir M. Visvesaraya, an eminent Indian engineer and administrator has put it, 'Industrialize or perish'.

Rural Industrialization in Asia

The rural areas in Asian countries like their counterparts in other developing countries have tremendous difficulties to overcome. Often there is only subsistence farming which has a very low productivity yield. There is very little capital available and, in some cases, a great lack of skills. An additional obstacle is the low population density which makes it more difficult to use human labour as an effective national resources. The main problems are acquisition of knowledge and capital accumulation. These are the real obstacles to progress. Very little capital can be brought in from outside and because practically the whole nation has the same needs, it is quite inadequate. Capital accumulation is a central problem in village development in all the countries of the region and the income of the villagers is so low that they cannot enlarge production. They simply cannot afford machines, fertilizer etc., neither can they pay for experts.

Indeed, the most important element for the development of industry is knowledge. Although some traditional industries in Asian countries have been highly developed in the past, some of them are on the decline today. The development of skills, rather than the provision of physical facilities, is the bottleneck.

The most attractive method to develop these skills is indeed education. The gradual training process is then a productive period, instead of a too costly investment because there are only limited resources to draw from. The existing elementary subsistence farming creates little surplus available for investment.

One of the major problems facing many of the Third World countries today is how to create a strategy which will lead towards rapid economic development and industrialization. It is to be realized that the industrialization of the rural areas plays a vital role; mechanization of agricultural production and rural industry will have to develop together. This line of argument appears self-evident given the conditions of many Asian countries. Yet, in reality what is actually happening is with minor exceptions, quite the opposite: industrial growth has tended to hug the city areas and the industries have tended to be capital intensive, large-scale monopolies. The villages and towns in the rural areas are rarely increasing in wealth and in some places there is an actual decline.

All the countries of Asia are committed to rural development although different strategies are followed. Rural reform community programmes and rural industry schemes have received increasing priority in all the countries. Although the rapid social and economic changes in most Asian villages certainly offer escape routes for a small number of enterprising individuals, it should be borne in mind that the objective of rural development is the social development of the community rather than the individual[1].

The level of poverty and technical knowledge in many rural areas of the region remains extremely low by any measurable standard. While no self-respecting nation will emphasize this point, it remains an indisputable fact which has failed to disappear. Moreover, with rapid population growth of the last five decades, the overall level of poverty has increased too. The future capital of the Third World can only come from the labour of the people in the community itself. This is the only form of political strategy which can conceivably bring the people out of their poverty.

With these conditions in mind, it is argued that the future prosperity of agricultural countries in the Asian region lies in the working hands of the villagers, who are a hidden resource which needs to be mobilized. Investment in rural areas does not, in this view, require foreign capital for finance, it requires the release and nurturing of the technical skills of the people to face and overcome the problem of production and development for themselves. The rural industries have been growing steadily over the past few decades in the Asian countries, playing a vital role in the economic structure of these countries, contributing significantly to the GNP and also generating employment for a large number of people.

Unfortunately however, in most of the countries in Asia reliable statistics on rural industries are not available. The variations in the criteria for definition employed in different countries, together with the non-availability of adequate and accurate statistics make international comparison difficult, if not impossible, while one endeavours to trace the growth of rural industries.

The Kind of Industrialization

There are as they are organized and operated today, large-scale, medium and small-scale industries besides cottage industries and the new type that has been recently conceptualized and added to the categories, the tiny sector. The large and medium industries have their place depending on the nature of the product, raw materials, locational advantages, national requirements, priorities, transportation and the interests of the general public. But the large and medium industries are only a partial answer to the socio-economic needs and problems of the developing countries. The promotion of small industries and supporting and sustaining the traditional cottage and village industries in rural areas plays a much-needed complementary role in balanced development.

Disadvantages of Large-Scale Industrialization

Industrialization in any country is to be viewed with reference to the local context, the economic, demographic and social conditions. There cannot be a blind imitation of small or large industry. Ideas, programmes and technology are to be adopted suited to the indigenous conditions. While the large industries have a place and play a vital role in the national economy, they suffer from certain disadvantages in the context of developing countries. These disadvantages are relative in nature. They are in a way associated with the political and economic systems, nature of the population, and the resources with which the country is endowed. Briefly some of the disadvantages of large-scale industrialization are:

- It requires large capital resources beyond the capacity of developing countries to raise on their own.
- It involves substantial foreign exchange which is not available in adequate amounts from the export earnings of these countries.
- The large-scale units take longer gestation period resulting in immediate inflationary trends in the economy.
- Because of the sophisticated nature of technology and techniques adopted, it has to depend for quite some time on technical know-how from abroad.
- Employment potential per unit of capital investment in large-scale industries is too small to afford much relief to the growing unemployment problem.
- Centralized large-scale industrialization creates various social problems associated with overcrowded industrial urban centers.
- Most often, large-scale industrialization has resulted in concentration of economic power in fewer hands,

it failed to provide solutions to regional economic imbalances and generated monopolistic tendencies.

Under the foregoing disadvantages of large-scale industrialization, the prudent policy and approach could be dispersal and decentralization of industries which has, in large measure, the following advantages:

- Developing countries generally lack know-how and workers skilled in technology, small-scale and cottage industries, normally, do not require a high level of technology.
- Small-scale and cottage industries are labour-intensive and do not require large amounts of capital. The energy of the unemployed and underemployed should be used for reproductive purposes in an economy in which capital is scarce.
- Small-scale industrial projects can be undertaken in a short-span of time and hence can increase production with direct implications both in the short and long run.
- Most of the developing countries are rich in certain agricultural, forest, extractive, mineral and marine resources, hence small-scale and cottage industries can be based on the processing of locally available and produced raw materials.
- It is possible to save and earn foreign exchange by producing and exporting goods processed from local resources employing local unutilized and under-utilized labour.
- Small-scale industrial enterprises, whether traditional or modern, provide a training ground for local entrepreneurs for upward movement. The knowledge and managerial skills gained through small-scale

industrial enterprises can be transferred to other sophisticated enterprises.

- By creating opportunities for the small businessmen, small industrial enterprises can bring about a more equitable distribution of income.
- The growth of small-scale and cottage industries in the developing countries will help to create economic stability in society by diffusing prosperity and by checking the expansion of monopolies and concentration of wealth in a few hands.
- The development of small-scale and cottage industries will create employment opportunities in the rural areas of the developing countries where unemployment and underemployment are relatively high. This will tend to reduce the exodus of workers from the rural to the urban areas in search of jobs.
- The development of small-scale and cottage industries will make possible a transfer of manufacturing activities from the congested urban centers to rural areas. This dispersal and de-concentration of manufacturing away from the urban areas is a policy pursued by most of the developing countries.
- Apart from the linkages between agricultural or rural development and small-scale industrial enterprises, there is an essential linkage between large and medium-scale industries and small-scale industries in the sense that the former create opportunities or facilities for the growth of the latter. Certain large-scale industries create work subcontracted to ancillaries and even to very small units as in the case of Japan.
- The development of small-scale and cottage industries in rural areas will contribute to balanced regional development and a relative local self-sufficiency and

social justice. It also contributes to rehabilitation of displaced persons.

- Small-scale enterprises have their own place in a country's economy. Imperfect competition which characterizes most of the economies of the developing countries protects the small firm's markets and enables them to exist even where they are not efficient in terms of cost. The imperfection may be due to rational factors like transport cost, which can hardly be eliminated. It may be due to differentiations in taste, that is, there may be an individuality of product to which the consumers really attach significance and to irrational factors which are also important in determining demand.

And so, industry alone with a wider spread embracing all rural communities can draw the hidden unemployed off the land into production and so long as they are left on the land, agriculture cannot increase its efficiency. Industrialization must jolt the agrarian sector out of its deep sleep. This transformation is to be brought about in a phased manner with systematic and realistic planning schemes carried on by a rightly orientated and trained administrative and developmental personnel.

The Role of Industry in Integrated Rural Development

Integrated Rural Development (IRD) though connotationally sounds comprehensive, operationally it aims at redressing and alleviating the problems of the poorer segments of the rural population.[2] In the series of approaches, strategies and methods towards rural development during the past five decades, the IRD is the latest, and purportedly, the most effective approach in bettering the lot of the rural poor and yet its operationalization suffers from shortcomings at the community level. The concept of integrating and mobilizing the material and human resources at the community level is wanting.

Some rural development efforts in terms of political overtones, economic objectives, organizational process, plan formulation and programme implementation are a new kind of experience for the people and the development agencies. We are in the process of finding, learning, new and better ways of doing things. There is always a need to look back and take stock of things, so that we can have a clearer perspective of the situation, avoid the pitfalls, overcome the barriers and discover effective approaches and alternatives towards substantial and sustained development in rural areas.

In the meaningful and substantive development of rural areas, along with other sectors of economic and social development, industry must be accepted as an important component of any integrated rural development programme.[3] The nature and pattern of rural industrialization, both small-scale and cottage or handicraft industries will, however, depend on the material and human resources of the area concerned. In the formulation and execution of an integrated rural development programme, the role of rural industrialization has not been adequately recognized, in spite of its importance, nor is it always reflected adequately in the rural development programme of the developing countries.

Industrialization, in general, is also of great significance to rural development. Industry helps develop the skills and disciplines necessary for modern economic society. It is looked upon as the principal means of breaking the traditional barriers to growth.

Though it is rather obvious, we may briefly look into how industry supports rural development even at the cost of repeating some aspects mentioned earlier in support of rural industrialization.

Industry Supports Rural Development

Industry supports integrated rural development in several ways. First, in almost all countries there are cottage or handicraft industries producing a variety of articles for rural and urban consumption and for export. The traditional and socially inherited skills on which these industries are based can be further developed and upgraded. Secondly, there are manufacturing industries that are closely linked with agricultural development, industries producing fertilizers, pesticides, agricultural machinery, equipment and tools (mechanical, hand-operated and animal-drawn) and industries in respect to the maintenance of machinery and transport equipment. Some of these industries are operated on large and medium-scales and although they may be located outside the rural areas, they contribute substantially to increasing agricultural productivity by supplying inputs for rural development which largely means agricultural development. Thirdly, there are industries based on the processing of local raw material from agriculture and fisheries - food processing, leather and textiles; and from forestry construction and furniture. There is enough scope to develop many small-scale enterprises in the rural areas. Lastly, other industries not included in the types mentioned above, but satisfying some of the basic needs of the rural population or linked with infrastructural development may be developed in the rural areas as part of the policy of decentralization of industrial development.

Industrial Development Programmes as a Component of Integrated Rural Development

A certain geographical area is usually taken as the unit for integrated rural development, selected on the basis of criteria formulated in the light of the objectives of government policy on rural development. The criteria may vary from area to area in a country, depending on the needs and resources of the area, both material and human. An industrial potential techno-economic survey is essential to obtain information on the size of the area, the composition of the population by sex and age; employment and unemployment and the main occupations; actual and potential resources for economic and social development; and infrastructural facilities. As the purpose for collecting all this information is to prepare an industrial development programme for the area, one has to look for the kind of viable nonagricultural and other industrial enterprises in the light of the available resources of the area such as raw materials, the supply of labour, technical know-how, entrepreneurship, the availability of finance and the internal and external demand for the products that maybe produced in the area. National machinery at different levels is necessary to prepare, coordinate and implement rural development programmes. Several countries in the Asian region have such machinery for providing institutional support.

Elements of a Rural Industrialization Programme

In view of the interrelated nature of development a broad, integrated approach should be adopted for rural industrialization. Mere credit facilities for small-scale industrial promotion are not enough though necessary. Development of small-scale enterprises in rural areas is limited by such factors as lack of technical knowledge, inefficient marketing, poor design of products and lack of skill in planning and managing industrial enterprises. A programme for developing industries in the rural areas should consist of measures to deal with the numerous limiting factors simultaneously.

A rural industrialization programme as a part of integrated rural development may, therefore, encompass the following elements:

- The selection of an area on the basis of the desired criteria;

- A survey to assess the human and natural resources of the area;
- Identification of potential enterprises for incorporation in the industrial development programme for the area;
- Project preparation and evaluation;
- Financial or credit support;
- Industrial research and advisory services;
- Procurement of raw materials and equipment;
- The establishment of industrial estates or centers with basic facilities;
- Industrial training;
- Marketing support in the initial stages.

Almost every developing country in Asia has a programme for developing small-scale and cottage industries, but these programmes seldom constitute a significant part of integrated rural development.

Broader Implication of Rural Industrialization

While the role of small-scale and cottage industries is important in rural industrialization, it is not sufficient by itself to lead to the desirable scale of industrialization to deal with the problems of the disadvantaged and weaker segments of the population in the rural areas. Rural industrialization traditionally associated with small-scale and cottage industrial enterprise, should really imply a mix of industrial enterprises which may be large-, medium-, small-scale or handicraft in character, depending on the availability of or access to requisite infrastructural facilities and the cost of providing such decentralized infrastructure, raw material and markets.

Though the emphasis in rural industrialization is on small-scale and cottage industries, since they meet the situation which exists in rural areas, there is nothing preventing the rural population benefiting entrepreneurially and industrially through the location of large- or medium- scale industries in the rural areas. Whether industrial location is rural or urban, the core question is to what extent and in what ways, would it enable the rural people to benefit in terms of increased employment and income and a better quality of life? The answer is, clearly, that it would lead to improved rural development.

REFERENCES

1. Rizwanul Islam, ed., "Rural Industrialization and Employment in Asia", *Asian Employment Programme* (New Delhi: ARTEP, 1987).
2. E. Desingu Setty, "Field Approach to Integrated Rural Development", *Journal of Rural Development*, Vol. 7(6) (Hyderabad: National Institute of Rural Development, 1988), pp.675-688.
3. United Nations Economic and Social Commission for Asia and the Pacific (UN/ESCAP), "Administration of Rural Development in ASEAN Countries", *Proceedings of the Colloquium* (Jakarta, 1983), pp. 189-240.

12

Rural Industralisation in India

India provides an example of consistent and progressive industrial policy measures beginning 1948 and upto the present. In gradual succession these policy measures were aimed at rural industrialization, promotion and development of overall socio-economic development of rural as well as urban population. These measures encompass organizational and institutional support in terms of identification of viable small-scale enterprises, potential entrepreneurs, and institutional credit, a variety of incentives, infrastructure, training, common facilities, supply of raw material, machinery and equipment and support for marketing of products. The small-scale industries have been accorded a priority status in terms of reservation of certain products to be exclusively produced by the SSI units and preferential bulk and higher quantum of purchase of SSI products by the governmental and quasi-governmental organizations. The Government of India through the Ministry of Industry, the State Governments and a plethora of national and state level organizations with diverse functions coordinate the promotion and development of small-scale and cottage enterprises in the country. In the pages that follow a brief profile on the development of small-scale and cottage industries in India is attempted.

Industrial Development Policies

Industrial Development Policies as a significant and set

of progressive measures for industrial development, the Government of India has successively formulated industrial development policies right from 1948 down to 1991 as shown below:-

The nucleus for the industrial policy measures in India is enshrined in the 'Directive Principles of State Policy' of constitution of India. In view of the imperative need to promote and develop village and small industries, the Government of India, soon after attaining independence, came up with its first industrial policy resolution in 1948 which had the following emphasis:

Cottage and small industries have a very important role in the national economy. These industries are particularly suited for better utilization of local resources and for the achievement of local self-sufficiency in respect of certain types of essential consumer goods. The hearty expansion of cottage and small-scale industries depends upon a number of factors like the provision of raw materials, cheap power, technical advice, organized marketing of their produce and where necessary safeguards against intensive competition from large-scale manufacture. Most of those fall under the provincial sphere and are receiving the attention of the government of the province and the states.

In pursuance of this policy measure, a significant place for promotion of cottage and village industries was accorded in the First Five Year Plan (1951-56). During the period of First Five Year Plan the government had launched industrial pilot projects in selected community development blocks and had set up all India level Boards for Handlooms, Handicrafts, Sericulture, Coir and Khadi and Village Industries to advise and assist in the formulation of development strategies for them. Certain degree of protection to the small-scale sector in terms of reservation of certain spheres of production, exclusively for the village and small industries sector, non-expansion of capacity of and imposition of cess on large-scale sector and also arrangements for preferential supply of raw material to the decentralized industries was accorded.

The Industrial Policy Resolution of 1956 reflects the experience gained in the First Five Year Plan and had a slight shift. It stated that while some basic and heavy industries would be set up, simultaneously Government of India would stress the role of cottage and village and small industries in the development of the national economy. It aimed at dispersal of small enterprises all over the country to make use of the local resources, to develop and upgrade local skills, to meet the local consumer demands and to avoid unplanned concentration of population in urban areas, migrating from rural areas.

In 1970, prior to the announcement of the third Industrial Policy Resolution of February 1973, the Government of India formulated special schemes of incentives in favour of small industries such as subsidy on investment, subsidy on transport of raw materials and finished products and schemes of concessional finance from banks and also certain fiscal concessions to industries that are started in the backward areas selected for this purpose. These concessions are operative up till now.

In 1977, there was change of government at the centre and the new government announced its own industrial policy. Besides several policy measures, one highly significant outcome of the new policy was the creation of District Industries Centre, one for each district in the country. It was envisaged that the DIC would function as a 'single roof' providing the entrepreneurs of small-scale and village industries with all the services and support required by them for starting and successfully running their enterprises. The DIC is headed by a General Manager assisted by a team of technical staff covering economic, credit, raw material and machinery and equipment, extension and marketing and other special activities wherever they existed.

The policy in general, envisaged that the thrust of the new industrial policy would be an effective promotion of cottage and small industries widely dispersed in rural areas and small towns and whatever can be produced by small and cottage industries must only be so produced. It paid attention to the tiny sector within the small sector with an investment of Rs.100,000 on plant and machinery, located in towns with a population less than 40,000 and villages. It further said that the government would consider introducing special legislation for protecting the interest of cottage and household industries with a view to ensuring that those activities which provide self-employment in large numbers get due recognition in industrial development. It also indicated that the focal point of development for small-scale and cottage industries will be shifted from big cities and state capitals to the district headquarters. This last component of the policy resulted in the creation of District Industries Centres all over the country. The policy also has laid emphasis on the promotion of ancillaries as linkages to nucleus plants and large industries.

The announcement of the Industrial Policy of July 1980, coincided with the formulation of the Sixth Five Year Plan (1980-85). The policy statement sought to harmonize growth in the small-scale sector with the large and medium sectors. The emphasis was on fostering complementarity between the large and small sectors so that the dichotomy between the two sectors does not impair the economic pattern. An important element in the new policy was the raising of investment limits in respect of tiny and small-scale industry.

Establishment of nucleus plants in backward districts

was another salient feature of the policy statement. It was envisaged that this would foster ancillarization and functional linkages between large and small industries and bring about economic federalism. Other measures proposed in the policy included the strengthening of the existing arrangements for the provision of credit facilities, establishing of buffer stocks of essential and critical raw materials for the use of small units, providing the benefits of research and development in order to facilitate easy flow of technology, modernization and establishment of an early warning system to prevent sickness and to take appropriate and timely remedial measures.[1]

The same tenor of emphasis on village and small-scale industries continues in the Seventh Five-year Plan document (1985-90). It says that provision of village and small-scale industries will continue to be an important element in the national development strategy particularly because of its very favourable capital output ratio and high employment intensity and this sector would: (a) assist in the growth and widespread dispersal of industries; (b) increase the levels of earnings of artisans; (c) sustain and create avenues of self-employment; (d) ensure regular supply of goods and services through use of local skills and resources; (e) develop entrepreneurship in combination with improved methods of production through appropriate training and package of incentives; (f) preserve craftsmanship and art heritage of the country. The plan document adds that the strategy for achieving the above objectives would consist of upgradation of technology and modernization, supply of adequate inputs promoting specialization in production and export oriented industries, strengthening and enlarging skill profile and entrepreneurial base and management practices to increase opportunities for self-employment and strengthening the programmes of ancillarization to establish and improve linkages between large and small industries leading to harmonious growth of the total industrial sector.[2]

In the Industrial Policy of 1990, the Government have been considering the need to take measures for promotion of small-scale and agro-based industries and to change procedures for grant of industrial approvals.

- The policy focuses on re-orienting industrial growth to serve the objective of employment generation, dispersal of industry in the rural areas, and to enhance the contribution of small-scale industries to exports it has been decided to take the measures enumerated below.

- The investment ceiling in plant & machinery for small-scale industries (fixed in 1985) would be raised from the present Rs. 35 lakhs to Rs. 60 lakhs and correspondingly, for ancillary units from Rs. 45 lakhs to Rs. 75 lakhs. In order to enable small-scale industries to play an important role in the total export effort, such of the small-scale units which undertake to export at least 30 per cent of the annual production by the third year will be permitted to step up their investment in plant & machinery to Rs. 75 lakhs.
- Investment ceiling in respect of tiny units would also be increased from the present Rs. 2 lakhs to Rs. 5 lakhs. However, with regard to their location, the population limit of 50,000 as per the 1981 census would continue to apply. Steps will be taken to ensure better inflow of credit and other vital inputs and to improve the infrastructure support to the constituents of the Tiny Sector.
- Presently, 836 items have been reserved for exclusive manufacture in the small-scale sector. Efforts would be made to identify more items amenable to similar reservation. Encroachment and violation by large-scale units into areas reserved for small-scale sector will be effectively dealt with.

- A new scheme of Central Investment Subsidy exclusively for the small-scale sector in rural and backward areas capable of generating higher level of employment at lower capital cost would be implemented.
- With a view to improving the competitiveness of the products manufactured in the small-scale sector, programmes for modernization and upgradation of technology would be implemented. A number of technology centres, tool rooms, Process and Product Development Centres, testing centres, etc. will be set up under the umbrella of an apex Technology Development Centre in Small Industries Development Organization.
- To ensure adequate and timely flow of credit of the small-scale industries, a new apex bank known as SIDBI has already been established. One of the major tasks of SIDBI and other commercial banks/financial institutions would be to channelise need-based, higher flow of credit, both by way of term loan and working capital, to the tiny and rural industries. A targeted approach will be adopted to ensure implementation and to facilitate monitoring this objective.
- The existing regime of fiscal concessions will be reviewed both to provide sustained support to the units in the small-scale sector and to remove the disincentives for their graduation and further growth.
- All new units upto an investment of Rs. 25 crores in fixed assets in non-backward areas and Rs. 75 crores in Centrally notified backward areas will be exempt from requirement of obtaining licence/ registration.
- For the import of Capital Goods, the entrepreneur would have entitlement to import upto a landed value

of 30% of the total value of plant and machinery required for the unit.

- For imports of raw materials and components, imports will be permissible upto a landed value of 30% of the ex-factory value of annual production. The ex-factory value of production will exclude the excise duty on the item of production. Raw materials and components on OGL will not be included within this 30 percent limit. For all licensable items of raw materials and components, import-licensing procedures will continue to operate.
- 100% export oriented units (EOUs) and units to be set up in export processing zones (EPZs) are also being delicensed under the scheme upto an investment limit of Rs. 75 crores.
- The above proposals will be applicable to all manufacturing items in a specified list. The list shall follow the nomenclature of the Indian Trade Classification based on the Harmonized System. In such section of the classification, apart from positive mention of approved items, those not permissible shall be specifically excluded from the benefit of the proposals listed above. Approval for excluded items will be as per the existing industrial policy regime and procedures.

The latest Industrial Policy of 1991 which briefly refers to the earlier industrial policies as mentioned below:

The Industrial Policy Resolution of 1948 was followed by the Industrial Policy Resolution of 1956 which had as its objective the acceleration of the rate of economic growth and the speeding up of industrialization as a means of achieving a socialist pattern of society. In 1956, capital was scarce and the base of entrepreneurship not strong enough. Hence, the

1956 Industrial policy Resolution gave primacy to the role of the State to assume a predominant and direct responsibility for industrial development.

- The Industrial Policy Statement of 1973, inter alia, identified high priority industries where investment from large industrial houses and foreign companies would be permitted.
- The Industrial Policy Statement of 1977 laid emphasis on decentralization and on the role of small scale, tiny and cottage industries.
- The Industrial Policy Statement of 1980 focused attention on the need for promoting competition in the domestic market, technological upgradation and modernization. The policy laid the foundation for an increasingly competitive export base and for encouraging foreign investment in high technology areas. This found expression in the Sixth Five-Year Plan which bore the distinct stamp of Smt. Indira Gandhi. It was Smt. Indira Gandhi who emphasized the need for productivity to be the central concern in all economic and production activities.
- These policies created a climate for rapid industrial growth in the country. Thus on the eve of the Seventh Five Year Plan, a broad-based infrastructure had been built up. Basic industries had been established. A high degree of self-reliance in a large number of items-raw materials, intermediates and finished goods had been achieved. New growth centres of industrial activity had emerged and had a new generation of entrepreneurs. A large number of engineers, technicians and skilled workers had also been trained.
- The Seventh Plan recognized the need to consolidate on these strengths and to take initiatives to prepare

Indian industry to respond effectively to the emerging challenges. A number of policy and procedural changes were introduced in 1985 and 1986 under the leadership of Shri Rajiv Gandhi aimed at increasing productivity, reducing costs and improving quality. The accent was on opening the domestic market to increased competition and readying our industry to stand on its own in the face of international competition. The public sector was freed from a number of constraints and given a larger measure of autonomy. The technological and managerial modernization of industry was pursued as the key instrument for increasing productivity and improving our competitiveness in the world. The net result of all these changes was that Indian industry grew by an impressive average annual growth rate of 8.5% in the Seventh Plan Period.

- Government is pledged to launching a reinvigorated struggle for social and economic justice, to end poverty and unemployment and to build a modern, democratic, socialist, prosperous and forward-looking India. Such a society can be built if India grows as part of the world economy and not in isolation.
- While Government will continue to follow the policy of self-reliance, there would be greater emphasis placed on building up our ability to pay for imports through our own foreign exchange earnings. Government is also committed to development and utilization of indigenous capabilities in technology and manufacturing as well as its upgradation to world standards.
- Government will continue to pursue a sound policy framework encompassing encouragement of entrepreneurship, development of indigenous

technology through investment in research and development, bringing in new technology dismantling of the regulatory system, development of the capital markets and increasing competitiveness for the benefit of the common man. The spread of industrialization to backward areas of the country will be actively promoted through appropriate incentives, institutions and infrastructure investments.

- Government will provide enhanced support to the small-scale sector so that it flourishes in an environment of economic efficiency and continuous technological upgradation. (For further details of Industrial Policies, please see Appendix-II(A) & II(B)).

Basic Approach Znd Measures Initiated

The basic approach towards development of small-scale industries as outlined in various policy resolutions and national plans can be summed up as to create employment opportunities with relatively low investment, to meet a substantial part of the increased demand for consumer goods and simple producer goods, to facilitate mobilization of resources of capital and skill which may otherwise remain unutilized, to help in raising the levels of earnings and standards of living of a large number of artisans, craftsmen and entrepreneurs, to promote entrepreneurship widely with focus on villages and small towns, to make small industries export-oriented and to help upgrade quality of products, and to remove regional disparities through a deliberate policy to encourage growth of non-farm occupations in villages and small towns. The development strategy, all through, comprises of: (a) protective discrimination; (b) integration between small and large-scale industries; (c) elaborate schemes of assistance and incentives administered through a large number of government departments, agencies and institutes; (d) modernization of technology without displacing labour; and (e) adoption of an area approach in development planning.[3]

In order to translate the above strategies into action, programmes on some aspects of small-scale industries are being implemented. They comprise the following:

1. Reservation of items for manufacture in the small-scale sector: The policy of reserving certain lines of manufacture for exclusive production in the small-scale sector has been pursued since 1967 to provide protection to the small-scale sector against competition from medium and large industries. A standing committee of the Ministry of Industry reviews the list periodically to ensure that production in the small-scale sector is economical and of acceptable quality. As new products and new processes capable of being manufactured in the small-scale sector are identified, they are added to the reserved list. Beginning with 46 items in 1967-68, it rose to 869 items by March 1988. Reservation of items for production in the small-scale sector is covered under section 29B of the Industries (Development and Regulation) Act of 1951 with an amendment passed in 1984.
2. Reservation of items manufactured in the SSI sector for Central Government Purchases: The policy of reserving certain products for exclusive purchases from the small-scale sector under the central government purchase programme was introduced in 1956 by identifying 16 items. It was only in 1976-77, that the number was increased to 241. As of March 1988, it stood at 409. In addition, four categories of handicraft products (14 items) and 14 items from handlooms were also listed for exclusive purchase from the village industries category. Two other categories introduced sometime back for purchases

from the small-scale sector are: purchase to the extent of 74 per cent (14 items) and purchase to the extent of 50 per cent (28 items). The list is periodically reviewed.

3. Referred items and items of mass consumption selected for intensive growth during he Sixth Plan period (1980-85): One hundred and fourteen products were identified for this purpose. They include products reserved for manufacture in the small-scale industry as well as others. These products have growth potential and offer greater scope for employment generation.
4. Items banned for manufacture in the small-scale industry sector: Items banned for manufacture in the small-scale sector announced periodically by the Small Industries Development Organization (SIDO) refer to products where capacity is saturated and further expansion is not considered advisable. The number of such banned items as of January 1987 was 11.

EDP though primarily it depends on the individual interest and initiative in view of the need and complexity of several enterprises individuals alone cannot meet the requirements for promotion and sustaining their enterprises. In this context, the State comes forward with comprehensive industrial development policies from time to time. Wherein it focuses the kind of role that is to be played by the state by the financial institutions and the kind of reservation, enterprises need these small scale sectors and also detailing the kind of incentive in terms of that the state should provide to the entrepreneurs, the industrial policy stands as a guideline, a support system, encouragement and helping the neo-entrepreneurs, thus contributing to industrial activity generating employment, income and thus taking the state economically and socially forward to higher levels of living. The issuing of industrial policies by Govt. of India began in 1948 and periodically upto 1991. Each industrial policy spell-out in detail the role of the state and other institutions in the state.

PLAN OUTLAYS AND PROGRESS OF VILLAGE AND SMALL-SCALE INDUSTRIES

The emphasis on the promotion and development of small-scale and village industries is reflected in the outlays earmarked under public sector in the Five Year Plans. Though in terms of percentage the outlays appear small, in financial terms, the allocation appears to be substantial.

Though the progress of small-scale and village industries is not attempted here either fiscal year-wise or the Five Year Plan-wise, it may be mentioned here that the increase in the number of SSI units has been significant. At the end of March 1988 there were a little over 1.06 million registered small-scale units and 0.52 million unregistered small-scale units. Ninety per cent of establishments registered under the Factories Act were small-scale units with investment on plant and machinery not exceeding Rs.2 million (Annual Survey of Industries, 1984-85). This figure and the following facts are based on the earlier definition of small-scale industry with an investment on plant and machinery not exceeding Rs.2 million over 5,000 products are being manufactured by small-scale industrial units (SIDO industries). Village and small-scale industries (unregistered manufacturing sector) account for about 39 per cent of the total value of production of the manufacturing sector (national income computation for 1986-87 at 1980-81 prices). Small-scale factory establishments, with 90 per cent of units account for 5.3 per cent of the total fixed capital of all factories, provide employment to 33.7 per cent of the total, have share of 20.4 per cent of the total output and contribute to 16.6 per cent of the value added by manufacture.

Employment generated in small-scale factory is nine times that of large establishments for an investment of Rs.100,000 in fixed assets. Small-scale industrial units provide employment to about 11 million persons.[4]

INSTITUTIONAL FRAMEWORK

Prior to looking into the institutional framework across several levels in the country to carry on multiple tasks of a complex and stupendous programme of small industry development, we may briefly look into the concept and definition of the subcategories within what is called small industry. The concept and definition of small-scale industry have changed over years with the changing circumstances and pressing problems of the Indian economy. Currently, a small industry is defined as an industrial unit with investment on plant and machinery not exceeding Rs. 3.5 million and not exceeding Rs. 4.5 million if it were to be an ancillary unit. Within this sub-sector, there is a separate category of tiny units. A tiny unit is defined as a unit with an investment on plant and machinery not exceeding Rs. 200,000 and located in villages and small towns. These definitions have been formulated for implementing the composite loan schemes for providing loans which include fixed and working capital and for implementing specific development programmes. Table-I shows actual plan outlay for village and small-scale industries.

TABLE-I

Plan Period	*Public Sector outlay for village and small-sale industries*	*Total Public Sector outlay*	*Share of village and small-scale industries in the*
	(Rs. Million)	***(Rs. Million)***	***total outlay (%)***
First Plan: 1951-52 to 1955-56	430	19,600	2.0
Second Plan: 1956-57 to 1960-61	1,750	46,000	4.0
Third Plan: 1961-62 to 1965-66	2,410	85,770	2.8
Annual Plans: 1966-67	430	21,650	2.0

1967-68	420	20,850	2.0
1968-69	410	23,760	1.7
Fourth Plan: 1969-70 to 1973-74	2,430	157,790	1.5
Fifth Plan: 1974-75 to 1978-79	5,925	394.262	1.5
Annual Plan:1979-80	2,557	121,765	2.1
Sixth Plan: 980-81 to 1984-85	19,451	1,092,917	1.8
Seventh Plan: 1985-86 to 1989-90	27,527	1,800,000	1.5

Source: Small Industry Bulletin for Asia and the Pacific, No.23, p. 95.

We may just have a glance at plan outlay of States and Union Territories under Village and Small Industries. The following Table No.2 provides figures from 6th Plan to 9th Plan.

TABLE 2*

(Rs. in Crores)

States	*Sixth Plan Outlay*	*Seventh Plan Actuals*	*Eighth Plan Agreed Outlay*	*Ninth Plan Agreed Outlay*
Andhra Pradesh	30.00	107.15	141.60	394.48
Arunachal Pradesh	2.75	7.73	13.00	34.32
Assam	30.00	55.00	109.68	174.77
Bihar	47.00	87.86	120.32	197.65
Goa	*	5.21	16.80	28.55
Gujarat	61.50	208.18	435.00	369.65
Haryana	19.46	48.95	135.19	111.83
Himachal Pradesh	9.05	12.78	47.50	80.00
Jammu & Kashmir	34.70	46.77	101.50	**
Karnataka	74.00	163.95	756.31	565.00
Kerala	49.80	69.29	304.00	509.00
Madhya Pradesh	33.40	76.38	105.87	314.82
Maharashtra	60.26	88.53	225.78	362.30
Manipur	12.50	14.62	22.00	42.84
Meghalaya	4.00	6.78	11.11	32.00

Mizoram	4.00	16.37	37.50	59.73
Nagaland	5.00	8.83	18.00	85.28
Orissa	27.00	68.39	114.00	68.70
Punjab	20.61	17.79	119.92	24.16
Rajasthan	19.50	25.69	170.94	300.63
Sikkim	3.60	3.32	8.80	25.00
Tamil Nadu	80.00	276.62	269.00	600.00
Tripura	8.50	13.42	34.50	37.99
Uttar Pradesh	125.23	162.41	261.20	204.47
West Bengal	60.00	69.04	223.52	213.06
Total States	**821.07**	**1,661.06**	**3,803.05**	**4,836.23**
Union Territories				
Andaman & Nicobar Islands	1.00	2.64	6.90	38.00
Chandigarh	0.60	1.56	2.64	3.09
Dadra & Nagar Haveli	0.55	0.90	3.25	5.74
Daman & Diu	2.50	0.24	2.76	1.28
Delhi	25.64	45.15	27.00	59.90
Lakshadweep	0.30	1.21	3.40	9.16
Pondicherry	4.60	13.20	27.20	78.00
Total UTs	**35.19**	**64.91**	**73.15**	**195.17**
Total (States & UTs)	**857.05**	**1,725.97**	**3,876.20**	**5,031.40**

Note: 1). * : included in Daman & Diu.

2) **: Not yet finalized.

Further, Table No.3 provides details plan-wise right from 6th Plan to 9th Plan outlay for other than Village and Small Industries.

TABLE NO.3 *

(Rs. in Crores)

(Other Than Village & Small Industries)				
States	*Sixth Plan (1980-85) Outlay*	*Seventh Plan (1985-90) Outlay*	*Eighth Plan (1992-97) Outlay*	*Ninth Plan (1997-2002) Outlay*
Andhra Pradesh	75.66	219.30	130.90	567.65
Arunachal Pradesh	7.51	2.75	13.94	11.78
Assam	24.75	53.10	214.25	205.27

Bihar	51.65	146.60	339.00	140.97
Goa	@	@	19.70	6.00
Gujarat	99.60	129.44	233.50	835.35
Haryana	11.40	20.55	85.33	32.85
Himachal Pradesh	9.00	16.27	28.70	70.00
Jammu & Kashmir	38.07	38.75	93.20	131.90
Karnataka	88.68	95.00	228.44	461.00
Kerala	109.70	131.00	506.52	616.86
Madhya Pradesh	35.55	56.35	360.27	798.15
Maharashtra	131.90	302.00	588.68	540.30
Manipur	7.50	10.30	18.00	83.67
Meghalaya	5.50	13.10	32.06	70.00
Mizoram	0.58	2.35	7.25	9.19
Nagaland	7.00	20.20	32.00	35.74
Orissa	38.00	100.35	671.94	54.79
Punjab	61.07	88.71	43.00	257.14
Rajasthan	64.09	144.64	365.07	1,452.75
Sikkim	2.94	5.42	12.00	45.00
Tamil Nadu	91.77	155.00	281.00	802.91
Tripura	5.46	6.25	30.50	41.35
Uttar Pradesh	198.12	429.03	308.35	322.18
West Bengal	213.34	226.00	853.96	1,113.23
Total States	**1,378.84**	**2,412.46**	**5,497.56**	**8,706.03**
Union Territories				
Andaman & Nicobar Islands	0.00	0.00	0.00	0.00
Chandigarh	0.49	0.19	0.20	0.00
Dadra & Nagar Haveli	0.00	0.00	0.00	0.00
Daman & Diu	6.00	11.85	0.02	2.32
Delhi	1.98	12.00	3.50	50.10
Lakshadweep	0.00	0.12	0.46	0.00
Pondicherry	1.74	3.34	21.69	107.00
Total UTs	**10.21**	**27.50**	**25.87**	**159.42**
Total (States & UTs)	**1,389.05**	**2,439.96**	**5,523.43**	**8,865.45**

Note: 1) @: included in Daman & Diu.

**Source:* http://planningcommission.nic.in/plans/planrel/fiveyr/10th/volume2/v2_ch7_1.pdf

In the Indian context, it is relevant to look at the small-scale sector as distinct from the village industry sector. The village and small-scale industry (VSI) sector has been divided into different sub-sectors for administering assistance programmes and specialized institutions have been set up to look after each of the sub-sectors at the national level. These cover sub-sectors of Khadi (Handspun and hand-woven cloth) and village industries, handlooms, handicrafts, power looms, sericulture, coir and other small-scale industries. Categorization of the VSI sector based on the national level organizations implementing the promotional and assistance programmes is given below:

Categorization of the VSI Sectors

S.No.	*Commission / Board*	*Implementing Agency*
1.	Khadi and Village Industries Commission (KVIC)	KVIC at the Centre and KVI Boards in the states
2.	All India Handlooms and Handicrafts Board	Development Commissioner (Handlooms)
3.	All India Power loom Board	Textile Commissioner
4.	Central Silk Board	Central Silk Board
5.	Coir Board	Coir Board
6.	All India Small-Scale Industries Board	Small Industries Development Organization (SIDO) with Development Commissioner (Small Scale Industries - DC (SSI) - as the headquarters organization.

Power looms and small-scale industries are referred to as the modern sector and all the others as village/rural traditional industries are the decentralized sector. The tiny units can also be included under the decentralized sector. The concept of rural industrialization thus encourages village and tiny units located primarily in rural areas. As stated above, village industries cover those industrial units falling under the purview of the organizations listed at 1,2,4,5. Modern small industry sector coming under the purview of the All India Small-Scale Industries Board is thus given a residuary status, by having jurisdiction over all industries falling outside the purview of the other all India boards and at the same time falling within the stipulated investment ceiling on plant and machinery.

Khadi & Village Industries Commission (KVIC)

A brief special mention may be made of the All India Khadi & Village Industries Commission (KVIC). The apex organization located in Mumbai and its constituents in the states carry on very significant promotional programmes in the field of Khadi and other traditional 26 village industries. The KVIC network comprises 26 State Khadi and Village Industries Boards, 1114 Registered Institutions and about 30,008 Industrial Cooperatives of Artisans covering about 150 thousand villages.[5] *(Please see Appendix-II(B)for a brief profile of KVIC)*

Under textiles, the KVIC covers cotton, silk and woolen handspun and hand-woven fabrics. The village industries under its purview comprise:

1. Bee-keeping (Apiary)
2. Cottage match, manufacture of fireworks and incense sticks
3. Pottery
4. Soap
5. Flaying, curing and tanning of hides and skins and ancillary industries connected with the same and cottage leather industry

6. Ghani oil industry
7. Handmade paper
8. Manufacture of canegur and khandasari
9. Palmsugar and palm products industry
10. Processing of cereals and pulses
11. Manufacture and use of manure and methane gas from cowdung and other waste products (such as flesh of dead animals, night soil, etc.,)
12. Limestone, lime-shell and other lime products
13. Manufacture of shellack
14. Collection of forest plants and fruits for medicinal purposes
15. Fruit processing and fruit preservation
16. Bamboo and cane work
17. Blacksmithy
18. Carpentry
19. Fibre other than coir
20. Manufacture of Household utensils in aluminium
21. Manufacture of gum resins

Most of the above village/cottage industries are located in the villages. The value of the products under KVIC during Sixth Five Year Plan was Rs.9290 million and it provided employment to 3.7 million persons. During the Seventh Plan, the value of output of this sub-sector is targeted to increase from Rs.9,290 million in 1984-85 to about Rs. 20,000 million by the terminal year 1989-90. The employment coverage in this period is likely to increase from 3.7 million persons to 5 million persons. The targets set for Khadi and for village industries would account for growth rate of 7.1 per cent for Khadi Production and 17.5 per cent for village industries output.

India has developed a most comprehensive network of institutions in the public sector for the promotion of small and to some extent, medium industries. These institutions cater to the different needs of these industries, and taken together, they have schemes and programmes to attend to virtually all types of problems. As mentioned earlier, the components of this institutional framework are at national, state and district levels. This is necessitated by: (a) India being a large and diverse country; (b) industry being a concurrent subject between the union and state governments; and (c) small industry being geographically widely scattered and dispersed.[6]

The comprehensive institutional network involved for the promotion of small-scale industries in the country is presented in the following tables:

INSTITUTIONAL SETUP FOR SMALL-SCALE INDUSTRY DEVELOPMENT IN INDIA

1. National Level - Ministry of Industry, Department of Industrial Development

(a) Small Industries Development Organization (SIDO)

- Policy formulating, coordinating and monitoring agency;
- Maintains close liaison with the central ministries, Planning Commission, state governments and other organizations concerned with small-scale industry development and serves as the secretariat for the All India Small-Scale Industries Board;
- Provides a comprehensive range of industrial extension services including technical, managerial, economic and marketing assistance through its network of 26 small industries services institutes,

32 branch SSSIs, 41 extension centres, 4 regional testing centres, 1 product and process development centre, 2 footwear training centres and 4 production centres. In addition, 20 field-testing stations are being established in areas of concentration of specific industries for providing testing facilities to small-scale industries.

(b) National Small Industries Corporation (NSIC) with four regional offices

- Supply of machinery on hire purchase basis;
- Registration of units for participation in the purchase programmes of the Central and state governments, and other central institutions;
- Marketing assistance - internal and export;
- Development of prototypes of machinery and equipment, and other facilities
- Basic and advanced training in selected trades and technologies through its four-prototype development and training centres.

(c) Commissioner for Industrial Cooperatives Coordination of policies for industrial cooperatives.

(d) Specialized Institutions

(i) National Institute of Small Industry Extension Training (NISIET), Hyderabad-Interdisciplinary approach in the areas of training, research and consultancy relating to development and management of small-scale and village industries (earlier known as Small Industry Extension Training Institute - SIET)

(ii) National Institute for Entrepreneurship and Small Business Development (NIESBUD), New Delhi-Coordinates research and training in entrepreneurship development and devises specific training programmes suited to various categories of entrepreneurs specially from the weaker section of the society.

(iii) Central Institute of Tool Design (CITD), Hyderabad- Training in the design and manufacture of tools, jigs, fixtures, dyes and moulds;- Advisory and consultancy services including assistance in the design and development of tools;- Recommend measures to standardize tools, tooling elements, components etc.

(iv) Central Tool Room and Training Centres (at Ludhiana, Delhi, Calcutta and Bangalore)- Provision of tool room services and facilities in designs, manufacture and training. Tool rooms at Delhi and Bangalore are owned by the respective state governments.

(v) Central Institute of Head Tools (CIHT), Jalandhar.- Provision of improved technology, raw materials, designs and testing for hand tools industry.

(vi) Institute of Design of Electrical Measuring Instruments (IDEMI), Bombay- Provision of technical consultancy in the design and development of electrical and electronic instruments, calibration and testing, tool design, tool fabrication, prototype fabrication and training.

(vii) Central Machine Tool Institute, Bangalore.

(viii) Central Institute for Plastics Engineering and Tools, Madras (Ministry of Petroleum and Chemicals)

(ix) National Institute of Foundry and Forge Technology, Ranchi.

2. **State Level**

(a) Directorate of IndustriesWith a network of District Industries Centres at the district level, industries officers at the sub-division level and extension officers at the block level.

- -- Registration of small-scale units and recommending cases of large/medium industries to appropriate authorities
- -- Raw material quota
- -- Import quota
- -- Financial assistance under the State Aid to Industries Act- Industrial estates
- -- Technical consultancy
- -- Training of entrepreneurs
- -- Industrial cooperatives
- -- Compilation of statistics
- -- Overall administration of the village and small-scale industry sector and maintaining close liaison with the central and state level organizations concerned with industrial development.

(b) Small Industry Development Corporation- Supply of scarce raw materials through raw material depots- Machinery on hire purchase- Marketing assistance- Joint ventures in the small-scale sector- Entrepreneurship development

- -- Trade centres
- -- Industrial estates

(c) Industrial Infrastructure Corporation; Industrial Area Development Board/ Authority

- -- Plans and develops industrial estates and industrial areas

(d) Industrial Development Corporation-
Promotion of industrial units in the medium and large-scale including joint and public sector ventures

- -- Planning and development of industrial estates and industrial areas (in some states)

(e) Industrial Investment Corporation

- -- Finances medium and large units up to a certain investment ceiling with direct participation in share capital and underwrites new issues

(f) Agro Industries Corporation-Supply of agricultural machinery / equipment on hire

- -- Development of agro-based industries
- -- Sale of agro-inputs like fertilizers and pesticides

(g) Electronics Development Corporation

- -- Promotion of industries in the field of electronics including joint sector and public sector projects.

(h) Leather Industry Development Corporation and other similar commodity corporations

- -- Development of specific types of village and tiny sector units relating to a particular trade

(i) Rural Industries Marketing Corporation

- -- Marketing of village industry products and provision of a variety of services needed by village and tiny units (Gujarat State has setup this corporation)

(j) Industrial and Technical Consultancy Organization (Sponsored by IDBI/IFCI/ICICI)

- -- Technical consultancy services to small and medium-scale projects)

3. Financial Institutions

(a) Reserve Bank of India (RBI)The country's central bank,

responsible for currency and monetary regulation and other central banking functions besides being banker to the government. Also responsible for supervision of all banking institutions, provision of rural credit exchange control.Entrusted with the administration of the credit Guarantee Scheme, under which government guarantee is provided for advances granted by banks and other credit institutions to small industrial units. The administration has since been transferred to the Deposit Insurance & Credit Guarantee Corporation.

(b) All India Term Lending Institutionsi.
Industrial Development Bank of IndiaCoordinates in conformity with national priorities the activities of institutions engaged in financing, promoting/ developing industry; operates with schemes such as:

- Direct assistance
- Soft loan scheme
- Technical development fund
- Refinance of industrial loans
- Automatic refinance
- Special refinancing facility
- Rediscounting of bills
- Seed capital assistance
- Subscriptions to shares and bonds of financial institutions
- Development assistance fundii.

Industrial Finance Corporation of India (IFCI)

- Long term loans to new industrial units and also for expansion, diversification, renovation or modernization of existing units both in rupees and foreign currencies, underwriting of equity, preference and debenture capital

- Risk capital foundation provides soft loans as part of equity capital to new entrepreneurs, particularly technologists and professionals
- Benevolent reserve fund provides assistance for development purposesiii.

Industrial Credit and Investment Corporation of India (ICICI)

- Currency loans to small enterprises under its Rupee Assistance Programme and foreign currency loaniv. Industrial Reconstruction Bank of India (IRBI)
- Provides financial and other types of assistance to sick or closed industrial concerns, and operates, in the case of small units, through state level agencies by way of sanctioning 'Line of Credit'
- Provides managerial assistance
- Guidance for renovation and modernizationv. Export Import Bank of India (EXIM Bank)
- Finances, facilitates and promotes foreign trade of India
- Coordinates the working of institutions engaged in financing export and import
- Finances export of consultancy and related services, assists Indian joint ventures in third countries, conducts export market studies, finances export oriented industries and provides international merchant banking services.vi. National Bank for Agriculture and Rural Development (NABARD)
- Refinancing the farm and non-farm operations in rural areas

- In the non-farm sector, village and tiny sector industries located in rural areas are supported through refinancingvii.National Cooperative Development Corporation (NCDC)
- Promotes and finances cooperative enterprises in processing, marketing, storage and export relating to agro-based industries
- Agro-service centres.
- Promotion of units for production of fertilizers, pesticides and insecticides

  Workshop for fabrication of agricultural machinery/ implements
- Margin money for processing units
- Technical training

(c) Other Financial Institutionsi. Export

Credit Guarantee Corporation (ECGC)

- Supports and strengthens export promotion drive (a) by providing a range of risk insurance covers to exporters against loss in export of goods and services, (b) by offering guarantees to banks and financial institutions to enable exporters to obtain better facilities from them.ii. Deposit Insurance and Credit Guarantee Corporation (DICGO)
- Operates four guarantee schemes: (a) small loans guarantee scheme, (b) small loans (small-scale industries), guarantee Scheme, (c) small loans (financial corporations) guarantee scheme, and (d) service cooperative society guarantee scheme

(iii) State Financial Corporation (SFC)

- Provides long and medium term loans for acquisition of fixed assets of small and medium-scale industries

- Guarantees payment for purchase of machinery from suppliers within India
- Guarantees loans raised by industries from commercial banks, cooperative banks etc.
- Foreign exchange loans under World Bank line of credit
- Special capital assistance upto Rs.200,000

(iv) Commercial Banks

- Provide term finance and working capital advances classified under cash credit, overdrafts, demand loans, purchased / discounted/ advanced against inland bills, purchased / discounted / advanced against import bills and clean advance.

(v) Regional Rural Banks (RRBs)

- Provide banking facilities in remote and unbanked areas among other places of the selected districts and provide credit to agriculturists, artisans and other self-employed persons belonging to weaker sections. The loans are given in kind.

(vi) Cooperative Banks

- Provide credit to farm and non-farm cooperative societies.

(d) Research Laboratories

- National laboratories coming under the purview of the Council of Scientific and Industrial Research (CSIR) and of other organizations and ministries of the Central Government
- Research laboratories established by state governments for research and development of new products / processes.The National Research Development Corporation (NRDC), New Delhi releases the patents

of new processes / products developed by national laboratories for commercial exploitation.

(e) Association of Small-Scale Industry Entrepreneurs

- Federation of Association of Small Industries of India (FASII)
- Indian Council of Small Industries (ICSI)
- National Alliance of Young Entrepreneurs (NAYE)
- State Small Industry Associations
- District small industry associations
- Associations at state and national levels for specific groups of industries
- Chambers of commerce & industry and their federations.

The All India Small-Scale Industries Board (AISSIB) with the Union Minister for Industry as the Chairman is the apex contemplative and advisory forum for the small-scale sector. As the Board meets only once or twice a year, it operates through a number of standing committees for detailed deliberations on various aspects. The standing committees operating at present are on policies and programmes; development of industries in the North Eastern region; ancillary development, quality improvement and marketing assistance including exports; credit facilities, taxation and modernization; and industrial sickness. The secretariat for the Board is the office of the Development Commissioner (Small-Scale Industries), headquarters of the Small Industries Development Organization (SIDO).

Central Organizations

The principal central institutions assisting the small-scale sector are the Small Industries Development Organization (SIDO) and the National Small Industries Corporation (NSIC) under the Ministry of Industry. The SIDO was established in 1954. It acts as a policy formulating, coordinating and monitoring agency for developing of small-scale industries. It coordinates the work relating to the development of small industries on an all-India basis by evolving an all-India policy and programme for the development of small-scale industries; coordinating the policies and programmes of various state governments, programmes and development of large and small-scale industries and programmes for the district industries centres, and development of industrial estates and ancillaries all over the country. It also acts as a liaison between different states and between the states and central ministries, planning commissions, the Reserve Bank of India and financial institutions.

The SIDO renders such technical assistance as may be required by the state governments for preparing schemes within the overall plan allocations. It assists the Ministry in regulating central assistance to the states for the development of small-scale industries.

An important function of the SIDO is to suggest a pattern of small-scale industries development for the country as a whole. This involves responsibilities for indicating the lines of manufacture which are suitable for the small-scale sector, and giving it all assistance in the form of promotion, procurement of raw materials and machinery, and other technical advice from time to time.

The SIDO provides a wide range of extension services through its network of small-scale industries service institutes, branch institutes, extension centres, regional testing centres and other institutions at the field level.

The National Small Industries Corporation was set up in 1955. Its primary function is to help small entrepreneurs in setting up small industries by providing both indigenous and imported machinery and equipment on hire purchase basis, assisting small units in marketing their products through participation in the Central Government Stores Purchase Programme. Through its prototype development and training centres, the Corporation develops prototypes of machinery for transfer of technology and know-how for commercial production and imparts training to skilled workers and entrepreneurs in various technical fields.

State Level Institutions

Prominent among the sate level institutions assisting the small-scale sector are the Directorate of Industries, Small Industry Development Corporation and State Financial Corporation. The Directorate of Industries is the executive agency for the village and small-scale industry sector. It acts under the overall guidance of SIDO and the concerned central institutions associated with various programmes of assistance. Its functions include regulatory and development activities. In the recent years, its emphasis is on utilizing the regulatory functions for more effective performance of developmental functions. It implements certain programmes of assistance and oversees the implementation of other schemes with the help of specialized agencies operating at the state level for village and small-scale industries. Its main asset is the extensive network of field offices in every district of the state, at the district, sub-division and block levels.

The main functions of the Small Industry Development Corporation are: supply of scarce raw materials to units in the small-scale sector, supply of machinery on hire purchase, provision of marketing assistance and promotion of entrepreneurship through various schemes. The State Financial Corporation provides long and medium term loans for acquisition of fixed assets of small and medium-scale industries.

Through various schemes of financing for small and

medium-scale units, it is actively involved in attracting entrepreneurs to backward and rural areas.

District Industries Centres

An important institution set up at the district level for industrial promotion is the District Industries Centre (DIC). It is a major structural innovation introduced in May 1978 to serve as a unified agency for industries under a single roof. Compared to the earlier pattern of district industries officer/ assistant director of industries, the institution has been upgraded and headed by a senior person designated as general manager. He is of the rank of joint director of industries and in certain cases deputy director of industries. There are in all 422 DICs in the country covering 428 districts. With a senior officer posted at the district level, powers have been delegated to him in a number of areas and many organizational innovations are either introduced or contemplated in various states to provide a wide range of services and support to entrepreneurs and artisans.

The general manager has four functional managers concerned with the functional areas of economic investigation, village industries, credit, marketing, infrastructure and raw materials. It is planned to augment the strength of functional managers with three project managers specialized in different product groups, based on the needs of a particular district. It is hoped that the team will be able to give area orientation and project orientation to its activities simultaneously for helping entrepreneurs in various ways. In many states, sub-divisional set up has come into being with an assistant director of industries and an industrial promotion officer posted at the sub-divisional headquarters. In addition, at the block level, an extension officer (industries) is in position. In the recent past there have been some changes in some states especially in Andhra Pradesh, the block as a unit changed to Mandal. In some states, he looks after two to three blocks. It is hoped that an extension officer will be given the jurisdiction of not more than one block in the near future, to cope with a number of developmental schemes for which he is held responsible as a field level functionary. Strong district and lower level teams are an important aspect of industrial administration in the country.

ECONOMIC INFORMATION SERVICE

In the package of services needed by entrepreneurs at the pre-investment, investment and post-investment stages, economic information service and technical and management consultancy are quite prominent. Some of the important consultancy needs of entrepreneurs at various stages are detailed below:

- To identify industrial potential of a region and suggest project ideas;
- To prepare project profiles, feasibility reports and other pre-investment studies;
- To prepare detailed project reports and when called upon, render turn-key services in project implementation;
- To identify potential entrepreneurs, provide them with technical and management assistance and train them to shoulder the entrepreneurial responsibility;
- To undertake the techno-economic appraisal of feasibility/project reports;
- To undertake market research and surveys for specific products;
- To undertake project supervision and follow-up and where necessary, render technical, management and administrative assistance;
- To undertake studies for expansion/modernization/diversification;

- To undertake diagnostic studies of sick units and monitoring of the rehabilitation programmes;
- To provide industrial and management consultancy services.

Economic information services are made available through a number of studies carried out by promotional and consultancy organizations. These are techno-economic surveys at the district/regional level, industry surveys, product profiles, feasibility studies, market surveys and surveys dealing with impact of specific programmes. These were initially undertaken by the SIDO on an extensive scale and gradually, at the state/district levels, by small industries corporations, technical consultancy organizations and district industries centres have pursued them. Training and research organizations like the National Institute of Small Industry Extension Training (NISIET) have prepared select studies on these themes and evolved guidelines for incorporating the foci considered relevant at various periods in the studies carried out by them from time to time.

Information service provided to entrepreneurs at the SISIs and at other institutions at state and district levels is based on the findings of studies of the type referred to above carried out by a number of agencies. This service helps prospective entrepreneurs in selecting suitable product lines. An existing industrialist is assisted to know about the competitive position of his industry and market, and guided in the expansion/diversification of his product lines.

The Small Enterprises National Documentation Centre (SENDOC) established at the NISIET is a storehouse of information on all aspects of relevance to the small-scale industry sector. The Centre has close links with all national laboratories, specialized research institutions and development agencies in the country, and prominent international organizations concerned with industrial development. It captures technological management and economic information from a variety of sources and disseminates the same to entrepreneurs and development functionaries. Dissemination of information attempted through various journals and ad-hoc publications as an anticipatory information service relates to specific products processes and regions.

Similar documentation centres have been established in a number of national level research laboratories to provide information on specific product groups to entrepreneurs and development agencies.

ENTREPRENERSHIP DEVELOPMENT

Entrepreneur being the kingpin of industrialization, emphasis was given to development of entrepreneurship of various categories as part of the small-scale industry promotional efforts. With the special programmes launched in 1971 to provide large-scale self-employment opportunities for the educated, unemployed, technically qualified, skilled and experienced persons, development of entrepreneurship became an important element in the strategy for stimulating industrialization. Entrepreneurs are trailblazers or innovators. They can be identified through certain demographic, social, economic and psychological tests and such characteristics can be developed through educational and training programmes. Thus entrepreneurship can be stimulated, increased, regulated and controlled.

The need for achievement, affiliation and power have been regarded as the most significant characteristics of successful entrepreneurs in the pioneering studies carried out by David C. McClelland and his team at the National Institute of Small Industry Extension Training (NISIET) in the mid sixties. Through these and subsequent studies, and experiments carried out by NISIET and a number of other institutions in the country, more insight was gained into the nature of entrepreneurship, and the ways and means of promoting and developing qualities of entrepreneurship relevant for small scale industries and small business.

Among institutions specialized in this field mention may be made, besides NISIET, Hyderabad, Entrepreneurship Development Institute of India, Ahmedbad; National Institute for Entrepreneurship and Small Business Development (NIESBUD), New Delhi; and Management Development Institute, New Delhi. Recently, the National Board for Entrepreneurial Development was established with the Union Minister for Industry as the chairman. At the operational level, Small Industries Development Organization through its network of SISIs have organized a large number of programmes all over the country. Financial institutions, particularly the State Bank of India and technical consultancy organizations promoted by the all-India financial institutions have organized a number of programmes on entrepreneurship development at the district level, taking clues from the patterns advocated by specialized institutions. The Indian Investment Centre, New Delhi, is another institution which has made a significant contribution in this field.

Intensive campaigns are organized extensively for attracting entrepreneurship. In the initial years, they were conducted at the state level and in recent years focus is on district and taluk level campaigns. All organizations concerned with small industry promotion come together in a particular location, publicize the opportunities available and facilities offered for starting small-scale units, and enthuse entrepreneurs through counseling. On the strength of the preparatory work done earlier, the campaigns enable a large number of entrepreneurs make up their mind on the product lines they intend to pursue. Clearances are given on the spot by the concerned agencies to entrepreneurs who are in an advanced stage.

As entrepreneurial development programmes gathered momentum in the seventies, more streamlined procedures were adopted for identification and selection of entrepreneurs, and to provide them techno-managerial training. Selection procedure evolved consists of administering psychological tests like TAT, risk taking, personal efficacy; finding out the socio-economic views. Among the states, mention may be made of Gujarat where systematic efforts were made to develop entrepreneurial qualities among employees, workers, merchants and all those who evinced interest in pursuing self-employment avenues in various vocations - industry service and business. The programme was not limited to small-scale industry alone nor to people with relatively high level of education, including technical education. People with smaller means and with low level of education were helped to become self-employed.

The integrated model for entrepreneurship development evolved by NISIET in the early seventies is the result of its experience and realization that entrepreneurship development is a multi-disciplinary and long-range plan executed through well orchestrated institutional support. The main components of this model are: (a) local agency to initiate and support potential entrepreneurs till the break-even stage; (b) inter-disciplinary approach; (c) strong information support; (d) training as an important input for entrepreneurial development, monitoring and evaluation; (e) institutional financing and counseling services. These steps may also be categorized as stimulatory, support and sustenance activities needed for development of entrepreneurship. The inter-disciplinary training programme of twelve-weeks duration include economic aspects of self-employment including industrial opportunities and acquaintance with the environment for establishing a venture; feasibility studies for selected product lines; management of new enterprises.

Programmes were organized for training the trainers who could in turn put across programmes at the district level. In this effort NISIET was instrumental in the establishment of the entrepreneurial motivation training centres in Assam.

The type of entrepreneurs selected by various agencies for the programmes organized by them included educated unemployed, science and technology graduates, technically qualified, skilled or experienced persons, women entrepreneurs, retired defence personnel, entrepreneurs from tribals and other economically weaker sections, entrepreneurs interested in ancillary units, those interested in industry, service and business (small enterprise and not necessarily small industry) and artisans. The nature of the programme was modified to suit the needs of specific categories.

One important direction in which programmes are being pursued is to look for entrepreneurship in smaller towns and rural areas. This needs to be intensified further through a cluster approach. Grouping entrepreneurial activities in different clusters and planning interrelated activities and services would be useful in the context of small towns and rural areas. Manufacture of products needing simple technology, and goods and services required in the neighbouring areas could be the focus for reaching smaller towns and rural areas through this programme.

In the context of rural areas, 'Training of Rural Youth for Self-Employment (TRYSEM)' is a scheme started in 1978 to cater to the age group of 18-35. Another scheme known as 'Providing Self-employment to Educated Unemployed' (SEEU) was started in 1983 with focus on educated unemployed persons with low level of education in the age group of 18-35 interested in self-employment ventures requiring total investment not exceeding Rs.25,000/-. Developing entrepreneurs through self-employment ventures has thus been one of the major goals of smalls-scale industry programmes for quite some time.

TRAINING

Training was visualized in its totality for the benefit of the small-scale sector right from the early years. Based on the needs identified, programmes of training and institutional framework were evolved at various levels. Technical and managerial training is an integral part of the extension services rendered by SIDO. Basic consideration in organizing these programmes is the scope for developing new enterprises and improving the productivity of existing ones. Over the years, small-scale industries have developed a greater degree of sophistication. Skills, managerial talents, technical know-how and entrepreneurship required for these industries are of a high order. New institutions have been established to provide specialized series including training to certain categories of industries.

SIDO conducts technical and managerial training programmes for small industries through SISIs, extension centres, and training and production centres. Short courses are organized on various aspects of management and technical areas. These include trade-oriented, process-oriented, and product-oriented courses. Mobile workshops are attached to SISIs visit areas of concentration of artisans for demonstration and training purposes. Training through mobile vans is imparted to interested artisans in areas such as blacksmithy, carpentry, leatherwork, general engineering, woodwork, etc.,

NISIET provides composite non-technological training in almost all aspects connected with small industry development, emphasis being on development, management and behavioural science programmes at national and international levels. It trains development and extension personnel of organizations associated with small industry development in the country and from a large number of developing countries, and existing and prospective personnel from various organizations are also organized periodically. It thus serves as an apex training, research and consultancy organization in the small-scale sector.

The National Institute for Entrepreneurship and Small Business Development (NIESBUD) coordinates the training and research activities for entrepreneurship development in the small enterprise sector. It also undertakes specific programmes to cater to the needs of various target groups. Its programmes are mainly for motivators, trainers and entrepreneurs.

Some of the central institutions which provide specialized training for technical personnel concerned with specific industry groups are Prototype Development and Training Centres of the National Small Industries Corporation, Central Institute of Tool Design (CITD), Hyderabad, Institute for Design of Electrical Measuring Instruments (IDEMI), Mumbai, Central Tool Room and Training Centres, Central Institute of Hand Tools, Jalandhar, National Institute of Foundry and Forge Technology, Ranchi and the Central Institute for Plastics Engineering and Tools (CIPET), Chennai.

To supplement these, the state governments have also developed training centres, tool room and testing facilities in certain line of manufacture. At the grass root level for development of skills needed for various industries, polytechnics and industrial training institutes are operating in each district. Training programmes are being closely monitored to ensure that they cope with the requirements of the industry from time to time.

TECHNICAL AND MANAGEMENT CONSULTANCY AND TECHNOLOGY SUPPORT

As part of the comprehensive extension service, technical and management consultancy services are quite important. Project consultancy is an integral part of this package deal. This indicates the need at various stages to conduct specific studies in the plant to improve productivity, efficiency and profitability with the help of effective consultancy services. Consultancy in this sense should have process orientation, i.e., a continuous consultant-client relationship where both are jointly involved in identifying and analyzing problems, finding solutions to problems and implementing them, with the major role being played by the client himself while the consultant would function more as resource person.

Key organizations providing consultancy services to small enterprises are as follows:

1. SIDO Network (SISIs, and its branch institutes, and extension centres) providing virtually free consultancy services and acting as promotional organizations;
2. Technical consultancy organizations (TCOs) promoted by all-India financial institutions (Industrial Development Bank of India, Industrial Finance Corporation of India and industrial Credit and Investment Corporation of India) providing consultancy services at subsidized rates;
3. Consultancy bureaus of banks established recently providing services free of charge to enterprises assisted by the respective banks;
4. Private consultants and management institutions mostly serving medium and large enterprises who can pay for the services rendered. To enable small enterprises avail of private consultants, financial support from governmental institutions becomes necessary.

SISIs and TCOs have a complementary role to play in providing consultancy services. They can pool their expertise and provide consultancy services in the respective states. A roster of private consultants is maintained by SISIs, TCOs and financial institutions. They solicit the services of consultants as and when they find it necessary. The cost of such services is subsidized by the government: SISI for the work entrusted by SISI and the concerned all-India financial institution for the work taken up or entrusted by a TCO.

Management consultancy involves study of specific aspects of the unit and in some cases study of a number of technical and managerial aspects simultaneously. The integrated plant studies encompass areas such as production, inventories, layout, designs, quality control, plant maintenance, marketing, finance, costing, industrial relations, inter-personnel conflicts, training etc. Packaging consultancy services bring out practical suggestions which can be pursued by the unit for implementation.

TECHNICAL CONSULTANCY

Small industries service institutes and industrial extension centres are equipped with workshops where small units can utilize engineering services such as machine shop, tool room, heat treatment facilities and furnaces. Laboratories are set up to provide testing facilities. Product and process development centre for glass and ceramics at Ranchi develops viable processes and products and introduces quality control measures. Prototype development and training centres of NSIC development prototype of such equipment and tools as are relevant to the small-scale sector and provide common facility services such as testing, machining, castings, electroplating, etc., and intensive job-oriented technical training. They also design, develop and produce improved tools for use by rural artisans. Footwear training centres offer training in improved methods of footwear technology.

Technical consultancy rendered by SIDO consultants can be grouped into the following areas:

- Advice on improvement of processes, use of modern machines, production planning, layout of the factory, and material handling.
- Assistance in better product design, preparation of drawings of machines and machine parts, equipment, tools, jigs and fixtures;
- Demonstration of use of modern technical processes through workshops;
- Research on proper use of equipment, improved designs of machinery;
- Training in various technical trades for the benefit of small industrialists and artisans;
- Preparation of product profiles, feasibility studies and projects reports;
- Guidance on proper selection of machinery and equipment, make or buy policy, sources of supply of machines, erection and commission of machinery, proper maintenance, etc.

Specialized institutions such as central tool room and training centres, Central Institute of Tool Design, Institute for Design of Electrical Measuring Instruments, Central Hand Tools Institute and National Institute of Foundry and Forge Technology, provide a variety of advisory, consultancy and common service facilities for existing and prospective entrepreneurs and for developing manpower in specialized areas through training to take to employment in small scale units.

Role of TCOs

Technical Consultancy Organizations (TCOs) promoted by all-India financial institutions provide a wide spectrum of reasonably priced consultancy services to small and medium scale units and to prospective entrepreneurs. They also provide consultancy services to government departments, commercial banks and other state level developmental and financial institutions concerned with industrial development. Sixteen TCOs (including the one promoted by the Government of Karnataka) started with major focus on technical consultancy. Preparation of product profiles, feasibility studies and project reports constitutes a sizeable part of the work. Gradually they are diversifying their activities into managerial consultancy, specialized studies needed at the district and regional levels and selection, motivation and training of entrepreneurs as part of entrepreneurship development programmes. They are also entering areas such as design engineering services, turn-key assignments, retainer consultancy services, putting up functional industrial complexes, adopting sick units and training barefoot consultants who can act as a link between the consultancy organization and entrepreneurs.

One of the technical consultancy organizations covering Gujarat state (GITCO) has introduced a number of innovative experiments in developing management consultancy services for small-scale industries which are:

1. Novel approaches for reviving sick units through the adoption or retainer systems.
2. Marketing consultancy clinics organized at various locations for benefiting clusters of small enterprises.
3. Marketing assistance either by undertaking direct sale or through counseling. In case of the latter, the effort involved is in developing the product concept,

identification of market segments, determination of marketing strategy in terms of price, promotion and distribution, and procurement of orders.

Modernization and Technology Support

The scheme for modernization of selected small-scale industries was introduced in 1975 with a view to identify the problems of productivity-efficiency and obsolescence, and keeping industrial units abreast of the latest trends in production processes, product design, technical and technological development and training facilities through an effective consultancy service and other forms of assistance. Salient features of the programme include motivational and educational activities like seminars, industrial workshops, industrial clinics etc., inplant studies for suggesting modernization methods, preparation of modernization guides and industrial study reports and conducting of modernization courses. All India industry study reports are prepared for specific industries for identifying the problems of industries relating to product design, technology, machinery and equipment, managerial aspects, etc., and for taking action to overcome the problems. Under this programme, 20 industries have been selected on an all-India basis and 38 industries based on state wise concentration of units. Selection of these industries was done on the basis of present status of technological obsolescence, potential for export and possibilities of import substitution.

Intensive inplant study of small-scale units registered under this programme is conducted free of cost by consultants/ SIDO officers. For studies conducted by consultancy organizations, SIDO bears the cost upto a maximum of Rs.2000 per study. For problem-oriented consultancy, 75 per cent of the expenditure upto Rs.500 per unit will be borne by SIDO. For units from backward areas, the service is free. For organizing study visits of entrepreneurs from one area to another to study advanced technologies, better design and testing facilities in the same industry, 50 per cent of the transport cost is borne by SIDO.

Interest subsidy scheme for modernization has been recently introduced to quicken the pace of modernization for implementing the recommendations of inplant study reports prepared by SISIs. For undertaking modernization, loan is made available at 7 per cent rate of interest per annum, the difference between this figure and the normal rate of interest charged by financial institutions for loans advanced by them being subsidized by SIDO, subject to a maximum of Rs.20,000 per unit per annum. The subsidy will be available for five years for a unit located in backward areas and for three years in other areas. In respect of all the above-mentioned schemes, SISI is the implementing agency at the state level.

As part of the programme of technology upgradation and testing, a number of institutions are operating in the field. Four regional testing centres of SIDO provide testing facilities and assistance to small-scale units in improving the quality of their products and enabling them to produce goods conforming to Indian Standards Institution specifications.

A chain of twenty field-testing stations is being established in areas of concentration of specific type of industries as part of the network of regional testing centres. Specialized tool rooms and training institutes including prototype development and training centres of the NSIC provide a variety of services to small-scale units in technology upgradation. Science and technology parks are planned to be established in a number of centres in the country to provide a window to the industry for new technologies developed in various fields which could be adapted by existing and prospective entrepreneurs. Establishment of pilot plants for enabling entrepreneurs to try out processes developed in research laboratories to test their commercial viability is also planned in these parks.

INDUSTRIAL ESTATES

Availability of factory accommodation with a package of facilities and services has been an important attraction for small-scale units. This is provided through industrial estates and industrial areas in locations identified for intensive promotion and those where prospects for industrialization are bright. Provision of such facilities in anticipation of demand obviates the need for the entrepreneur to get clearances from a number of agencies for establishing his enterprise, which is often a cumbersome and time consuming process, and conserve his capital for production purposes rather than utilizing it for land and buildings.

The industrial estates programme of India which was started in 1955, expanded rapidly in certain periods of planned development. The main purpose of the programme was two-fold: promotion of small-scale industries and entrepreneurship on an extensive scale; dispersal of industries to less developed or backward regions, smaller towns and rural areas.

The programme also serves other purposes such as promotion of specific category of industries, relieving congestion in cities, promotion of export-oriented units, attracting foreign investment through promotion of industries, and integrating industry with urban and regional planning.

Types of Estates

Industrial estates can be categorized from three angles: (a) sponsorship; (b) nature of industrial activity; and (c) location.

Industrial estates in most cases have been sponsored by state governments. Either the Department of Industries or government corporation have developed them.

Another pattern of estates promoted is on cooperative lines. In the states of Maharashtra and Gujarat in the western part of the country, cooperative pattern is preferred as it involves the entrepreneurs to a considerable extent by pooling their own resources right from the conception of the estate proposal. The idea is to enable entrepreneurs develop the estate, construct factory buildings and make them available to its members. Land is acquired and given by the government on lease to the society. The financing pattern followed in a cooperative estate is 20:20:60. In the total project cost of the estate including building construction, members' share capital contribution is 20 per cent, and equal amount is contributed by the state government and treated as a long term interest free loan, and 60 per cent is obtained as long tern loan from a financial institution. Life Insurance Corporation of India provides finance to cooperative estates.

In many locations, industrial estates are of general-purpose type judged by the nature of industrial activity. All types of industries are permitted in them except noxious and hazardous ones. In such estates, provision is made for custom built factories where manufacturing operations demand special type of facilities. Ancillary estates are promoted for attracting ancillary units either for one parent large-scale unit or for a few parent units located nearby. Clusters of ancillary units thus promoted help parent units to provide the required services such as supply of raw material, technical guidance, quality control, etc. Single trade estates are designed to attract units of the same trade or a cluster of units belonging to a homogenous group. A functional estate is one in which the functions of one industry are sub-divided among a number of small-scale units located at one place, each functioning according to a coordinated manufacturing programme. Both single trade and functional estates offer opportunities for planning the technical and common service facilities to a greater degree and facilitate arrangements for joint purchase of raw materials/sale of finished goods. These two patterns are very often used as synonyms and referred to as functional complexes. Many states are promoting functioning complexes for leather goods, ceramic products, light engineering goods, hosiery, agro-industries, etc.

Another categorization attempted is by location: metropolitan, urban, semi-urban estates refer to places from 50,000 to one million population; semi-urban estates refer to urban settlements upto 50,000 population; rural estates are situated in rural settlements, of generally below 5,000 population.

By March 1981, there were 799 industrial estates sponsored in the country out of which 659 were functioning and 140 were at various stages of development. At the aggregate level, more detailed picture is available as at the end of March 1979. The data relate to industrial estates and do not include industrial areas. The accent on development of industrial estates in small towns, rural areas and less developed regions is conspicuous by the large number of estates sponsored during the Third Plan period (1961-66) which could start functioning only during the Fourth Plan period. Hence, rightly, the emphasis from the fourth Plan period has been on consolidation and making the existing estates function effectively. By March 1979, the number of functioning estates was 633 as against 796 sponsored. Sheds constructed were 19,368 of which 17,451 were occupied, resulting in the occupancy rate of 90 per cent (72 to 84 per cent from 1961 to 1975). On the other hand, the occupancy position of developed plots was only 70 per cent in 1979 (75 per cent in 1975). In the 18,241 units functioning in allotted sheds and plots, production was Rs.8,030 million and employment of 286,000 was generated. Out of the completed estates of 705, there were 316 in urban locations, 179 in semi-urban and 210 in rural settlements. Occupancy rate of semi-urban and rural estates was less than that of urban estates, indicating the slow response from entrepreneurs in these locations.

Lessons of Experiences

With wide diversity in the levels of industrialization and development, the degree of effectiveness and success of industrial estates in various locations has varied.

Development and management of estates in various centres should be related to the potential and pattern suited to the locations. In centres where industrialization is of a high order, industrial areas could be the answer. Ancillary estates, functional complexes and estates needed for specific categories of entrepreneurs may be planned. Wherever possible estates may be sponsored by cooperative societies or associations of entrepreneurs.

In semi-urban and rural areas, assessing entrepreneurial response is necessary to decide on the size and type of estates. Building construction is to be attempted in consultation with the entrepreneurs to ensure that it meets their needs. In smaller towns, linking the units of estates with the resource and demand picture of the region and developmental plans envisaged promotes inter-sectoral linkages. In bigger centres objectives such as catering to institutional purchases, demand of a larger region, meeting inter-firm demand can certainly be kept in view while selecting product lines. In each of these locations entrepreneurship development of a pattern that is considered advisable for a region has to be pursued. Attracting outside entrepreneurs and technical talents from elsewhere to a less developed region is necessary to trigger off industrialization of that region. Guided entrepreneurship needs to be pursued in less developed regions.

In the units functioning in existing industrial estates, monitoring of performance is necessary for identifying the reasons for some of them not working up to optimum capacity and devise strategies to improve their performance.

REFERENCES

1. D. Nagaiya, "Small-Scale Industry Development in India: Policy, Programmes and Institutional Support" in Victor Sit Fung-Shuen, ed., Strategies for Small-Scale Industries Promotion in Asia (Hong Kong: Longman: 1984), pp. 8-42.
2. Planning Commission, Government of India, Seventh Five Year Plan 1985-90: A Summary (New Delhi, 1985), p. 25.
3. Manas Bhattacharya, "Planning and Development of Small-Scale Industries in India" in Small Industry Bulletin for Asia and the Pacific, No.23,(New York: United Nations, 1988), p. 89.
4. D. Nagaiya, Small-Scale Industries in India: Handbook of Statistics (Hyderabad: National Institute of Small Industry Extension Training, 1989), pp. 10-11.
5. Planning Commission, Government of India, Seventh Five Year Plan, Vol. 2, p. 101.

13

Strategies for Developing Entrepreneurship

When we speak of developing entrepreneurship among women, we cannot think of this effort and programme in isolation. One can think of developing entrepreneurship among women only through creating an environment which would motivate and facilitate women coming forward to take to certain enterprises. This necessitates developing entrepreneurship in rural areas. The present chapter focuses on developing entrepreneurship towards rural industrialization. Such a measure will pave the way and create conditions which will help the women folk from different ethnic segments and economic background to gradually move and shoulder up industrial activity by themselves or with their family members.

As we have pointed out earlier, promoting and developing small-scale and cottage industries inclusive of handicrafts and artisan enterprises in rural areas is not for their own sake, nor is it simply a political strategy to appease the low-income groups in the community, but it is an indispensable measure, whatever be the approaches and methods employed towards the use of the material and human resources at the disposal of the rural communities. So long you have the choice to ignore rural industrialization and that you have better alternatives to it, you are free to pursue such a course of development. But such alternatives are few in view of the enormity of population in some countries, literacy and technological levels out-weighed by material and human resources that could be gradually harnessed and utilized to meet the minimum needs of the people.

We can safely say, irrespective of certain limitation in respect of the whole class of small-scale and cottage industries in terms of productivity, quality of products, profits and poor management of these enterprises, that there is no argument against rural industrialization and development of small-scale and cottage industries.

Promotion and development of small industries will involve, both directly and indirectly, the development of entrepreneurship. The approach and strategies for achieving industrial development may vary from those for entrepreneurship development. Perhaps, the strategies vary accordingly as emphasis is placed on either of the two. Needless to say that industrial development cannot be achieved without entrepreneurship development. Depending upon the emphasis, one becomes the by-product of the other. They are indeed two facets of the same activity.

The inadequacy of entrepreneurship is an inhibiting factor to accelerate the process of industrialization in the newly developing communities. Although there is no such thing as a zero level of entrepreneurship, the absence of an appropriate industrial and entrepreneurial climate and an industrial base, coupled with lack of access to relevant technology, has acted as a handicap for such communities, to achieve rapid industrial development. The inadequate availability of entrepreneurial talent particularly affects the development of modern small manufacturing and processing enterprises for, while large industries can be set up with expatriate capital and entrepreneurship, small industries need to have a domestic entrepreneurial base. The development of indigenous entrepreneurship especially among the rural-tribal populations is, therefore, a key issue and an imperative need on the part of the countries embarking on small industry development programmes.

Our focus in this discussion is on entrepreneurial development in rural communities. Development here means a basic, partial or total transformation, a socio-cultural change in the client community. Entrepreneur in this context is defined as one who would start an industry or take to a new enterprise which is a deviation from his traditional family occupation or profession. Further, entrepreneurship may be defined as a creative activity, the entrepreneur being an innovator who introduces something new into the economy: a method of production not yet tested by experience in the branch of manufacture concerned, a product with which the consumers are not familiar, a new source of raw material, or of a new market hitherto unexploited and other similar innovations.

The approach suggested here is field approach which may be defined s a holistic approach to development comprising the study of the social structure and socio-cultural processes that operate in a given client community. It envisages a thorough understanding of the target community in all its aspects and attempts entrepreneurial development in it, manipulating simultaneously all the key elements in the total system such as physical and human resources, institutions, infrastructure and the entrepreneur himself.

Prior to the advent of entrepreneurial development agencies, entrepreneurship grew as a spontaneous economic activity among certain traditionally entrepreneurial communities wherein this activity was institutionalized. Besides, there has been sporadic emergence of entrepreneurship among other groups based on needs and wants of people, natural resources, innovativeness, managerial and risk-taking abilities on the part of individual entrepreneurs. The rate and volume of spontaneous emergence of entrepreneurship is far behind the desired national, social and economic objectives of entrepreneurial development. Attempts during the past few years have been towards induced entrepreneurship. This was restricted to selective, sporadic and isolated approaches and the results have not been commensurate with the time and money spent on these programmes. It is relevant here to look into some sociological aspects of entrepreneurship citing India as an example.

SOCIOLOGICAL ASPECTS

Entrepreneurship as an economic activity emerges and functions in a sociological and cultural setting. It could be conceived of as an individual's free choice activity or a social group's occupation or profession. In the Indian context, the supply of entrepreneurship in the past was mostly from some functionally designated communities or individual families. The ancient Hindu Varna order and its later ramifications called the caste system were partly based on the division of functions in the Hindu society. Thus we had and have the Brahmin, Kshatriya, Vysya and Sudra with innumerable sub-castes and sects in the first three and hundreds of castes or endogamous groups among the Sudra. Of the four Varnas traditionally, it was the Vysya community that was assigned the entrepreneurial activity comprising farming, trade, commerce and industry. Over the years, trade and commerce became characteristic of them. Further, the caste system, which was the later complex social stratification of the Varna order, was predominantly associated with diverse occupations and professions in a given territorial community. This stratification of Hindu society resulted in the birth of a new institution called the Hindu Jajmani system. It is a service relationship between the service or goods receiver (Jajmani) and the service and goods supplier (Kamin). The rendering of service or supply of goods on the part of a caste has become over centuries hereditary and closely associated with the caste system. The Jajmani system is a complex network of socio-economic relationship and still prevails all over rural India. Thus we had the functional groups such as priests, carpenters, blacksmiths, goldsmiths, potters, dairymen, washer-men, gardeners, water bearers, cobblers, barbers, sweepers, scavengers, oil-mongers, vegetable growers, weavers, traders and scores of others with distinct functions. An occupational or servicing group rendered service or supplied goods as the case may be and received remuneration mostly in kind annually or periodically.

In the jajmani system the farmer was the central figure and other groups served him and served each other. This kind of barter economy and socio-economic relationship streamlined and institutionalized the castes and their distinct functions, as a contrast to the Japanese society where in there has been negligible division of labour or functions. Since it became institutionalized over a period of time, it tended to be rigid, each caste pursuing its traditionally designated or customary function. Thus, as a sequence of the jajmani system, activities relating to industry, trade and commerce and small enterprises such as handicrafts made by artisans and their counterparts elsewhere in the country (Agarwal, Marwari etc.), the smith and artisan groups are examples of those who are predominantly engaged in trade, commerce and small enterprises, manufacturing, processing, the supply of entrepreneurs was sociologically and culturally limited to the traditional entrepreneurial groups. That is, only certain caste groups forced by the value system and tradition entered the field of entrepreneurship. Alongside the traditional entrepreneurial caste groups, in a sporadic way, a few individual pioneers and innovators drawn from the non-traditional entrepreneurial groups have taken to entrepreneurship.

During the past two-three decades in the context of India and other developing countries in Asia, as a consequence of a combination of factors such as increase in education, forces working against the institution of caste (in India), democracy as an ideal and value, territorial mobility, urbanization, increase in population, new impetus in science and technology, the state's intervention and emphasis on industrialization, new economic policy and diversification of occupations, a climate is being created inducing and encouraging development of entrepreneurship both among traditional and non-traditional groups.

ASSUMPTIONS

In our approach to the problem of developing entrepreneurship in rural communities, a basic question needs to be answered. Does promotion and development entrepreneurship depend on inherent entrepreneurial ability or quality of individuals in a given community? If the answer is 'yes', and since the inherent factor is a constant in all societies, it ceases to be a significant change-inducing factor. We may grant that entrepreneurial ability as a consequence of social and environmental background is distributed in a given population to a smaller degree. Assuming that, how do we explain and account for the transformation of agrarian societies into industrial societies. Almost the whole western society and Japan are examples of this transformation. In the case of Japan, which lacks most of the natural material resources, it was the human resource, the quality of man and the entrepreneurial climate it has built-up that put it on the map of highly industrialized countries in the world. The kind of transformation that has taken place in once-agrarian countries leads us to make the following assumptions:

1. We assume that agrarian societies could be transformed into industrial societies. The chief element in this change process is 'time', provided that factors such as finance, technology, marketing of the product and organizational machinery - necessary concomitants of industrialization are taken care of.
2. We assume that physical and institutional infrastructure could be provided with comparative ease in developing entrepreneurship.
3. We assume that conditions could be created and talented persons could be trained to become successful entrepreneurs.

We realize that the real problem we encounter in promoting entrepreneurship in the client community is the 'human factor', the individual in society, his network of relationships, his aspirational level, his attitudes and his group norms. This leads us to the study and understanding of the target community wherein we have to locate and develop entrepreneurship. We may call this a field approach or a total systems approach to the development of entrepreneurship.

This approach does not ignore the individual or selective approach by the use of projective tests and other psychological tools. Field approach is employed to see that the potential entrepreneur secures encouragement and support from the local institutions and environment of which he is a constituent. This modus operandi requires an understanding of the clientele community.

ASPECTS OF THE CLIENT COMMUNITY TO BE STUDIED

In the field approach, we take the entire community, be it a village, a cluster of villages, a mandal, a block, an occupational or a professional group as a unit of action. We study all aspects of the client system, physical, economic, human resources, cultural patterns, social, political and ecclesiastical structure, local institutions and institutional leadership. The study of the client system precedes the programmes related to entrepreneurial development. The data that are already available in respect to a unit of action (industrial potential surveys, lead bank surveys, techno-economic surveys, monographs, census reports etc.) will be made use of. The gaps in the aspects of the clientele group will have to be studied afresh. The major aspects to be studied of a client group may be described briefly.

Physical Conditions

It includes the physical resources that the area is endowed with, such as rainfall, terrain, quality of soil, the kind of farm activities that are in practice and enterprises that can be undertaken in the locality. This part of the study subsumes the industrial potential survey, as to how the people in the area have interacted with the given resources such as agricultural, horticultural, mineral, forest, marine etc., in the past and the resultant economic and industrial activities of the people and the related skills the people are proficient in. It will give us an idea of the ongoing activities, skills, attitudes, preferences on the part of the people and the kind of entrepreneurial activities that need modernization and innovative enterprises that could be introduced in the area.

Economic Structure of the Community

In the economic field, we study the types of production within the community, the organization of producing units, capital and labour resources, the ratio in which labour and capital resources are used, occupational structure, the functioning of the local marketing system, farm organization and land tenure. In this area, we also study the network of economic relationships the community has with the outside world.

Human Resources

Usually, the industrial potential surveys or techno-economic surveys that are undertaken by different agencies connected with industrial development pay a meagre attention to human resources. The requisite emphasis on human resources has not been there. The focus has been on economic resources and the potential thereof and not on the man and the group behind him. In the field approach, man or the human resource is at the centre. He is the starting point. Under the human resources, we go in for a census enumeration of literate population, skilled workers, technically qualified people, educated unemployed and various native skills available in the community. Another human resource is the leadership in the client group which is to be studied, promoted and utilized for introducing changes in the community. We will further deal with the resources aspect in the following pages.

Women constitute a potential human resource, untapped and underutilized and there is a need to make special efforts to promote entrepreneurship among women.

Cultural Patterns

A Community or a social group has history, a value system and tradition in terms of its occupation and or profession and choices or preference for economic activities. Individuals in the group when intend or motivated to take to some entrepreneurial activity look in for sanction and support from within the group. And so, in the field approach we make a historical analysis of the community and the patterns of diffusion and change. We look in for the direction and trend of change taking place in the community. The understanding of the cultural patterns of the group lends us some insight into the group's ethos and it will serve as a lead for further action in the filed of entrepreneurial development.

A study of the cultural patterns of the community takes us to the other intimately associated aspect of it - its social structure. In a general sense, entrepreneurship may be taken as an individual's free choice affair, but when the development of entrepreneurship comes to a rural-tribal community, it ceases to be purely an individual's affair. Here it is the group's choice. And hence the need for understanding the social structure of the group, the network of relationship between various sub-groups and institutions, and the dynamics of the group's influence over the individual and vice-versa.

In social structure of the community, we study the various constituents and the institutions in it. We may begin with the basic constituent of the society - the family, its structure, the decision-making process in the family, functional aspects of the family, and the typology of the families based on occupation and division of functions. Around the family is the kin-group with a set of consanguineous and affinal kin shaping, and influencing the individuals' decision making and behaviour. We study the kin-group in the client community, its structure and functions, intraclan, inter-clan, inter-tribal relationships and the role of certain kin in kinship circles.

Ethnic or tribal councils are significant and viable social institutions. We may say that tribal councils are almost universal among the tribes in the world. Despite the influence of Christianity, western styles of life and new politico-administrative institutions among certain tribal groups at the village-community level, the tribal councils still continue to be significant and functional in the life of a tribe. For instance in India, we find a high incidence of caste councils among the so-called lower castes. These are village or settlement-based and community-based in a region. Though caste councils are sporadic among middle-ranking and higher castes, we come across among some of them formal caste associations at town, district and regional levels. These caste associations (Sanghams) are a kind of foundations to promote the education of the children and other welfare activities of the group. Wherever the caste-tribal councils obtain, whatever may be their strength and influence over the individual and group today, they are to be reckoned with as factors of influence, Positive and negative. Further, ethnic groups in a multi-ethnic community maintain or enjoy certain social balance, a particular group being predominant over the other, a particular group subservient to the other, a group dependent on another for leadership and guidance or a group blocking changes or progress in the other. In the Indian context, in the rural-tribal settings, inter-caste and caste-tribe relationships matter while attempting planned changes among them. This takes us to the study of caste-tribal council, its constitution and functions, the role and influence of the chief of the council, the council's influence over its members, and the degree of their dependence on the council in the matters economic and social. Further, we study the nexus of relationship between tribals and non-tribals.

The traditional village council (non-statutory) is another ancient social institution still in vogue in most of the villages. It chiefly deals with village affairs, celebration of local deities, sundry civil and criminal issues and divorce cases. The office of the chief of the traditional village council is either hereditary or elected. In some cases, the caste/tribal council itself functions as the traditional village council. Despite the advent of statutory village council in some communities, the traditional one, still enjoys status and influence over the local community. It is also to be studied and its relationship utilized for entrepreneurial development.

Besides the traditional institutions referred to above there are the modern associate or feeder organizations viz. Farmers' Forum, Youth Club, Women's Club, and recently organized users committees in the rural areas in Andhra Pradesh etc.

which do matter as sources of influence, guidance and leadership in the entrepreneurial development programmes.

While studying the social structure of the client community we may also take into account the sacred institutions in the community, the temple, church, mosque and the sacred specialists or the religious leaders associated with the sacred institutions. Though their domain is religious/spiritual, they are significant people in the community. The entrepreneurship developer may work through them to clear the way and secure sanction and support for the potential entrepreneur to go about his enterprises.

Further, the schoolteacher also considered a friend, guide and philosopher to the local folk is a force to be reckoned with and he plays the role of a catalyst and his services may be utilized in the programme. Mention may be made of the local medical practitioner and he sometimes as a source of influence for the programmes.

The Political Structure of the Community

Entrepreneurial development or introducing of any change in the client group depends on the political leadership, power structure and the politico-administrative institutions at the village, and district levels. In other words, it has a bearing on the initiative, lead and encouragement given by the local leaders. Under the political structure we study the leadership patterns in the community. At the village level we can think of five different kinds of leaders:

(1) Hereditary leaders such as village level officials (in some cases), Chiefs of Caste-tribal councils and traditional village councils;

(2) Functional leaders who matter in specific areas;

(3) Sectional leaders who represent a class, tribe, a neighbourhood or a locality;

(4) Elected leaders of the statutory council and cooperative; and

(5) Professional leaders who are from outside the community, officials of different developmental agencies operating at the village level.

In the field approach we identify the different kinds of leaders in the community and work through them towards entrepreneurial development. Wherever the existing leadership is inadequate for entrepreneurial promotion, new organizations are to be developed. It may be noted here that a potential entrepreneur in the community may tend to look for some nodding approval and encouragement from the people whom he considers significant in the group. If the potential entrepreneur is convinced of his project or enterprise and if he can venture into action on his own, we need not bother about his environment and referent groups. But the situation in the rural and tribal areas is not so. Even if he is sure of his project and ready to take the risk and thinks that he could manage his enterprise, he has sometimes an obligation to seek the opinion and secure the approval from the significant members in the group. And so, the entrepreneurial developer enters the client system through the local leaders, expose to them the idea and prospects of some entrepreneurial activity, try to convince them so that either they encourage the potential entrepreneurs to go ahead with their ventures or do not stand in their way of movement. There is every likelihood of the local leaders sometimes playing a negative role.

On the institutional side in this field, the elected council at the village level, and village cooperative may be used as sources of information and as levers to influence potential entrepreneurs in the community.

In sum, it may be observed here, that institutions and organizations in the community may or may not have a direct bearing on or a functional relationship to entrepreneurship or economic activity. The tribal council, the caste council, the religious institutions for example, deal mostly with social aspects of the community, but as traditional and deeply rooted institutions, they influence and control the behaviour of people. The change agent tries to make use of these existing institutions and customs to communicate to the people. The leadership in all spheres of communal activity will be utilized to bring about desirable changes in the client community.

BARRIERS AND STIMULANTS TO CHANGE

We may pose here a basic question. What is the supply position of entrepreneurship in developing countries today? The field experience and the rate of growth of entrepreneurship in the area of small-scale industries in most of the developing communities show that the supply of entrepreneurship (the number of entrepreneurs that take up some enterprise) in a given period of time is short of what the Industrial Development Agencies demand or in a position to support and promote. When there is spontaneous emergence or adequate supply of entrepreneurship, then the problem is to meet the new entrepreneurs' needs and providing them with physical and economic infrastructure to help them start and run their enterprises successfully. But unfortunately, the State as the chief promoter of entrepreneurship wants to, within the constraints of scarce resources, promote entrepreneurship. In this process of inducing entrepreneurship among the rural-tribal people we meet with shyness and resistance on the part of individuals and groups to go in for some enterprises. Entrepreneurial development is a basic complex change. It is met with different kinds of resistance and so it leads us to identify the barriers (areas of resistance) and stimulants (promotional factors) to change.

Foster (1973, 82-146) discusses at length the different kinds of barriers and stimulants to change. All societies are constantly in a state of relative tension. Each society can be thought of as a host to two kinds of forces - those that seek to promote change, and those that strive to maintain the status quo. These forces are locked in perpetual combat, the former trying to throw the latter off balance in order to gain ascendancy and the latter trying to prevent this from happening. [1]

It is necessary on the part of the entrepreneurial development agency to identify the areas of resistance and the factors that contribute to change, here the entrepreneurial development.

We can think of three kinds of barriers - cultural, social and psychological. These are interrelated in any community. Here, basically we go in for an understanding of the value system of the client community, the factors that inhibit or promote change. On identifying the barriers, we work toward loosening their grip over the potential changees, simultaneously using the positive factors available from within the client group.

Despite barriers changes do take place in all spheres of life-religious, political, ideological, economic and social. When a group is faced with the prospect of change, there exists a balance of forces. On one side are those forces which are against change, viz., conservatism, apathy, fear and the like; on the other side are the forces for change such as dissatisfaction with the existing conditions, pride of new occupation, profession, new status or economic and social benefits that are anticipated in the new activity. Successful entrepreneurial development consists largely of choosing those enterprises where the balance is almost even and then trying to lighten the forces against change or to increase the factors that promote change.

Some of the positive factors that could be used for inducing change are motivating people to change through education and demonstration of the usefulness of the new activity, working on the desire of clients for economic gain and prestige, making use of a competitive situation obtaining in the client group, using the positive forces of authority and timing and sequencing the programmes in such a way that the total effort and process results in entrepreneurial development.

One crucial factor in working with tribal groups is their value system. The change agent needs to have a knowledge of the dominant values in the culture of the group, and working through these values, gradually bring about desirable changes in the group. The two constants to community wide changes are the tribe's identity and the tribe's moral beliefs. It is important for them to know that they can maintain their identity while making changes in their value system. It may be noted here that an important value of a tribal group is: "what they want to be".

Another important factor that is to be taken into account in our approach to bring about entrepreneurial development among tribal groups is to know what agencies have worked so far with them, what programmes have been attempted, and with what results. This leads us to an understanding of the tribe's perception, attitude and experience of the agencies and developmental programmes. For instance, community development agencies, Christian missionaries and several voluntary organizations have been working with tribal groups for their development for sometime now. An understanding of the tribals' reactions and experiences vis-à-vis the development or change agencies, whatever may be their sphere of activity, will give us an insight into their problem, and help us in avoiding the pit-falls. This will help us formulate our strategy in a manner that will make the process of change smooth and gradual.

Social change relating to entrepreneurial development is a complex phenomenon. It requires an integrated approach, a sustained effort on the part of the organizations that promote industrial development.

PROBLEMS

In developing entrepreneurship, we are confronted with several problems. The barriers we referred to earlier relate to the client community which are of general nature, but we may also look into some specific kind of problems in promoting entrepreneurship in rural communities.

The problems of entrepreneurial development are of individual, group and of institutional nature. Ultimately, it is the individual who has to take the initiative to decide on, start and manage his enterprise. He also needs the approval and support of his kin-group or community. The individual and the group constitute the client system. The institutions are to stimulate the client system towards entrepreneurial activity. The institutions are the various governmental and autonomous agencies that are concerned with entrepreneurial development. They are the source of several commissions and omissions that impede and slow down the process of entrepreneurial development. We may briefly look into some of the problems that centre around the individual, group and the institutions.

Individual

1. Lack of motivation.
2. Shyness and inhibition.
3. Ignorant of opportunities that he can avail himself of.
4. Lack of requisite managerial skills to start and manage his enterprise.
5. Lack of finance for initial investment.

6. Lack of familial and community support for his enterprise.
7. Is scared of the cumbersome and time-consuming process in establishing the enterprise.
8. Even if he starts the enterprise, he is not sure of sustained support from the promotional agencies in terms of timely and adequate credit and marketing of his products.

Group

1. Lack of awareness.
2. Preference for traditional occupations and professions.
3. Don't think of alternative avocations.
4. Apathy, sense of fear and insecurity towards government initiated and sponsored programmes.
5. Ignorant of their own potential: material and human.
6. Economically and politically weak.
7. Lack the freedom to choose and pursue their choices as a consequence to the power-sway of the local elite or the dominant caste.
8. They are more tradition-bound, and their values are, to continue with their institutionalized familial occupations.
9. They prefer to be what they want to be.

Institutional

1. Vague and unrealistic policies, and policies not supported by action.
2. Lack of teamwork and internal coordination in the agencies.
3. Lack of inter-agency coordination.
4. Bureaucratic style of working.

5. The functions of the personnel are not vested with the requisite power and authority.
6. Overlapping and duplication of functions both at the apex and operational levels.
7. A multiplicity of agencies performing a more or less similar task.
8. The field-level personnel are not supported in their promises and performance by the higher-ups in the organizations.
9. Lack of work motivation and commitment to their task.
10. Lack of relevant training on the part of the EDP personnel.
11. Lack of appreciation of the importance of human factors in development.
12. Lack of knowledge of technical know-how on the part of the personnel.

Other problems of entrepreneurial development are in respect of provision of infrastructural facilities, including finance and marketing.

The problems mentioned above though are stupendous and complex, are not insurmountable, an inter-disciplinary and multi-pronged approach is required to find solutions to these problems.

The problems listed above are not inherent or unchangeable. Through gradual entrepreneurial education, organizational and institutional support provided to the people in terms of motivation, incentives, infrastructural facilities, supply of certain inputs, credit and market support, the neo-entrepreneurs will gain confidence through their experience and success and they would be the factors creating congenial entrepreneurial climate. These problems are interrelated and they are to be looked at by the industrial development agencies and the community leaders. As mentioned above, entrepreneurial education through entrepreneurial activity and training provided to the development personnel and potential entrepreneurs would gradually create conditions favouring a positive change in the problems listed above.

CONTRIBUTING FACTORS

In the foregoing discussion of field approach to entrepreneurial development, the focus and emphasis has been on the understanding of the client group and using the physical, economic and social resources. But when we look at the entire gamut of entrepreneurial development in terms of an action programme, we find four factors significantly contributing to entrepreneurial development. They are (1) Resources, (2) Organizations concerned with entrepreneurial development, (3) Infrastructure and (4) The entrepreneur. We may briefly examine them.[2]

Resources

The resources of a client community are of two kinds: material and human. The material side consists of the natural resources, primary (nature given) and secondary (man-made) that the community is endowed with viz., climatic, geographic, agricultural, horticultural, mineral, marine, forest, animal, textile, etc. Here we examine how a given community living in a region has interacted with the resources it is endowed with. What kind of economic and industrial activities and associated skills have been generated as a result of people's interaction with the resources. This will give us an idea of the enterprises that the people in the area carry on with, and which have become a part of their culture. Based on the ongoing economic activities, we can demarcate the enterprises that need modernization and the areas in which innovation can be introduced based on the available resources. Here we move from the familiar (to the people) to the unfamiliar but associated entrepreneurial activities. What is envisaged here is that the entrepreneurship development agency should examine the potentialities of the material resources, in what manner they could be developed making use of the human material available in the target community.

A word here about analyzing resources. A resource is truly a resource in the economic sense only if it can help to produce something which somebody wants at a cost that he is willing to pay. In analyzing the resources of an area from the point of view of the area's suitability for various kinds of enterprises we cannot count among today's resources like timber located in the middle of the jungle or minerals so far underground or so far from transportation that the labour of getting them out-costs more than the materials are worth. The cost factor is all important in appraising the industrial usefulness of an area's resources. The resources need not always be available in the immediate local community and they can be obtained from elsewhere so long the enterprise would be profitable. In fact, successful manufacturing areas rarely have a complete supply of the resources they use.

The existence of certain very evident resources, especially raw materials, within an area does not necessarily mean that enterprises based on these resources will be economical and beneficial in the area. Other resources not quite as evident may even more important than this raw material in determining the total cost of resources that go into the manufactured product, for example, technical labour, supervision and capital equipment. The total cost of all the input items is the important thing on the resource side. Also factors on the marketing side may pull enterprises to a location quite far from the origin of the most conspicuous material.

In the analysis of an area's industrial potential it is necessary to make a systematic inventory of al types of resources in the area that might be usable in some enterprises. The purpose is to determine the presence or absence of specific kinds of resources required in different kinds of enterprises and to ascertain their location, quality, abundance and probable cost. This information, when fitted together with information about the resource requirements of different industries and the market demand for the products of these industries, will enable an intelligent preliminary choice to be made of enterprises most suitable for promotion and development in the area.

The analysis of the resources can be conducted with almost any desired degree of comprehensiveness in detail. It can be merely a quick survey for general orientation based on information available in published materials or readily obtainable through quick surveys. Otherwise, it could be a comprehensive and detailed assessment of potential and usable resources based on industrial potential surveys.

Speaking of natural resources, we may think of a particular natural resource, how it is being utilized in a given area, in how many ways and how the same resource is utilized or processed in another area, or what kind of industries are based on a particular natural resource. Let us take for example, the coconut. It is cultivated in abundance in Assam (India), but it is chiefly used as a food article as it is and for ritual and ceremonial purposes, but whereas the same coconut is used in over a hundred different ways in Kerala. Coconut constitutes a base in Kerala's economy. Similarly bamboo is used in multiple ways for handicrafts in Tripura but its economic or industrial use elsewhere in India is limited to a couple of utilities. Another example is the abundant cultivation of ginger in Mizoram (India) but a total absence of any industry based on this resource in the state.

As we have pointed out earlier, industrial resources are not solely material. In the ultimate analysis it is the area's human and social resources - labour, management and organization are the key to successful industrial development. Japan and Switzerland are the most striking examples wherein the human resources have been the dominant factor in their tremendous advancement in industrial development[3].

It is the human resources that shape and control the material resources in industrial development. Ways can be found to overcome many material deficiencies if the human talents are highly developed and if environment of social, political and economic institutions is favourable. But if the human skills and institutions which make for effective industrial production are not available in an area, then no amount of material resources will bring a successful industrialization. It is the reason all the more to lay emphasis on entrepreneurship development which is the human side of industrial development.

In sum, it is the responsibility of the industrial development agencies to assess the resources available in the area, the possible industrial uses they could be exploited for and the kind of technology and infrastructure required for the newer uses of a resource and thus guide the potential entrepreneur and his group.

Organization

In a basic sense, entrepreneurial/small enterprise development is based on the individual initiative and when it is either lacking or meager, it is to be induced and promoted by the state. The situation in many of the Asian countries demand an induced entrepreneurial development and consequently we find several organizations figuring in the realm of entrepreneurial development. These are governmental, quasi-governmental and some are voluntary organizations.

The nomenclatures, structure, functions, area of operation, size and number of such organizations vary from country to country. For instance, in a medium-sized state in India there are about twenty-five organizations or departments that are in a way connected with industrial development. The kind of their functional responsibilities and the degree of their involvement in industrial promotion vary. Again, India may be taken as an example which largely represents the role responsibilities of development organizations in other Asian countries. Based on the way the organizations are related to entrepreneurial/industrial development, they may be categorized into three groups.

The first group of organizations have a primary function and a direct responsibility in entrepreneurial development. They are chiefly organizations such as: (i) Directorate of Industries, (at the State level), (ii) District Industries Centres, and (iii) Small Industry Service Institutes (SISIs). These primary small industry development agencies are supposed to carry on both stimulatory and supportive kind of activities in respect to entrepreneurial development. It is the Directorate of Industries and more especially the District Industries Centres (DICs) which are charged with the task of identifying technically feasible and economically viable enterprises and identifying, motivating, selecting and training the small-scale entrepreneurs. They are to do the primary job of bringing in the entrepreneurs to the threshold of entrepreneurship. But in many of the cases, we find that the stimulatory part of their job is lacking and they are more at ease and successful in supportive kind of activities such as financial, infrastructural and technical. Concerted and persevering efforts are necessary in the filed of stimulatory activity in generating an entrepreneurial climate to bring in new entrepreneurs.

The second group of organizations which may be called secondary consisting of different corporations of finance, infrastructure, raw materials and machinery, banking and marketing mostly carry on supportive and sustaining kind of activities. These organizations are partly or distantly related to the primary function of development of entrepreneurship in the small-scale sector.

The basic task of finding an entrepreneur or responding to a potential entrepreneur lies largely on the first category of organizations.

We may call the third group of organizations as tertiary which are mostly governmental development departments or line agencies which are indirectly or remotely connected with industrial-entrepreneurial development. Departments of agriculture, horticulture, sericulture, sylviculture, pisciculture, animal husbandry, mineral, power, irrigation, highways, transport, communications, education, both basic and technical, textile and so on, fall under this category. Though these departments or agencies are not directly connected with industrial-entrepreneurial development, any improvement or expansion in them contributes to industrial development. They are the sources, feeder and support agencies which generate the potential for industrial development and ultimately contribute to its promotion.

The purpose of this brief preceding discussion is not just academic but it is to emphasize that the functions of organizations charged with industrial-entrepreneurial development are to be clearly demarcated and well defined in order to avoid or reduce overlapping or duplication of activities and ensure a synergetic effect on small industry promotion. A periodic examination of the functions of these organizations, their strengths, needs and shortcomings and the coordination among them is necessary. The whole promotional machinery is to be streamlined to deliver the goods, taking into account the institutional problems that have been listed out earlier. In other words, there is an imperative need to build up functional linkages and relative accountability among the three categories of organizations at the State (provincial), and the district levels, which should finally facilitate a rapid entrepreneurial development.

Infrastructure

We mostly relate infrastructure to physical facilities such as land, site, building, power, water, transport and communication facilities for starting an industry or an enterprise. Some of the infrastructural requirements are enterprise specific and some are of general nature and further we may consider the enterprise-specific infrastructural facilities as primary and other facilities such as schools, hospitals, housing and marketing for day-to-day requirements for the entrepreneurs, their families and workers as secondary. But the latter facilities gradually emerge and get established once the enterprises are started. In the induced and planned entrepreneurial-industrial development provision of infrastructural facilities is a necessary primary condition. Some of the facilities may be managed by the entrepreneurs themselves but some such as power, communications, sometimes, land and work-sheds are beyond the capability and affordability on the part of the small-scale entrepreneurs. Such a provision solely rests on the government development agencies.

Usually, infrastructure as pointed out above is mostly taken to be the physical and material facilities, but it constitutes only a part of the infrastructure in a comprehensive sense. We may think of two kinds of infrastructure for industrial-entrepreneurial development. They are: (a) physical and economic infrastructure; and (b) social infrastructure. The first one comprises the items noted above plus finance and marketing facilities. The social infrastructure consists of clear-cut industrial development policies, political commitment, an able and well-trained, motivated and committed industrial development personnel, a well-coordinated institutional support, positive attitudes, values and preferences of people and an entrepreneurial climate for developing entrepreneurship. Another significant social infrastructure is the entrepreneurial leadership in the target community. One could see that the provision of physical and economic infrastructure is in the hands of and under the purview of governmental agencies. Most of these agencies fall under secondary and tertiary organizations, discussed above. The state regulates the provision of these facilities. Again in a relative sense, the physical and economic infrastructure could be provided by the State with comparative ease. But the question arises: whose responsibility is it to educate the community and the potential entrepreneurs and generate an entrepreneurial climate? It falls largely on the primary set of organizations which have the task of creating the entrepreneurial climate in the communities. The role of other agencies in building up or providing the social infrastructure directly for entrepreneurial development is rather marginal and peripheral. However, it may be noted that the presence or provision of any physical infrastructure is a likely inducement to the population in the area to gradually venture into some enterprises. But there is no denial of the fact that physical and economic infrastructure is a necessary condition but not sufficient for entrepreneurial development. The physical and social infrastructure contributes to the growth of one another and they are complementary to each other, but undeniably it is the social infrastructure which is paramount. Once it is strong, once it is generated both on the part of the development agencies and the people, the physical and economic infrastructure would follow. It is here that the primary industrial development agencies are to play a vital role apprising the client community of what its resources and potentials are, in what direction and ways it could harness and develop its material and human resources, what local consumer needs and external market it could respond to, and the ways and the extent to which the agencies could extend their help to the community in entrepreneurial development.

The approach envisages an intimate and continuous dialogue between the clientele group and the development agencies. It is obvious that some of the material resources (finance, power, transport) are scarce and they are to be allocated judiciously for industrial development, but the more scarce material is the entrepreneur himself. How to identify him, how to motivate, encourage and assure him so that he takes the initiative and ventures into some entrepreneurial activity. What may be called the human-end product (the entrepreneur) in entrepreneurship is the function of the social infrastructure or the entrepreneurial climate. This leads us now to the entrepreneur.

In this context, we may briefly look into the concept and characteristics of successful entrepreneurs as defined and interpreted by social scientists.

CHARACTERISTICS OF ENTREPRENEURS

When we try to conceptualize the term entrepreneur, we note that though it originated in the west, it has undergone many changes from time to time. In the early 16th century, it was used to denote a dealer who bought a thing at a certain price and sold it at an uncertain price making a profit out of it. A sort of social stigma was attached to this concept. Towards 1961, Schumpeter redefined entrepreneur 'as an agent for change'.... an innovator. Subsequently, it took on the meaning of 'an efficient manager'. In the Indian context and in the context of other developing countries, however, a new concept emerged i.e., 'a person who undertakes to organize, own and run an enterprise'.[3]

Various attempts have been made to understand the emergence of entrepreneurship. Sociologists analyze the phenomenon of entrepreneurship in terms of caste, social status, values, migration, family socialization pattern, etc. Psychologists attempt to explain it on the basis of personality traits or characteristics such as, need for achievement, creativity, propensity to take risk, independence and leadership. Economists consider it from the point of view of occupational background, access to capital, technical experience and insight to exploit economic opportunities and attain economic gains. From these different approaches, it becomes evident that a strict compartmentalized approach will not be of any help in understanding the emergence of entrepreneurship. Since entrepreneur is an individual who lives in a society, both individual and social factors have to be taken into consideration. Similarly, when we talk about a woman entrepreneur, she should be regarded, as an individual who takes up a challenging role in which she wants to adjust her personality needs, family life, social life and economic independence. Such an integrated approach may help us visualize this phenomenon more adequately.[4]

Some of the basic or inherent characteristics may be there in the beginning but as the entrepreneur moves forward with expansion and success in promoting his enterprise other kinds of characteristics are born or emerge in the individual. In a sense, it is a learning kind of thing on the part of the entrepreneur. As he moves forward the essential characteristics which stand for success in entrepreneurial activity emerge and grow over a period of time. The entrepreneur learns on the job, through his success and failure in his venture.

A review of the available literature on the factors contributing to successful entrepreneurship supports the contention that certain personality characteristics are associated with successful entrepreneurs.

McClelland and his associates have reported that entrepreneurs are characterized by (1) unusual creativeness (2) propensity of risk-taking and (3) strong need for achievement. They have also reported that persons high on need for achievement have some specific characteristics. While research has established that achievement motive contributes largely to entrepreneurship, it has also been observed that though achievement helps one to become an entrepreneur, it is not the only factor in making him successful. It is also found that an entrepreneurial manager should have a high need for influencing others (need for power), a low need for affiliation and a large capacity to discipline one's self (inhibition). An entrepreneurial manager is also found to possess flexibility in style and displays high psychosocial maturity. Further, it is also to be noted that entrepreneurs decision to start an industrial unit was not influenced by level of education, income differences, risk-taking ability and need for achievement, but rather an ambition, social prestige, social responsibility, economic gain and perception of demand for a particular product.

The most significant characteristics associated with entrepreneurs are need for achievement, support, independence and leadership. On the basis of the information given by participants of a symposium on Development of Entrepreneurship, the following appear to be the characteristics:

1. Perseverance and hard work
2. Risk-taking ability
3. High aspiration
4. Willingness to learn
5. Dynamic and creative
6. Adoptable
7. Innovative

8. Good Salesmanship
9. Ability to make friends and overcome losses
10. Initiative
11. Self-confidence
12. Will-power
13. Determination to succeed
14. Pleasing personality, composed and tactful
15. High integrity
16. Responsible
17. Excellence in work
18. Perception of time

The research available clearly reveals that an entrepreneur is certainly different from the non-entrepreneur in terms of his psychological and social dispositions. The available evidence only points to some dominant traits in successful entrepreneurs; the optimal combination of characteristics needed for success has not yet been arrived at.

Further, some researchers have come up with another set of characteristics listed below:

1. Drive
2. Self-confidence
3. Long-term involvement
4. Money as a measure
5. Persistent problem-solving
6. Goal setting
7. Moderate risk-taking
8. Dealing with failure
9. Use of feedback

10. Taking initiative and seeking personal responsibility
11. Use of resources
12. Competing against self-imposed standards
13. Internal locus control
14. Tolerance of ambiguity and uncertainty

Further, the following eight (8) aspects are described as entrepreneurial role requirements.

EIGHT ENTREPRENEURIAL ROLE REQUIREMENTS

1. Accommodation to venture
2. Total immersion and commitment
3. Creativity and innovation
4. Knowledge of business you want to launch
5. People and team building
6. Economic values
7. Ethics
8. Integrity and reliability

By and large, characteristics that differentiate entrepreneurs from non-entrepreneurs are: confidence, perseverance, determination, hard work,, general knowledge, dynamism, risk taking, optimism, technical knowledge, information gathering ability and initiative.

Entrepreneur

The entrepreneur may be likened to the fourth factor in production-organization (the rest being land, labour and capital). He is as significant as 'organization' in production. Interestingly, these two factors - entrepreneur and organization are intimately associated. What happens when you have the required resources, promotional organizations, physical and economic infrastructure and lack the entrepreneur? To a considerable extent, this is the situation in many of the Asian countries. We are looking for the right kind of entrepreneurs. They are not born as such, but they could be made as such.

There are two kinds of entrepreneurs, the ongoing and the potential ones. The ongoing entrepreneurs are those who are in the field already, some who have taken to entrepreneurship on their own in a spontaneous sense and others who have been induced to this activity. The industrial development agencies in their initial enthusiasm and under pressure of targets for putting a certain number of individuals in the field of entrepreneurship, brought in some entrepreneurs and fulfilled their paper targets. But a considerable number of them are left in the lurch. They are at various stages with varying problems struggling to reach the take-off point in respect to their enterprises. Some are struggling to complete the formalities for final registration of their units, some are held up for want of adequate raw material, working capital, or the requisite machinery and equipment, some waiting for power, some finding it difficult to market their products, and some being tossed over for X or Y licence to go about their business. In a word the entrepreneur who is already in the field faces some problems. Unless the industrial development agencies assess the problems of the ongoing entrepreneur and assist him in ameliorating his condition, we cannot go in for a new entrepreneur. Every satisfied and well-served entrepreneur is a positive force in generating a conducive entrepreneurial climate which in turn motivates, induces and encourages a potential entrepreneur to enter the field.

On the other hand a dissatisfied, not-very-much-cared for left-in-the-lurch-entrepreneur is a potential source of demotivation and discouragement to the new entrepreneur. We do not advocate here that the entrepreneur should be spoon-fed and that he should be a protected child. But he needs a prop in the initial stages in his growth and development. It is not wrong to say that a well-attended to and successful entrepreneur is equal to several professional agents of entrepreneurial development when it comes to motivating people to take to some entrepreneurial activity. If we take care of the ongoing entrepreneurs it would be easy for us to bring the new entrepreneurs into the field.

Identifying, selecting, motivating and training the new entrepreneurs constitute a major task for the entrepreneurial development agency. The promotion or development of entrepreneurship may be undertaken in five phases and we may briefly look into each phase.

Phase I

The first phase relates to the basic physico-psycho-socio-cultural and economic study and understanding of the area where the programme is to be implemented as detailed earlier. Industrial potential survey focusing both on material and human resources of the area will be the basis, based on which feasibility studies are to be prepared for each viable candidate industry covering technical, economic, financial, demand and marketing aspects of the enterprise. Such a study will serve the purposes of developing an action - programme for identifying viable enterprises either resource-based, demand-based or footloose and potential entrepreneurs.

Here the emphasis is to be laid on starting small-scale enterprises where the people are living now, cheap enough so that they can be created in large numbers without calling for an unattainable level of capital formation and imports, with relatively simple production methods, so that the demands for high skills are minimized not only in the production process itself but also in matters of organization, raw material supply, financing, marketing, and the production mainly based on local materials and for local use. With such a purpose, initially to make use of the local resources and the local consumer demands, we are not to look for highly talented, sophisticated entrepreneurs, but people with some interest, with some investment capacity, who are partially unemployed or totally unemployed, people who are looking for some avenues to increase their income, people who are likely to take certain amount of risk in venturing into some entrepreneurial activity. Highly achievement-oriented individuals seek opportunities, create conditions, need less propping and venture into industrial activity. Such people can take care of themselves with minimal support from the development agencies. But our task is to gradually shape the common man into an entrepreneur. Against this objective, potential entrepreneurs in the client community may be drawn from the following segments: (a) artisan groups, (b) high school dropouts, (c) educated unemployed, (d) merchant-trading groups, (e) farmers who are in the process of or likely to partly shift to some enterprise, (f) farm-labourers who are likely to take some small business or enterprise and (g) woman entrepreneurs.

In the first phase as a constructive approach and strategy, the entire client community is to be exposed to the idea of entrepreneurship development. No segment in the community should feel it is isolated or ignored and the programmes are meant only for certain sections. The general exposure of the entire client community to the idea and prospects of entrepreneurship will create awareness, interest among them which will gradually motivate the potential entrepreneurs to move into action.

The creating of awareness, preparing the community, motivating and facilitating some individuals in the community to take decisions, secure the sanction of their families and opinion leaders, that is cutting through the socio-cultural barriers may be done through entrepreneurship-extension education through individual and group methods and through the mass media, always reinforced by personal contacts and counseling. One of the foremost things in the process is raising the aspiration level of the people. They have to be told convincingly of the social and economic advantage inherent in industrial activity. The rise in their standard of living as a result of successfully running an enterprise has to be projected and brought home to them. These ends can be achieved through what is called 'intensive campaign' technique. It is a package of activities comprising an industrial potential survey, publication of the survey findings, holding of small group meetings explaining to people in the community, the kind of enterprises that are feasible in the area, the requirements for starting the recommended enterprises, who can undertake them, the kind of assistance they can expect from the various industrial development agencies and in such a type of campaign, the industrial development personnel and the selected local and political leaders will be involved. The inclusion of influential local and district leadership would build and reinforce confidence and morale on the part of the potential entrepreneurs in the local community.

It may be in order to mention here the steps that may be taken in identifying the viable enterprises and potential entrepreneurs in the client community.

The Steps

1. Identification of the natural resources the community is endowed with.
2. Listing out the ongoing economic and industrial activities carried on by the community based on the resources at its command.
3. Listing out the associated skills available with the members of the community (or the target population).
4. Listing out the kind of new enterprises technically

feasible and economically viable that could be promoted based on the available resources and skills.

5. Listing out the existing and required infrastructural facilities in view of the new enterprises suggested.
6. Appraising the client system of:
   - -- the kind of new enterprises they could take to;
   - -- the financial, managerial, technical and marketing requirements in respect to each enterprise;
   - -- the kind of people who can take up the suggested enterprises;
   - -- specifying in general the qualifications, personal aptitude and abilities and investment capacity on the part of the prospective entrepreneurs.
7. Appraising the client system of:
   - -- the kind of help the multiplicity of agencies connected with entrepreneurial development can extend to the prospective entrepreneurs, which may cover questions like What? When? To what extent? How often? To what purpose? etc.
8. Final identification of potential entrepreneurs and matching their interest with the enterprises.

A word on identification of potential entrepreneurs. Depending on the extent of response, the level of candidates, the potential and the capabilities that are sought among the candidates, the optimum number that the resources and schemes could support and sustain, one may go in for psychological tests such as: (a) Achievement Motivation, (b) Risk Taking, (c) Value Orientation, (d) Adoption Propensity, (e) Level of Aspiration, etc. These projective or psychological instruments are rather complementary to the information provided on the application that the candidate fills in, concerning his family background, his educational attainment, work experience, his choice of enterprise, his experience if any in entrepreneurial activity, his investment capacity and his socio-cultural affiliations.

Importantly, the means employed for identification are the application, interview and if need be, the tests mentioned above. One invaluable resource for identifying potential entrepreneurs is the client community itself.

When it comes to identification and selection of potential entrepreneurs, more often, we ignore the local community. The people in the local community may not be conversant with attributes or traits that are contributive to successful entrepreneurship, may not have any idea and understanding of some of the projective techniques used sometimes to measure the strength of need for achievement, value orientation, risk taking and adoption propensity on the part of the prospective entrepreneurs, but they will have a fairly good understanding of the people in the community as to who would do what and to what extent one would fair well and who is innovative and who would manage an activity effectively. This kind of knowledge of individuals is based on the day-to-day observations irrespective of an individual's profession or occupation. And so, one can, to a large extent depend upon and make use of the local community, the small groups in the community for identifying and selecting potential entrepreneurs. As we have pointed out earlier, once the viable enterprises have been identified based on industrial potential survey, one may list out the personal requirements that one is looking for or in other words the kind of people who can answer these requirements in order to respond to the recommended enterprises. Once this information is communicated to the community through individual contact and small group meetings, it is possible for the local community to indicate the names of individuals who are likely to be successful as small entrepreneurs. This could be in addition to individuals themselves coming forward to take to some entrepreneurial activity. The stress here is that the local community could well serve as a source and guide in selecting potential entrepreneurs.

Phase II

It consists of training various categories of personnel who will be involved in locating and developing entrepreneurship in the area under question. A general but comprehensive course of three to four weeks is to be prepared keeping in view the earlier work-experience of the personnel. The participants will be familiarized with the prospects and problems of entrepreneurial development in the area of operation. Further, the programme will include inputs on feasibility studies, techno-economic surveys, preparation of industrial profiles, entrepreneurial development, marketing, etc. (See Appendix for a model training programme). Representatives of financial institutions in the area may be associated with the training programmes. By the end of the second phase, the agency will be in readiness with the knowledge of the area of operation, and also trained personnel to select and train entrepreneurs.

Phase III

It consists of selection and training of potential entrepreneurs in the client community by the agency. The training of the entrepreneurs will be arranged at district or sub-district headquarters. The personnel of the development agency who have already undergone training will conduct the training programme. The duration of this training may range from two to six weeks. It depends on funds and the category of candidates trained. In some cases, inclusive of in-plant studies, the courses are run for 14-20 weeks. The training inputs will include elements that would enable the entrepreneur-trainees acquire basic knowledge, skills and motivation to establish their units and manage them successfully. The training will be both theoretical and practical. Towards the end of their training, the candidates will go back to their villages and make a mini-market survey concerning their enterprises, or prepare project reports. They bring back the field data, and work these into project proposals for securing funds from financial institutions.

Phase IV

It consists of the agency collaborating with other functionally associated agencies to guide and help the trained entrepreneurs in establishing their enterprises, either individually, in small groups or through industrial cooperatives.

Phase V

In the final phase, which will be taken up after a lapse of six months after the training of entrepreneurs, the training programme will be evaluated. The objective of the evaluation is to find out as to how many of the trained entrepreneurs were able to establish their enterprises and the problems they faced in setting up their ventures. In the light of this experience the training programme for other batches of entrepreneurs will be restructured if necessary.

Support for Marketing of Products

More often, the entire success of small enterprise promotion in rural-tribal communities hinges on marketing of products of the neo-entrepreneurs. In the initial stages and also, in some cases on the sustained basis, the promotional agencies should help in marketing of the products. The induced and emerging entrepreneurs may be too weak to organize the marketing of their products on their own. The promotional agencies may go in for internal or external export of the indigenous handicrafts and products through a network of marketing channels. Such a support would sustain the ongoing entrepreneurs and also motivate the potential entrepreneurs to ventures into the field.

In sum, we may say that the women constitute a significant segment in the population. Till now, they have not been the focus of entrepreneurial development. The need today to develop entrepreneurship among them is imperative, the development of entrepreneurship among men and women being simultaneous. The question of EDP among women is a question of choice, priority and organization.

REFERENCES

1. Somsak Tambunlertchai and Utis Kaothien, "Thailand's Industrial Transformation and Regional development: Situational Review and Policy Evaluation" (Paper presented at the International Conference on Industrial Transformation and Regional Development in an Age of Global Interdependence, 18-21 September, 1989, Nagoya and Tokyo), p. 1.
2. United Nations Economic and Social Commission for Asia and the Pacific (UN/ESCAP), *Entrepreneurship Development for Small and Medium-Scale Industries in Selected Developing Countries* (New York, 1989), pp. 2-3.
3. Dr. Asghari Mohiuddin, Entrepreneurship Development Among Women - Retrospects and Prospects, SEDME, Hyderabad, Volume X, Number-1, March, 1983.
4. Medhi Krongkaew, 'The Development of Small and Medium Scale Industries in Thailand" in *Asian Development Review*, Vol.6, No.2, (Manila: ADB, 1988), p. 90.

14

Participation of Women in Socio-Economic Development

There are two issues of global nature or call them problems or challenges, one currently facing the entire mankind and the other a few societies or distinct cultures; environment and gender development. Environment encompasses what man has done to nature, the way he has exploited, fouled and abused it resulting in threats to the health and survival of future generations of mankind and other species - plants and animals which have been a source of man's survival thus far. The gender question revolves around what man has done or doing to woman, the other half of the mankind. The environment problem is physical, economic, industrial, technological, avarice and senseless short-sightedness on the part of the modern man whereas the gender question is complex steeped deep in history influenced by prejudices, discriminatory religious and social codes of behaviour imposed on women, and man's audacity in arrogating to himself a superior status and treating the woman his subordinate. The status, freedom and respectability accorded to and enjoyed by women in society is a mark of wisdom and civilization of that particular society. We can conceive of a continuum wherein at one end of the continuum women enjoy equal rights, respectability and are equal partners in economic pursuits and social positions and at the other end, one finds women treated inferior to man, deprived of freedom as enjoyed by man. The gender question is a perennial question. The world body may declare equal opportunities and rights for women and men but it is the nation states and the religious and ethnic groups that have to translate such a principle into reality. One is forced to come up with a statement that so long a man does not treat a woman his equal, he is not civilized. Looked at from any angle, political, economic, social, religious, spiritual or moral, woman is an equal partner and should be an equal partner in all pursuits of life.

The purpose here is not to carry on the debate over feminine rights but to look into women's participation in development activities especially in entrepreneurship development. Their participation, the variety, extent, and mode of participation and the activities in which they participate is influenced by religious sanctions (mostly mistaken and misinterpreted by ignorant and selfish men), economic conditions, ethnicity, occupations, professions, social status and personal endowments like literacy, knowledge and skills. Of all the forces that keep women off the economic and social activities as equal partners is religion. Unfortunately and lamentably sanctions and tenets of some religions are unquestionable. That is, you cannot question the logical inconsistency and irrationality in those sanctions and tenets. It is highly sensitive and explosive.

The women in such religious groups, in most of the cases are confined to their homes just to carry their housekeeping, child-bearing and child rearing roles. Quite lamentable, what forces, what authority, what revolution would emancipate the women in these groups so that they contribute economically, benefit socially, grow individually and advance spiritually?

In order to make women as equal participants in all development activities, it is not enough that you bring in constitutional and legislative measures ensuring equal rights and opportunities for women, but what is wanted is creating a right type of awareness and change of attitude both on the part of men and women, and dissolving of age-old arbitrary, deeply crusted prejudices and biases against women.

As democracy is a desirable system of government, women's participation in all development activities is a desirable thing. Everything about women is not dark and dismal. They have been in the forefront in several fields and emerging as substantive partners in economic and social activities. Woman has been an economic, political and ritual partner with man, only in certain designated activities which vary from society to society. We may have a brief historical perspective of women and society.

WOMEN AND SOCIETY

In the historical evolution of mankind, woman has been an economic partner to man, besides her biological and social roles. It is said that it was the woman who discovered the possibility of domesticating plants for food and beginning the rudiments of hoe-culture. It was so when man was in the hunting and gathering stage. Since then, through agricultural and industrial revolutions, she has been an economic partner in the family of man. She started the enterprise of food cultivation and later adopted bartering the food articles for other necessities of life.

Over a period of time, certain patterns of life and the division of labour changed. She worked on the farm, kept the house and reared the children. Further, in the Indian (Hindu) context, when social stratification (caste-system) and occupations became institutionalized, the womenfolk confined themselves to the chores assigned to them and assumed by themselves in their respective occupations or professions. Again over a period of time, class distinctions emerged, accompanied with restrictions, norms or social sanctions and certain freedoms enjoyed by women. In the general society, high and middle class women tended to confine themselves to the biological and social roles of rearing children and keeping the house. But in the case of economically lower class women, besides their bio-social roles, they had equal or more than equal share in the economic activities of the family.

In the recent past, the increase in women's education, industrialization, urbanization, social and occupational mobility, the emergence of nuclear families, westernization, politico-social movements and changes in the value system, some educated women have taken to certain careers. Some compelled by economic necessity, have taken to small business and trade (Setty, 1985).

WOMEN'S PARTICIPATION IN DEVELOPMENT

Importance and Role

Historically, women have at all times and in all types of economies made a substantial contribution to the production and distribution of their community's resources. The role of women in the development process has been widely investigated in different cultures of various countries. By now, it has become an established fact that women have been stepping out of their traditional status of being confined to the environment of their homes. They perform dynamic roles in enabling their society to advance towards development and prosperity. Women's productive efforts and their capability to shape family life and thus society have convinced more and more men of the need to recognize women's equal right and status (Shahand *et at.*, 1986).

In an ESCAP document (1989) containing an analysis of the women's contributions to the economy, it is stated that:

"Women's participation" in so-called informal sector

activities such as petty trade, brokering, shop-keeping and other small-scale enterprises help to lubricate the developing commercial market economy, performing many functions which are not profitable enough to attract or support larger modern businesses, yet are necessary to serve the local consumption needs of the population at large, particularly lower income groups. It is significant that women are frequently the only members of the indigenous population who can compete with minority immigrant groups in such activities.

Thus women's employment or self-employment in market production makes an important direct contribution to economic growth, and particularly to the development of certain "modern sectors" and industries which could not survive without them and have proved especially important to the balance of payments. But women's non-market activities also play an important though largely unrecognized and unrewarded role.

Women's subsistence agricultural production, for example, subsidizes many rural workers' families and thus lowers the real wage that employers have to pay them, increasing the surplus available for reinvestment and growth. It includes not only the cultivation of staple grains, but also poultry rearing, vegetable farming, collection of forest products and other supplementary activities. Women's craft production for the household use has the same effect. And in many areas, the time-consuming and backbreaking tasks of fetching and carrying water, and gathering firewood, are assigned to women, as is household marketing and the transport of goods often for considerable distances on foot. Child rearing, including the teaching of household and farm production tasks, which largely devolves on women, daily housekeeping and cooking, and general household management, including budgeting and financial management, complete the wide range of activities which comprise women's reproductive duties.

It has become common to describe women as invisible to depict a situation in which planners of development strategies have failed to pay serious attention to the differential roles and functions of women. The differentiation between men and women's role and work may be classified as follows (ESCAP, 1989).

(a). *In agricultural process:* A sexual division of labour assigns to women specific tasks. For instance, in rice cultivation, women are involved to a greater extent than men in transplanting, weeding, harvesting and in some post-harvesting process.

(b). *In industry:* Women have provided the bulk of the labour force in light industries which in many developing countries have spearheaded industrialization programmes, eg., industries such as electronics, textiles and garments, food processing and pharmaceutical. Within this industry there is an uneven distribution of sexes within employment hierarchies, women dominating the lower wage, unskilled or semi-skilled production process. This means that women are vulnerable to particular occupational hazards in the operations in which they are concentrated.

(c). *In domestic roles:* In addition to the unsubstitutable function of child bearing, women are the main providers of basic family needs: food, water, clothing, domestic energy and maintenance of family shelters. They bear the major responsibility of child-care, thus functioning as the principal transmitters to future generations of attitudes and values. In their hands is the burden of the health and well-being of present, past and future generations of the enumerated labour force. The performance of these tasks, particularly in rural areas, is inefficient in the use of resources of time, labour and energy. It is these talks which account for much of women's labour, resulting in an imbalance in which women's work-hours exceed those of men.

In maintaining and nurturing the family, women frequently find ways to add to household income. Their entry or exist from market activities are sometimes flexible, dependent on contingency. This activity occurs mostly in the "informal sector" and is commonly small-scale, requiring low levels of skills, and earning low returns.

In most parts of the developing world, the major benefits of economic growth have failed to reach women. Women have also paid a steep price for the modest glimmerings of modernity that have reached them. In different places around the world, women's labour obligations have multiplied, their independent resources have shrunk, and their autonomy and cultural worth have often diminished as development has unfolded.

Failure to develop women's resources and skills undermines development as a whole. Women's labour, whether paid or unpaid, is essential. Women everywhere are primary care-givers for their families and children. Decisions women make and skills women have materially affect the health, nutrition, attire, cleanliness and emotional equanimity of all family members. With the sharpening recognition that development hinges on the fulfillment of basic human needs and the quality of life, as well as on the transfer of capital and technology, women have at last found their way onto the international development agenda, though the resolution of these problems has barely taken shape (March and Taqqu, 1986).

Manifestation of Women's Problems

Women's special problems manifest themselves across the board but can in large measure be traced to three main areas: the data base for development planning; education and training including extension services; and technological change, not least its social implication.

In the bookkeeping system of development plans, women (and girls) have generally been seen as consumers, not as producers. Moreover, women's work in particular rural women's work, is often not counted statistically.

A primary reason for not including women's work in the computation of the gross national product (GNP) is that so much of it is performed in the family setting. Additionally, it is often of a subsistence nature. On both counts such work, when performed by women, tends to be excluded from official statistics. In many countries such work is recorded, in many others it is not fully recorded or omitted entirely. The reason for non-recording is usually that the societal ideal is that women should not perform such work, in particular, not field work. It should be done by men or, in parts of India e.g., by hired lower-caste women (UNDP, 1980).

Because so much of development efforts has been deficient in its attempts to reach the common people, there is now wide spread agreement that the revised development strategies need to be broad-based and people-oriented. For such strategies to succeed, they must combine two basic principles. On the one hand they must provide for a wide distribution of benefits and services like health care, education and training, productive employment, credit, marketing, fuel, water, sanitation and protection against environmental degradation, in particular the loss of cultivable land through erosion. On the other hand, to make such policies a realistic alternative, a greater mobilization of people as productive agents must be achieved. Their labour, capability, motivation and enterprise in bettering their own conditions must be stimulated. In both respects, women's role in development, not least in rural areas, deserves special attention (UN, 1982).

UNDP (1980) summarized its evaluation of the rural women's participation in development reaching the conclusion:

"If the poor are to be given a fair opportunity to participate in the development effort, there is every reason to consider the participation by women as full and equal partners as a major factor in this effort. In other words, as there are two systems of social stratification, there are two problems of integration, that of the poor and, especially within but also beyond this problem, that of women. No strategy is going to succeed within the foreseeable future".

In India, it has been observed that in Kaira district of Gujarat, where the cooperative movement started, women's status has not improved as a result. While in the past, production and marketing were in women's hands, in the new modern dairy industry management its rewards have been taken over by men.

"Of the more than 2000 persons employed in the Amul (Anand Milk Union Limited) complex, there is only one woman veterinarian and a few telephone operators and secretaries. Not even one woman has been given the mastery over the new technology that has taken over the women's traditional tasks of making butter and cheese". (Brandtzaeg, 1979).

With respect to membership in the cooperative, data from 481 societies show that women only constitute from 2 to 15 per cent of the members. Moreover, the majority of woman members are successors to husbands who have died or are dummy members to enable individual families to control a larger number of shares. With the exception of one all-women society, all the other societies are run by men (Brandtzaeg, 1979).

In the less developed countries the labour force is more evenly distributed among the three categories of workers:

employers and own-account workers (self-employed), employees (wage labourers) and unpaid family workers. The distribution of female workers tended to follow this pattern, with the notable variation of a larger proportion of women than of men being employed as unpaid family workers. Indeed, in most cases, including in the more developed countries, females accounted for disproportionate share, often a large majority of the unpaid family workers. Conversely, they accounted for a disproportionately small share of employers and own-account workers. In short, women tend to be under-represented at the higher and over-represented at the lower levels of the labour force (ESCAP, 1989). Let us look at the situation in India as an illustration.

EXPERIENCE OF WOMEN'S PARTICIPATION IN DEVELOPMENT IN INDIA

India's economy and also the status of her women remained stagnant for a long time. They started to change for the better slowly with the advent of the British education system but women are still victims of the basically exploitative mechanism operating against them. In fact, like the resulting development pattern of the Indian economy, the Indian woman has suffered a dualism in status on her way to play effectively her economic and social role (Sen, 1989).

Shyam (1989) in his study of the India framework for Rural Development stated that:

> "Women labour force constitutes about half of the unorganized labourers in rural areas. In addition to their 10-12 hours per day engagement in household work, women's role in agriculture, animal husbandry and other allied activities is very important. A large number of women labourers are engaged in marginal occupations to supplement the family income. Their contribution, however, is

> yet to be quantified in terms of working hours as well as in terms of income generated. The green revolution has aggravated the plight of woman labourers in rural areas".

In the history of the country's planned development, women have remained invisible except for the Sixth Plan in which for the first item, a chapter was devoted to the integration of women into the development process. The main challenge in women's development has been the means of mainstreaming women into the development process.

Indian planners (Planning Commission, 1985) have recognized the fact that:

> "The Green Revolution has led to increased demands for casual labour, dispossession of small land holders from their land and consequently, pushing out women from such small land holdings to become wage earners. Though many of the tasks performed by males are mechanized, women continue to toil in labour intensive jobs like rice plantation, cleaning and storage of grain in post-harvest operations, picking of leaves, fruits and hand shelling of groundnut and picking of seeds etc. Women got limited job opportunities in modern occupations / trade as they do not have access to the training required for new technologies. In many areas where multiple crops are grown, the workload of women has increased. In industry, women continue to be employed mostly on unskilled jobs. The average earning of a regular salaried woman worker continues to be less than that of a man".

CONCLUSION

Empowering, enabling and facilitating women to

participate in all development programmes is a stupendous task in view of differential freedom and status enjoyed and the roles performed by women and the importance accorded to them across the diverse societies in the world. It is a task so massive and the efforts should also be multi-dimensional and at multi-level wherein the educational institutions, the media, the writers, leaders of all description, the extension personnel and above all the enlightened public should carry on the job of bringing about a change in the value orientations and the psyche of both men and women that the women are not only biological partners in procreation, but equal partners in social and economic development.

REFERENCES

- Brandtzaeg, B.(1979), "Women, Food and Technology: The Case of India", *Economic and Political Weekly*, Vol.XIV, No.47.
- ESCAP (1989), *"Status of Women in Asia and the Pacific Region"*, United Nations Economic and Social Commission for Asia and the Pacific, Bangkok, p.113.
- March, K.S. and R.L. Taqqu (1986), *"Women's Informal Associations in Developing Countries: Catalyst for Change?"*, Westview Press, Boulder; p.154.
- Planning Commission (1985), *Seventh Five Year Plan*, vol.I and III (1985-90), Government of India, New Delhi.
- Sen, R.K.,(1989), "The Nature of Women's Role in Economic Development". In Mahajan (ed.) *Women's Contribution to India's Economic and Social Development*, Deep and Deep Publishers, New Delhi; pp.58-73.
- Setty,E.D.(1985), "People's Participation in Rural Development: A Critical Analysis", *The Indian Journal of Social Work*, Vol.XVI, No.1; pp.73-85.
- Shahand, A., M.A. Tekie and K.E. Weber (1986), "The Role of Women in Slum Improvement: A comparative Study of the Squatter Settlements at Klong Toey and Wat Yai Sri Suphan in Bangkok, Thailand, *Studies on Human Settlements Development in Asia*, HSD Research Report 10, Asian Institute of Technology, Bangkok; p.161.

- Shyam, R. (1989), *"India's Framework for Rural Development"*, Commonwealth Publisher, New Delhi, p.112.
- UNDP (1980), "Rural Women's Participation in Development", *Evaluation Study No.3*, United Nations Development Programme, New York, p.225.
- United Nations (1982), *"Poverty, Productivity and Participation: An Analysis of some Recent Experiences", Bangkok: UNESCAP.*

15

Mini-Entrepreneural Initiatives by Women Self-Help Groups in Andhra Pradesh

The following details speak of some attempts made by the Government of Andhra Pradesh in organizing and helping the women folk below poverty line to collectively venture into some income-generating activities.

This chapter covers programmes under DWCRA and some entrepreneurial initiatives undertaken by some NGOs like Project Shakti of Hindustan Lever Limited, Padmavathi, Rashtriya Seva Samithi, Swayam Krushi, etc.

The main objective of the programme for the Development of Women and Children in Rural Areas (DWCRA) is to improve the lot of rural women through the creation of income-generating activities in a district. It is a programme sponsored by the Government of India. Districts to be covered are selected keeping in view low-literacy rate and high infant mortality rate. It envisages formation of groups of 15-20 rural women each for carrying on income-generating activities. Each group is sanctioned a 'revolving fund' of Rs.15,000/-. In the case of states, the amount is shared equally by the Centre, and State Government and the UNICEF while in the Union Territories, the Central Government bears Rs.10,000/- per group and the balance is borne by UNICEF. UNICEF also bears the expenditure on staff component which is fully reimbursed. The programme has made considerable progress since it was launched in 1982.[1]

Availability of credit is the basic requirement to any citizen, more so, to a poor person. Credit, should be timely as well as easily available. Formal institutions, including nationalized banks are unable to meet the micro credit requirements of the poor people, as normally credit for income generation has been institutionalized rather than micro credit for various purposes. This has left the poor persons with no option except to depend on moneylenders for credit. Moneylenders with abundant common sense offer timely - but an exploitative credit, which acts as a poverty trap for the poor. Various studies have shown that in rural India, a person taking credit from moneylender for health or for a marriage sinks down the below poverty line.

Poverty as we understand is a complex phenomenon and it cannot be solved only by providing income generating assets but through comprehensive human resource development of poor person enabling him/her to meet various needs.

Self-Help is the best approach:

> Experiments in various developing countries proved that the poor can be helped by organizing them into small self-help groups. Hence women self-help groups (SHGs) have become the ray of hope to the development personnel. Government of Andhra Pradesh having realized the power and potential of self-help groups in alleviating the poverty has started mobilizing the poor women into self-help groups. It is a unique step the government has taken in mobilizing the poor into self-help groups.

A typical SHG constitutes 10-15 poor women below poverty line. Members of SHGs save equal amounts as decided in their groups. The movement of SHGs started with a slogan 'save a rupee a day'. Of course there are number of groups who save more than Rs.2/- or Rs.3/- a day.

WOMEN'S SELF-HELP GROUPS (SHGS)

Self-Help movement through savings has been taken up as a mass movement by women - a path chosen by them to shape their destiny for better. Development agenda of the State in the last few years of placing the people, especially women, in the fore -front has enabled formation of a large number of Self-Help Groups (SHGs) throughout the State where the women are saving one rupee a day.

There are about 4.53 lakh women SHGs in Andhra Pradesh covering nearly 60.95 lakh rural poor women. Andhra Pradesh alone has about half of the SHGs existing in the country. Up to 1994, only 10,000 groups were functioning and in the last seven years, there was a massive scaling up in SHG activities. The SHGs are not only resorting to thrift but are also taking small loans out of the corpus available with the group. An amount of Rs. 1494.04 crores is mobilized as corpus with these groups so far and it is estimated that it would increase to Rs.2000.00 crores.

District-wise SHGs, Members and Corpus

S.No.	*DISTRICT*	*Total groups*	*Members*	*Corpus (Rs.in lakhs)*
1	2	3	4	5
1.	Srikakulam	22824	348291	5274.08
2.	Vizianagaram	14436	240369	3978.06
3.	Visakhapatnam	18930	272405	5135.09
4.	East Godavari	48154	607290	21193.17

5.	West Godavari	22330	293800	13509.17
6.	Krishna	25032	325420	6301.96
7.	Guntur	21062	246526	6506.42
8.	Prakasam	22010	288000	5056.00
9.	Nellore	17749	266285	5041.26
10.	Chittoor	19154	206874	5866.73
11.	Cuddapah	14473	154237	4653.94
12.	Ananthapur	18740	243620	6644.83
13.	Kurnool	19083	248580	5550.56
14.	Mahaboobnagar	25720	386000	8000.00
15.	Ranga Reddy	13102	182512	4968.92
16.	Medak	18000	269650	6800.00
17.	Nizamabad	14990	181125	2913.30
18.	Adilabad	14510	176553	2972.51
19.	Karimnagar	21602	325935	8691.00
20.	Warangal	24526	343364	7639.31
21.	Khammam	19055	209605	4707.91
22.	Nalgonda	17577	279045	8000.00
	Total	453059	6095486	149404.22

Socio-economic survey of such SHGs conducted by District Rural Development Agency (DRDA) in different districts has indicated that the scheme has helped women earn additional income of around Rs.2000/- per month depending on the economic activities taken up. In addition, women have taken initiative in improving their socio-economic status by participating in governmental programmes such as family welfare, promoting their nutritional and educational status, awareness on environment, public health through sanitation and clean drinking water.

Special programmes have been designed for training and capacity building of the SHGs. Training for skill development and awareness generation through exposure visits was taken up in all the districts. Around 10,000 volunteers in the state have been working and guiding the SHGs.

Marketing support is provided to the SHGs through DWCRA Bazaars (market outlets) which have been set up in all the districts. Products worth more than Rs.100.00 crores were sold through DWCRA Bazaars so far.

It has been planned by the government to bring all the rural poor women under SHGs in the next 4 to 5 years. It is programmed to cover at least one woman from a BPL (Below Poverty Level) family as a member of SHG in next two years. So far, all the habitations in the State have at least one SHG.

ECONOMIC SUPPORT TO SHGS DWCRA/SGSY

SHG Groups have been assisted under DWCRA/SGSY scheme in the form of Revolving Fund @ 25,000/- to each group. DWCRA scheme was in implementation w.e.f. 1983-84 to 1998-99 and ultimately merged in SGSY w.e.f. 1999-2000. Groups assisted with Revolving fund so far are as follows:

S.No.	*YEAR*	*No.of groups covered*	*Expenditure (Rs.in lakhs)*	*Total women covered*
1	2	3	4	5
1.	1983-84	283	9.83	4484
2.	1984-85	712	69.05	12288
3.	1985-86	330	83.99	4618
4.	1986-87	65	85.66	794
5.	1987-88	280	70.56	5005
6.	1988-89	356	70.94	5885
7.	1989-90	504	100.73	8321
8.	1990-91	477	87.15	7705
9.	1991-92	601	91.71	8586
10.	1992-93	935	88.23	6694
11.	1993-94	5647	553.29	61517

12.	1994-95	25071	4306.52	378460
13.	1995-96	17164	2735.43	246923
14.	1996-97	17737	3544.99	277319
15.	1997-98	7178	1288.34	100876
16.	1998-99	3828	938.08	59753
17.	1999-00 Special Assistance	20867	5015.17	292138
	TOTAL	102035	19139.67	1481366
18.	1999-2000 (SGSY)	10698	2674.50	160470
19.	2000-01	9393	2348.28	140897
20.	2001-02	7043	1760.75	105645
21.	2002-03	6091	1522.75	85274
22.	2003-04 (May'03)	275	68.75	3575
	TOTAL	33500	8375.03	492286
	STATE TOTAL	135535	27514.70	1973652

(b) State Revolving Fund

For ensuring financial viability of SHGs, the state government is providing budgetary support every year with an amount of Rs.44.00 crores. During 2002-03, an amount of 40.00 crores has been released to assist 40,000 groups covering 6.00 lakh women @ Rs.25,000 (Rs. Rs. 10,000/- subsidy + Rs. 15,000/- loan) as revolving fund to each group. In the year (2002-03) 39668 groups have been assisted utilising Rs. 39.67 crores out of the releases and Rs. 59.50 crores credit has been mobilised. This is in addition to Government of India grant under SGSY.

Year-wise Progress

Sl.No	*Year*	*Achievement (Rs. In lakhs)*	*Achievement (Groups)*
		Financial	*Physical*
1	1998-99	551.98	5719

2	1999-2000	1514.55	18656
3	2000-01	5207.85	63808
4	2001-02	4474.30	51752
5	2002-03	3966.80	39668
	Total	15715.48	179603

An amount of Rs. 1500.00 lakhs is provided in the budget 2003-04 and released to assist 15000 groups. By May'2003, 16 groups have been assisted with Rs. 1.60 lakhs subsidy and Rs. 2.40 lakhs credit.

(c) SHG Bank Linkage

NABARD, Commercial Banks and Regional Rural Banks are providing direct assistance to the SHGs under the "SHG Bank Linkage". 3.32 lakh groups have been assisted so far and 1.20 lakh groups have been assisted with repeat finance and assistance per group ranges from Rs.20,000 to is Rs.1 lakh. Around Rs. 1046.52 crores have been provided by banks under the scheme so far. During 2002-2003 an amount of Rs. 476.76 crores is mobilised as credit covering 165093 groups.

Around 60000 groups of 4.42 lakh groups above have been given repeat finance more than once.

It is proposed to mobilize credit of Rs. 1000 crores covering 2.00 lakh groups during 2003-04. During the year 2003-04 as on May, 6364 groups have been assisted with bank credit of Rs. 18.39 crores.

Year-wise Progress

		Achievement	
S.No.	*Year*	*Credit mobilized (Rs. in lakhs)*	*Physical (Groups)*
1.	1998-99	4189.91	12270
2.	1999-2000	8662.77	43586
3.	2000-01	17338.17	103606

4.	2001-02	26195.31	117352
5.	2002-03	47676.00	165093
	Total	104061.26	441907

Capacity Building

Special programmes have been designed for training and capacity building of the SHGs. Training for skill development and awareness generation through exposure visits is taken up in all the districts. Regular skill development training programmes are being organized for value addition to DWCRA products for better packaging standardization of ingredients, pricing and to develop marketing skills among women. Women are exposed to best and relevant technologies displayed at Training and Technology Development Centres (TTDCs) in all districts. The information about their functioning is obtained on a quarterly basis for monitoring and evaluation. Well-known agencies like ORG-Marg are associated for evaluation and monitoring of SHGs and to suggest measures for their sustainable growth.

Starting of SHGs

Once the members come together, they open an account either in a bank or post office in the area of the group. The group authorizes any of the members (elected as group leaders) to operate the group account.

Group Processes

Thrift is a good entry point and a binding force for poor women. They see their future in their savings, the savings which meet their immediate needs, and also provide security in their old age.

The meagre savings of an individual may not be sufficient to meet her needs but all the savings of the group members put together can be of great help to one or two members of the group. In any of the best SHGs, the credit operations also start at the end of first month itself wherein the members pool their savings and sanction loan to a needy member. Every group will have its own set of rules and regulations like the amount of savings by members, interest rate on savings, basis on which loans are to be prioritized, interest on loans and penal interest on defaulted amount.

Groups are Disciplined

The basic pillar for success of SHGs is its discipline. Every group decides frequency of group meetings, when and where to hold meeting. Best SHGs meet once a week, but normally any SHG should meet atleast once a month. The frequency of meetings strengthens the group processes, higher the frequency better it would be. Best groups maintain their discipline through fining the absentee members and latecomers. The thrift as well as credit operations take plakhe in the group meetings. The meetings have specific agenda and the discussions take plakhe as per the agenda.

A poor woman coming out of her house and attending the meetings as a stakeholder itself is a step towards empowerment.

In the meetings various issues are discussed at length and members decide who should be given the loan. The discussions take plakhe in a democratic and transparent manner. In the best SHGs, each meeting is presided over by members in rotation and this helps to impart leadership qualities to all the members.

Accounts are written in the meeting itself. The standard items of account include attendance register, savings and loan ledger, cash book and individual pass books. The accounts are written either by members themselves or by a person employed by the SHG.

Best practices in SHG are being evolved continuously based on the following factors:-

- Regular meetings.
- Continuous savings
- Internal rotation of savings.
- Conduct of meetings with specific agenda.
- Thrift and credit operations taking plakhe in the group meetings
- Rotation of leaders
- Transparent and democratic decision-making.
- Non-exploitation of members' needs.
- One for all and all for one.
- Urge for increase of corpus.
- Determination for economic and social development

Marketing

Marketing support is provided to the SHGs through DWCRA Bazaars (Market outlets), which have been set up in all the districts. A permanent DWCRA Bazaar is being set up at Hyderabad. Products worth more than Rs.100 crores were sold through DWCRA Bazaars in the last two years.

The SHGs are assisted in many districts to develop branding of their products ex: Stree Prakasham in Ongole district, Mahila in Adilabad, East Godavari etc., Women are encouraged to participate in fairs taking plakhe at national level and in other states. Collaboration with Hindustan Lever Ltd., has been secured by SHGs of Nalgonda district where MACS have been appointed as stockist points and groups as sales points for marketing DWCRA products. Leading super bazaars like Food World, Apna Bazaar, Thrinethra super market have come forward to tie up with SHGs to market DWCRA products.

INSTITUTION BUILDING

SHGs are encouraged to come together as Cooperative Societies at the village level and mandal level by federating them under Mutually Aided Cooperative Societies Act 1995. Nearly 350 societies have been formed so far. These societies will be accessing credit from financial institutions, donor agencies, DRDAs and voluntary organizations and help the members of women SHGs in availing bigger loans for economic activities and also help in collective bargaining in marketing of products, purchasing raw materials etc. These societies are popularly known as "Mahila Banks". These societies have a share capital of Rs. 5.80 crores and a total corpus of Rs. 17.77 crores. These societies charge interest at 12-18 % per annum for giving loans. The recovery rate is around 98%.

GOVERNMENT INITIATIVES

- Sales tax exemption on the sales of all the products manufactured by the DWCRA / SHG beneficiaries and marketed through the district level marketing societies organized by the DRDAs.
- Stamp duty waiver on all loan documents to be executed by the DWCRA / SHGs for accessing loans from banks and other financial institutions.
- Special provision made in the state budget during last four years for state matching grant / revolving fund to support SHGs
- Established permanent marketing centers in all the districts.
- Established TTDCs in all the districts for skill trainings and capacity building and also to display technologies.
- Setting up of Sri Ramananda Teertha Rural Institute (SRTRI) for technology development, research, training

and to coordinate the training activities for all the districts.

- Appointment of DWCRA / SHGs as implementing agencies under Mid-day meals scheme.
- Support to groups to participate in fairs at National, State and district level.
- Support to form women's co-operative societies under MACS Act.
- 14.83 lakh L.P. Gas connections to DWCRA / SHG women.
- Setting up of one permanent DWCRA Bazaar at Hyderabad.

Due to this massive Self-Help movement, there is perceptible improvement in socio-economic status of rural women. Due to constant efforts of the government, women have become very active, assertive and are concerned with the issues relating to them and their surroundings.

The particulars mentioned below speak of the ways in which the government has been assisting the SHGs in furthering their moving into entrepreneurial domain.

- Channeling of various development schemes particularly concerning women and children - Convergence of development activities
- Networking amongst the group - Mahila Banks
- Providing a platform for women to discuss common problems
- Improve awareness level of rural women - on various development schemes and government agencies implementing them.
- Improving socio-economic well-being of the rural women through micro credit.

- Marginalizing the role of moneylenders in the rural areas through access to credit.
- Instilling a sense of self-confidence among rural women.

POLICY INITIATIVES

Entrustment of Civil Works SHGs

- Execution of civil works were entrusted to SHGS
- SHGs were given necessary technical training on execution of works and they were provided with detailed booklets.
- About 562 works worth of Rs. 376.00 lakhs were entrusted to the self-help groups from Panchayat Raj Department
- In the same way, Roads and Buildings Department entrusted 20 works worth of Rs. 3.29 lakhs and Irrigation department entrusted 3 works worth of Rs. 3.70 lakhs to the self-help groups

Supplies to Welfare Hostels Entrusted to SHGs

- All the welfare hostel supplies like provisions and commodities were entrusted to SHGs.
- There are 243 government hostels (SC-122, ST-70 and BC-50) in the district; the SHGs are carrying out business worth of 27.16 lakhs per month towards supplies to the hostels and generating an income of Rs. 3.00 lakhs per month.

Raising of Nurseries Entrusted to SHGs

- 68 groups presently raising about 40 lakh plants and earning Rs. 9000/- per group/season

Fair Price Shops Entrusted to SHGs

- 140 appointments were issued to SHG to run fair price shops

Punt Service contract was Entrusted to SHGs:

- At Mattampally on river Krishna 3 groups are managing and earning 1.5 lakhs per year by providing punt services i.e. carrying passengers from Nalgonda district side to Guntur district side across the river.

Non Timber Forest Produce - Contracts Entrusted to SHGs

- In 7 mandals 21 groups are collecting NTFP and earning Rs. 5000/- per group/season. Eg. Custard apple.

C. OTHER INCOME GENERATING ACTIVITIES

SHGs managing Hindustan Lever Limited (HLL) rural Distributorship

- Five MAC Societies are distributing HLL products to entire Nalgonda district rural retailers and to SANGHAMITHRA super bazaars managed by 10 MAC Societies. The profit margin is about 13%.

MACS Managing Nirodh Vending Machines

- At 82 plakhes covering 48 mandals SHGs & MACS are managing NIRODH vending machines. Net profit is Rs. 300/- per pack of 500 condoms.
- They are selling oral pills, while encouraging spacing methods, the SHGs earn 15% profit on sales

Cement Bricks

- 69 SHGs have taken up manufacturing of cement solid bricks and selling to DM (Housing) through NIRMITHI KENDRA

Super Bazaars

- 10 MAC Societies have started income generating activity under SANGHAMITHRA super bazaars. Each unit is established with an outlay of Rs. 2.00 lakhs.

The profit margin is 10% i.e. Rs. 4000/- to 5000/- per month

Sanitary Napkins

- To improve health and hygiene of rural women, sanitary napkin units at plakhes were established with an outlay of Rs. 7.00 lakhs. The product is sold at a profit of Rs. 5/- per pack under the brand name "SWETCHA MAHILA"

Wealth from the Waste

- 9 charcoal units were established in 9 mandals with an outlay of Rs. 1.00 lakh by using prosophis species and earning Rs. 5000/- per 10 Mt.

Agro Services

- SHGs are running a unit at Nakrekal with an outlay of Rs. 5.00 lakhs. Monthly income is at Rs. 5000/-

Land Lease

- 15 groups have taken about 100 acres of land on lease and raised vegetables, commercial crops etc.

D. Formation of New SHGs with Poorest of the Poor

Eligible Women Population

- Scheduled castes: 156893
- Scheduled tribes: 82855
- Total: 239748
- No. of groups that can be formed : 15983
- Women already covered: 60126
- Groups already formed: 4008

The Initiative

- New groups formed: 1948
- Women now covered: 29175

PROGRESS ON IMPLEMENTATION OF SPECIAL PROJECTS UNDER SGSY

(i) *Economic Generation Through Coir Production by Women SHGs in East Godavari District*

The Government of India have sanctioned special project of Economic Generation through Coir production by Women SHGs in East Godavari District with a total cost of Rs.1452.00 lakhs to be shared between central and state in the ratio of 75:25 and released Rs.1034.55 lakhs. The State Government has released their share of Rs.344.85 lakhs so far for implementation of the project.

So far an amount of Rs.1224.40 lakhs has been utilised and 11,800 beneficiaries have received training.

Production

1. 2 ply yarn making - 430 m. tons value of Rs. 60.20 lakhs.
2. Mat weaving 1.85 m.tons. Value of Rs.24.05 lakhs.
3. Brush making 0.185 m.tons. Value of Rs.1.85 lakhs totalling value of production is Rs.86.10 lakhs.

(ii) *Economic Generation through Fashion Designing & Garment Manufacturing by Women SHG in East Godavari District*

The Government of India have sanctioned special project on Economic Generation through Fashion Designing & Garment manufacturing by Women SHG in East Godavari District (2001-2002) with a total cost of Rs.1200.00 lakhs to be shared between central and state in the ratio of 75:25 and released 1st instalment of amount of Rs.360.00 lakhs in the month of March'2002. The State Government have released Rs. 120.00 lakhs. The Project Director, DRDA, East Godavari has identified the training centres and procured suitable machinery with the assistance of National Institute of Fashion Technology. Training has been given to 1000 SHG members and 2nd batch training is under progress. So far Rs. 375.80 lakhs has been utilised.

(iii) Development of Marine Fisheries in Srikakulam District

The Government of India have sanctioned special project on Development of Marine Fisheries in Srikakulam District (2001-2002) with a total cost of Rs.873.00 lakhs to be shared between central and state in the ratio of 75:25 . Funds have been released to a tune of Rs. 611.10 lakhs by Govt. of India and State Govt. so far.

Group loaning for 2233 beneficiaries with an amount of Rs. 132.33 lakhs. Revolving fund Rs. 72.73 lakhs, infrastructure for Rs. 51.50 lakhs, and training expenditure Rs. 8.10 lakhs.

(iv). Special Project on Employment Generation in Rural Areas of Nellore District

Govt. of India have sanctioned the special project to create employment in Rural Areas of Nellore District with a target of 10250 beneficiaries. The total cost of the project is Rs. 14.99 crores. The Govt. share is Rs. 12.01 crores to be shared by Central and State at 75:25 respectively. Govt. of India have released Rs. 360.36 lakhs as 1st instalment.

So far an amount of Rs. 122.13 lakhs has been spent under Minor Irrigation for desilting and improvement to the tanks.

(v) Income Generation of SHGs through imparting skills in Textiles Processing and Garment manufacturing in Visakhapatnam District.

Govt. of India have sanctioned the above Spl. project under SGSY for the benefit of 6080 families with a total subsidy of Rs. 726.72 lakhs and credit component of Rs.

489.60 lakhs. The Govt. of India have released the 40% of the Central Share of Rs. 218.02 lakhs as 1st instalment.

As the sanction is recently given (March'2003) the implementation of the programme is under process.

(vi) Development of Handicrafts clusters of Kalamkari painting at Srikalahasti in Chittoor District.

Govt. of India have sanctioned the above project under SGSY and envisages development of the craft through participatory mode of crafts persons for the benefit of 300 families. The total Govt. share is Rs. 298.74 lakhs and credit component is Rs. 60.00 lakhs. The Govt. of India have released 1st instalment of Rs. 89.624 lakhs,

As the sanction is recently given (March'2003) the implementation of the programme is under process.

(vii) Development of Tribal Jewellery Handicraft cluster in Nalgonda District:

The Govt. of India have sanctioned the above project with a total subsidy component of Rs. 48.40 lakhs, Credit component of Rs. 48.40 lakhs and beneficiary contribution is Rs. 3.49 lakhs for the benefit of 150 artisans. The Govt. of India have released Rs. 14.52 lakhs as 1st instalment.

As the sanction is recently given (March'2003) the implementation of the programme is under process.

ABSTRACT OF THE SGSY SPECIAL PROJECTS

Sl. No	*Name of the Project & Beneficiaries*	*Bank Component*	*Subsidy*	*Total*	*No. of Beneficiaries*
		(Rs. in lakhs)			
1	2	3	4	5	6
1.	Economic Generation through Coir production by Women SHGs in East Godavari District	0.00	1452.00	1452.00	13800

2.	Poverty Alleviation through use of Improved Agricultural Technology in Chittoor District	0.00	1500.00	1500.00	10000 Acres
3.	Action Plan to create technologically qualified Global Workers in Ranga Reddy, Medak, Nalgonda & Warangal districts	539.00	799.21	1338.21	12000
4.	"Economic Generation through Fashion Designing and Garment Manufacturing by Women Self-Help Groups in East Godavari District,	855.00	1200.00	2055.00	13680
5.	"Gollapalem Lift Irrigation Scheme on Aleru Drain in Inkollu Mandal of Prakasam District	0.00	295.00	295.00	1481
6.	"Economic Assistance to 6275 IAY (Innovative) Houses Swarozgaris in Madakasira Block Ananthapur district	361.00	621.00	982.00	6275
7.	"Development of Marine Fisheries in Srikakulam District	627.00	837.00	1464.00	6100
8.	Employment Generation in Rural Areas of Nellore District.	298.50	1201.20	1499.70	10250
9.	Providing Assistance to Self-Help Groups federated into mutually aided thrift and credit Co.op societies, Nalgonda	--	284.00	284.00	24111
10.	Income Generation of SHGs through imparting skills in Textiles processing and Garment manufacturing in Visakhapatnam District.	489.60	726.72	1216.32	6080 families
11.	Development of Handicrafts clusters of Kalamkari painting at Srikalahasti in Chittoor District.	60.00	298.74	358.74	300 beneficiaries
12.	Development of Tribal Jewellery Handicraft cluster in Nalgonda District	15.54	48.40	63.94	150 beneficiaries
	TOTAL	3245.64	9263.27	12508.91	88147 Beneficiaries 6080 Families 10000 Acrs.

LIST OF PRODUCTS MADE BY SHGS IN ANDHRA PRADESH

SRIKAKULAM	Mesta Products, Food items, Handlooms, Candles, Agarbarthis, Wooden toys, Home toys, Grooms, Brass, Bell metal, Pappads, Tamarind, Groundnut Kernel, Cashewnut, Dry Fish, Pottery
VIZIANAGARAM	Mango jelly, Leather & Rexene Bags, Wire Bags, Embroidery, Bobbili Veena, Banyans, Adda Leaf, Honey, Wool, Lakhe, Khadi, Soft Toys
VISAKHAPATNAM	Food items, Mesta, Etikoppaka Wooden Toys, Palm Leaf, Handlooms, Pickles, Coir, Tamarind, ginger, Mirabulum, Brass, Leather, Detergent Powder, Mango jelly, woollen Carpets
EAST GODAVARI	Kalankari, Coir Products, Wooden Toys, Sea Shells, Zari Sarees, Handloom Sarees, Lakhe Products, Dry Fish, Pickles, Coconut Products, Coir, Soft Toys, Seakoi, Soap Nut, Cane Products, Plaster of Paris, Non Veg. Pickles, Cloth bags, Candles, Croatia bags
WEST GODAVARI	Lakhe products, Food items, Pickles, Lungies, Blankets, Carpet, Kalankari, Soft toys, Mats, Printed sarees, Paper sweet (pootarekulu), Coconut brooms, Coconut oil, Readymade garments, Wire bags
KRISHNA	Dry Fish, Kalankari, Pickles, Wool items, Banians, Detergent powders, Palm Leaf, Rexene Bags, Ties, Pop corn, School Bags, Ready made Dresses
GUNTUR	Eatable items, pickles, Note books, Pads, Detergent Powder, Paper pulp toys, Leather Lampshades& Puppets, Peteru Sarees, Kalankari, Rold Gold Ornaments, Wire bags, Honey, Ghee, Wool items, Decorative articles, Hair Oil, jute bags, Khuresha wire bags
PRAKASAM	Leather bags, Pickles, Sarees, Dress material, Eatables, Crotia bags, Eatables, Fish & prawn, Readymade garments, Masala powders, Agarbathi, Dry Fish, Crotia wire bags, Zukad Sares, Chilli Power
NELLORE	Zari Sarees, Sea shells, Modern dress making, Kalankari, Croatia bags, Banana wire bags, Palm leaf, Cushion covers, Leather & Rexene bags, Leather chappals, Wooden cutlery, Carpets, Agarbathi, Masala powder, Pickles, Paturi sarees, Readymade garments, Soft toys
KURNOOL	Eatable, Soft toys, Embroidery, Wool items, Leather goods, Wool blankets, Sculptures, Furniture, Leather goods, Kalankari, Khadi, Fabri printed sarees Dyeng & Painting sarees, Silk sarees, Pickles, Bed sheets & towels, Rexene bags

ANANTAPUR	Leather lampshades & Puppets, Readymade garments, Dress material, Pickles, Masala powders, Gem stones, Agarbathi, Bamboo products, Eatables, unit cases, Nylon mats, Bags, Sarees, Soft toys, Kalankari products, Wool products, Silk cloth, Dress material
CUDDAPAH	Basket making, Wire bags, Broom sticks, Sweets, Ghee, Wooden sculptures, Pickles, Masala powder, Mosquito net, Towels, Cotton Sarees, Handlooms
CHITTOOR	Terrakota pottery, Kora toys, Leather goods, Wire bags, Zaree sarees, Lungies, Agarbathi making, Ariveni Handicrafts, Sea shells, Pen refill making, Copper vessels, Brass idols, Plaster of Paris, Furniture (windows), Wooden toys, Readymade dress material
RANGA REDDY	Banjara needle work, Pochampalli sarees, Dress material, Soft toys, Pot painting & wood painting, Palm leaf, Eatables, Pickles, Detergent powder, Napkins, Bed sheets, Petticoats, Photo lamination & paints, Decorative articles, Agarbathis, Candles
NIZAMBAD	Soft Toys, Food items, Readymade Dresses, Leaf plates, Ornaments, Pottery, Embroidery, Gollabhama Sarees, Chappals, Blankets, Toys, Medicine, Papads, Wool products, Jute items, Lambadi ornaments, Banjara toys, Eatables, Dry Fish, Cow Therapy medicines
MEDAK	Embroidery, Wool, Leather, Rexene item, Blankets, Toys, Medicine, Papads, Pearls, Jute items, Readymade garments, Camphor, Naphthalene, Incense sticks, Hindi crafts, Eatables, Detergent powder, Chappal, Leaf plates
MAHBUBNAGAR	Cotton & Silk sarees, Gadwal Sarees, Towels, Pickles, Hats, Kalankari bed sheets & towels, Soft toys, readymade garments, Eatables
NALGONDA	Bed sheets, Handlooms, Chudidars, Pillow covers, Diwan sets, Frocks, Cushion cover, Petti coats, Blouses, Plaster of paris toys, Lambadi ornaments, Fish Pickle, Leather chappals, Brass items, Turmeric, Chilli powder, Cloth bags, Bakery products, Food items
WARANGAL	Lungies, Towels, Kalankari, Sarees, Carpet, Chappals, Durries, Banians, Candles, Turmeric powder, Leather

	bags, Greeting cards, Honey, Ghee, Bakery products, Detergent powder
KHAMMAM	Handlooms, Sarees, Carpets, Brass items, Leaf Plates, Greeting cards, Dry Foods, Mats, Pickles, Readymade Garments, Kalankari, Candles, Eatables, Pickles
KARIMNAGAR	Silver Filgree items, Rexene bags, Velvet bags, Decorative items, Petti coats, Sarees, Shirts, Eatables, Pickles, Soft toys, Rexene Bags, Luggage bags, Papads, Bamboo products, Pillow covers, Purses, Towels, Banians, Detergent powders
ADILABAD	Handlooms, Agarbathi, Bamboo items, Brass articles, Mondas, Pickles, Adda Leaf Plates, Chappal, Toys, Paints, Cement products, Wooden furniture, Baskets, Petty coats, eatables, Lakhe items, Leather Chappals, Wool products, Chilli & Turmeric powder

DWCRA EVENTS IN 2003

	Exhibition	*Plakhe of Exhibition*	*Particulars Exhibition*	*Period of Exhibition*	*Total No. of Groups Participated*	*Total Sales (Rs. In lakhs)*
1.	All India Industrial Exhibition	Exhibition Grounds Hyderabad	Organized by Exhibition Society, Exhibition Grounds, Nampally, Hyderabad- CWE&SE Organised DWCRA Bazar in the site allotted by Exhibition Society in 63rd AIIE	01.01.2003 to 15.02.2003 (45 days)	75 groups	145.00 upto 10.02.2003
2.	Kakatiya Kalamaho tsavalu	Karimnagar	Organised by District Administration, Karimnagar - DRDA arranged DWCRA Bazar in the event	18.01.2003 to 20.01.2003 (3 days)	170 groups	100.00
3.	Kadapot-savam	1) Muncipal Stadium, Cuddapah, 2)JR Memorial Hall, Proddutur 3) MPDO office, Rajannapet	Dist Admn. Organiz-ed Kadapotsavam in three plakhes i.e. Cuddapah, Proddutur & Rajannapet, DRDA arranged DWCRA Bazar in three plakhes	28.01.2003 to 01.02.2003 (5 days)	88 groups	50.00
4.	India	Necklakhe	AP Tourism organized	01.02.2003	6 groups	15.00

Interna tional Travel Mart	Road, Hyderabad	India International Travel Mart at Necklakhe Road, Tank Bund, Hyderabad and allotted 3 stalls to DWCRA/SHGs	to 03.02.2003 (3 days)		
5. Grama Sree Mela	Bhuvaneswar, Orissa	CAPART organized Exhibition through DRDA Bhuvaneswar and allotted 2 stalls to DWCRA/SHGs from A.P	03.01.2003 to 12.01.2003 (10 days)	2 groups	1.60
6. Heritage Health Festival	Lalitha Kala Thoranam, Public Gardens, Nampally, Hyderabad	AP Tourism Dept. organized Heritage Health Festival at Lalitha Kala Thoranam, Public Gardens, Nampally, Hyderabad and allotted stall to DWCRA/SHGs food products	07.02.2003 to 09.02.2003 (3 days)	3 groups	1.50
7. Flemingo Festival	Sullurpet, Nellore	Dist. Admn.Nellore organized Flemingo Festival at Sullurpet, Nellore Dist - DRDA arranged DWCRA Bazar in the event	10.02.2003 to 12.02.2003 (3 days)		
8. Krishna Mahot-savam	Vijaya-wada	Dist. Administration, Krishna Dist. organized Krishna Mahotstav at Vijayawada and DRDA arrange DWCRA Bazar in the event	12.02.2003 to 16.02.2003 (5 days)		

Source: www.ap.nic.in/dwcra

MUTUALLY AIDED COOPERATIVE THRIFT SOCIETIES (MACTSS)

Introduction

The Government of Andhra Pradesh is marching forward towards social and economic empowerment of women through better access of women to economic resources, increased mobility, awareness, assertiveness, confidence, self-respect, self-esteem and gender equality. Net-working of SHGs at village, cluster and mandal level are emerging with the pro active role taken by the Government by way of introduction of MACTS Act, 1995 which is encouraging Women's Cooperative Thrift Societies. In the last 5-6 years the Government has been involving the women as active partners in the development process. Due to the best efforts and facilitation of State Government at present 350 MACTS are functioning successfully in A.P., consisting of 4.31 lakh members, having share capital of Rs.580.48 lakhs. The total corpus of 350 MACTS is Rs.1777.28 lakhs.

Savings and credit or income generation requires a holistic approach to human development, which ultimately leads to community development. The approach towards poverty alleviation should be self-help. Savings plus credit is a good starting point for group formation. Now in Andhra Pradesh the Self-Help Groups (SHGs) have become a forum for the collective unit of the poor against common expression and explanation, to understand individual and common problems and to improve their skills and capabilities to manage resources. These groups are highly cohesive entities. All members of the group conform strictly to the group standards and its leaders represent the feelings of the members.

Hence, it has become necessary to federate the groups bringing them under a statute, making them an economic group into a Cooperative Society, which can manage their own affairs, systematically follow the principles of cooperation formally. The groups in A.P. not only thrift-oriented but involved in several social and political activities at various levels.

In Andhra Pradesh such groups are federated under the provisions of A.P. Mutually Aided Cooperative Societies Act, 1995. MACTSs vary from 1 village to 15 villages covering of 50 to 100 groups consisting of 200 to 2000 women members. A MACTS is a community development financial institution with development consciousness and focus on poverty alleviation and empowerment of women. These MACTSs are also popularly called as 'Mahila Banks in Andhra Pradesh'.

Credit is an effective instrument of Social change and most critical need for survival. The Women's Thrift Credit Mutually Aided Cooperative Societies are voluntary, formed by the members of the SHGs. Both shareholders and directors belong to the women members of the society. These institutions are self-reliant business enterprises based on thrift and self-help and one controlled by the members for their economic and social betterment and is accountable to the members.

MACTSs provide easier, faster and higher access of credit to poor women at low rate of interest (Rs.1/- to Rs.1.50). Responsibility is placed on the groups to select the needy beneficiaries, disburse the loans and to ensure prompt repayments. An Executive Committee of 7 to 13 consisting of the representatives of the women helps to administer the bank.

Objective

The Objectives of MACTS are:

- Providing credit to poor women without security.
- Reducing moneylender exploitation at low rate of interest.
- Assets creation.
- To improve economic status of women.
- Creation of micro enterprises.
- Avoiding long loan sanction procedure and delay.
- To undertake sustainable employment generation activities.
- Generate livelihood to poor women.

Guidelines

The MACTS is formed with the following guidelines:

1. Thrift/DWCRA group Members only.
2. Minimum age of the members is 18 years and married women only.
3. Group savings of minimum one year.
4. Permanent Resident of the village.
5. Regular savings habit among all the group members.
6. Regularity in conduct of monthly meetings by the group.
7. Maintenance of Ledgers, Registers.
8. Internal lending among the Members.
9. Requiring the Thrift/DWCRA group to pay share capital of Rs.500/- or Rs.1000/-.
10. Entry fee Rs.20/- to Rs.100/- by each member.

Requirements to Join a Macts Are

- Seniority of the groups - minimum 1 year.
- Regular thrift.
- Level of internal lending.
- Level of repayment.
- Regularity of group meetings.
- Regular in maintenance of group records.
- Functional literacy level of groups.
- Family planning status of members.
- Participation in community programmers.

Key activities of these institutions:

Cultivating the habit of thrift and savings among the members. Loan to members with or without security for productive and asset formation and for consumption purpose.

1. Offer Credit and non-credit services in pursuit of women's economic prosperity through loan and credit.
2. Arrange for storage, grading, processing, value addition, packing, transportation and sale of the produce of the members.
3. Assist for enhancing the economic productivity and income of women and for asset formation.
4. Assist programmes promoting women self-employment, income generation, health, and education.
5. Gain collective wisdom in financial matters in organizing and managing their own finance and distributing the benefits among themselves.
6. Promote group production activities for gainful employment of women.
7. Providing technical and imparting training for its members.
8. Procure, pool, purchase, utilize and distribute inputs required for women in I.G.A. and consumer articles and articles required for household requirements.
9. Undertake any activity, which is incidental and essential for the attainment of the objective of the society.

Eligibility for Sanction of Loans

The criteria for sanction of loans are:

- Only for members in the MACTS.
- Loan application should be recommended by the group leader and by the director at the village level.
- They should not be loanees or defaulters for large amounts through any other sources as certified by group leader.

- Registers, passbooks should be regularly updated.
- Urgency, need and viability of loans.

TYPES OF LOANS

Sl. No.	*INCOME GENERA TING (60%)*	*ASSETS CONSUMPTION PURPOSES (40%)*
1.	Purchase of agrl. Land	1. Education
2.	Milch animals	2. Health needs
3.	Electric motors	3. Marriages
4.	Petty business	4. Accidents
5.	Flour mills	5. Festivals
6.	Grinders	6. House constructions
7.	Sewing machines	7. House repairs
8.	Cloth business	
9.	Fruit business	
10.	Land on lease	

Recovery of Loans

100% Loan Recovery is identified in all the MACTSs.

ENEFICIARIES

The Beneficiaries are all women, who are engaged in income generating activity and saving a min-amount of Rs.30/- per month regularly. They form into small self-help groups and in a group, on average as mentioned earlier, there are 15-20 members from different households, but residing in the some area. They are either SCs, STs, BCs and other caste members but basically they are all below poverty line. Occupation-wise they may be:

- Agricultural Labourers.
- Marginal and small farmers
- Non-farm wage farmers

- Unemployed or any disadvantaged groups, such as fisher women, petty traders and crafts women.

These people are made aware of their condition and importance of savings and credit and rotate the group's savings as their corpus and lend to their own group members to meet their immediate credit requirements. The external funding may be revolving fund provided to the women groups, grant-in-aid provided by the state Government for doing small business.

The group members are homogenous in terms of members' income, sex, social status, and place of residence and like-mindedness. Only one person or household is a member of the group. A member should attain the age of 18 years but not more than 60 years. Each member should be willing to accept the objective of the group. The group shall elect a representative/leader for a period of 3 years and she will be a member in the representative General Body of the Cooperative Society.

The groups conduct regular meetings - fortnightly or monthly and attendance of all members is compulsory. The time and place of the meeting is fixed and in the meeting members share their savings. All transactions are approved in the group meeting through resolution. At the group level, the group savings and loans issued to members will be maintained. The documents are in their simplest form and easy to write by a member who has simple numerical and writing abilities.

The self-help groups or DWCRA groups existing for more than one year and vibrant in doing credit and savings operations and who can manage them on their own independently can federate into a cooperative society under the provisions of A.P. Mutually Aided Coop. Societies Act.

Byelaws also are formulated to send the local requirements and got them registered.

Among other things, all the members of the group, will become members of the society. The committee is elected democratically and there is continuity of the elected management. The elected management consists of committee members.

Implementing Agency

The implementing agency at the state level is the Commissionerate of Women Empowerment & Self-Employment, Hyderabad. The Commissioner, Women Empowerment & Self-Employment will release the funds as per project outlay to the societies through the Project Directors of the concerned districts. The managing committee of the society in turn ground the scheme with and reports compliance. The unit for grounding the scheme is ultimately the cooperative society at the village or cluster of the villages level.

Role of Commissionerate

On receipt of funds the Commissionerate passes on the funds to the societies through the Project Directors of DRDA. It takes every step that the funds are strictly utilized for the purpose for which they were released. It obtains quarterly reports in a format and obtains utilization certificates. Besides quarterly reports, it evaluates independently the working of the society. Provides guidance to the DRDA and evolves a strategy for good working of the society.

The Commissionerate will see to writing and maintenance of accounts uniformly following standard formats' and procedures. It obtains statutory returns and audit reports and evaluates the working of the society. This evaluation work may be taken up by independent agencies also.

At the District level, the Collector and ROs implement

the scheme. The societies are supervised and they submit reports to the Commissioner, Rural Development. The DRDA basing on the local needs provides assistance and guidance for getting credit through banks and marketing their products of the members of the society. The training is provided to both members, group leaders, committee members of the society both in financial management. Accounting and capacity building. If necessary the DRDAs may arrange field visits to the group members to upgrade their skills.

TRAINING AND CAPACITY BUILDING

Special programmes have been designed for training and capacity building of the Presidents, Secretaries and members of MACATS. Training on Management and Maintenance of Accounts, Micro Credit etc., is organized for the members of MACTS. In addition to the above exposure visits are organized for awareness generation.

In a relative vacuum and rarity of interest, initiative, knowledge, skills and resources material and human on the part of the downtrodden women folk, the Self-Help Groups function as educational and enabling instruments to gradually elevate the life of the poor to minimum meaningful standard of life. This development is a journey and the destination will be moving forward on and on. The way in which the programmes are being carried on serves as training for the women folk. Entrepreneurial activities being carried on with assistance from different quarters, it is hoped that it would play a contagious role drawing people from other segments of the population. Here, we may presume though, the self-help groups are functioning collectively, over a period of time, individuals within the group are likely to graduate into successful independent entrepreneurs.

While speaking of entrepreneurial initiative on the part of the women, the district of Warangal in the State of Andhra

Pradesh presents an interesting and successful case as to how the woman members of SHGs were mobilized, encouraged and assisted to collectively carry on manufacturing and marketing of chilli powder.

EMPOWERING WOMEN THROUGH SELF-HELP GROUPS[3]

Andhra Pradesh Government has been vigorously pursuing the micro finance agenda for empowering poor women. DRDA, Warangal has made very conscious efforts to thoroughly internalize this new paradigm of development. As a result, organization of women into SHGs had really taken the shape of a movement in the district. Indeed it is a conscious path chosen by women to shape their own destiny. It is also believed that promotion of non-farm related micro enterprises is an integral part of planned strategy for securing balanced development of economy of the poor women. Steadfast efforts in this direction gave birth to some very spontaneous innovations of women in the district. In this regard, Chilli Processing Unit of 514 women is surely an inspiring story.

Of late, there is a paradigm shift in development process by incorporating the gender concerns as an important element of development strategy. Duly recognizing the importance and involvement of women in participatory model of development, Andhra Pradesh Government has taken up the theme of women's empowerment as one of the main agenda items to tackle rural poverty and socio-economic issues. With over 700 million women living in poverty globally, micro finance programming is seen as an essential tool in poverty alleviation. In recent years, micro finance programmes have been used as not only a tool for economic upliftment but also as an effective way to meet women's practical and strategic needs. In coherence with globally emerging development perspective, Andhra Pradesh Government has also been vigorously pursuing the micro finance agenda for empowering poor women. DRDA, Warangal has made very conscious efforts to thoroughly internalize this new paradigm of development and operationalise the same. As a result, organization of women into SHGs had really taken the shape of a movement in the district. Indeed it is a conscious path chosen by women to shape their own destiny. Concomitantly, several challenges emerged in terms of a variety of capacity building and further growth demands from women SHGs.

In Warangal District, 22836 groups are functioning with 3.10 lakh women with a corpus of Rs.85 crore. Out of 22836 groups, about 15000 groups are linked with various banks to avail credit facilities for production and consumption needs. Obviously, this is a clear indication of the quality and growth potential of SHGs.

As a logical step towards further development of women SHGs in the district, concerted and coordinated efforts are being made to sensitize and motivate women to undertake micro enterprises. Further, the interest in enterprise building is necessitated from the following local processes: (a) poor or dependent extremely on exploitative markets and have no control on their produce; (b) being non-enterprising, the poor are not well placed to take advantage of non-farm employment opportunities; and (c) lack of resource, capacities and opportunities. Hence are unemployed for several months. It is also believed that promotion of non-farm related micro enterprises is an integral part of planned strategy for securing balanced development of economy of the poor women. Our perseverance in this regard gave birth to some very spontaneous innovations of women in the district. In this regard, Chilli Processing Unit of 514 women is surely an inspiring story.

Chilli Processing Unit

Genesis of the Idea:- Senior women self-help groups in

Parvathagir Mandal have graduated to the stage of looking out for opportunities for profitable micro enterprises. Through a participatory process, opportunities available within the area were meticulously scanned and a list of feasible micro enterprises was prepared. Chilli being one of the major crops in the area, some women have started looking into the possibilities of setting up a Chilli Processing Unit (CPU). The proposal was further scrutinized and deeply analysed and found that it is a quite profitable venture. The local NGO and DRDA enabled the women SHGs to come together and develop necessary institutional linkages for putting their idea into concrete action form.

Favourable Conditions

Following conditions enabled women to set up their Chilli Processing Unit.

- Warangal district has about 62,500 acres of land under chilli crop.
- Warangal chapatta is a special chilli variety locally cultivated and which has high commercial value due to it's colour and moderate pungency.
- A project for organic production of chillies in 300 acres is already under implementation in close vicinity to these groups.
- Financial support available from the Spices Board for any spices promotion enterprises.
- Leadership and managerial capacity developed by SHGs by virtue of their experience.
- Financial capacity of the women SHGs to invest in-group enterprises.
- Good working relationship between SHGs and local service area bank.

Financial Sources

S. No.	*The unit has been set up with*	*Rs. 23.33 lakhs as under*
1.	Share capital from members (514)	Rs.05.14 lakhs
2.	Grant from Govt. of India (Spices Board, Kochi)	Rs.10.28 lakhs

3.	Grant from Infrastructure Fund of DRDA, Warangal	Rs. 07.91 lakhs
	Total	Rs. 23.33 lakhs
4.	Working capital loan: Rs.20.00 lakhs from Indian Overseas Bank, Parvathagiri.	
	NABARD has also extended managerial & technical support	

Organizational Process

Through an intensive process, women SHGs have reached an understanding that chilli processing unit is worth attempting to enhance their income and livelihood opportunities. The idea has been communicated to all the senior groups in a cluster of 10 villages in Parvathagiri Mandal and women SHGs which were strongly convinced came forward to invest and initiate this group enterprise.

Profile of the Chilli Processing Unit

- 2.3 acres of land with good water facility by the main roadside with all conveniences for transportation and future expansion.
- Building with good space for work shed, store, packing unit, rest & change room, office room, security outpost and toilets.
- Pulverizes (20 & 30 HP), Automatic pouch packing machine, electronic weighing equipment suitable for high quality of chilli powdering with installed capacity of 3 tons production per 24 hours.
- Roaster for quick removable of moisture from chillies.
- 500 square metres drying yard for hygienic chilli processing and drying.
- Electricity connection with 60 HP dedicated transformer.
- Agmark quality certification.
- Quality testing full-fledged laboratory available within the unit premises.
- Vermi and Nadep Compost units to convert bio-waste into compost.

514 women organized themselves into 'Srujana Mahilabhivridhi Upadhi Mutually Aided Cooperative Society (Srujana Women Development & Employment Mutually Aided

Cooperative Society). This society legally came into existence with 35 SHGs hailing from 12 villages. Total members are 514 of which 73 are from SC, ST, and BC communities. Each group has raised a share capital of Rs.15,000/- and demonstrate their conviction in the idea. This further enabled them to access financial support from the Spices Board, Govt. of India and DRDA, Warangal.

This has now become an example for women entrepreneurship on the one hand and demonstration of collective strength and wisdom of women on the other. It has become a model for *"Harvesting women's collective strength for poverty alleviation"*.

Organizational Setup

I. General Body: All the 514 women who have paid share capital and membership fee constitute the general body of 'Srujana'. It meets atleast once in a year and is the supreme body to decide on the affairs of the society.

II. Representative General Body: 35 women SHGs which are part of this 'Srujana' elected one representative from each group and they constitute the representative general body. They act as link between individual shareholders and the Board of Directors. On all critical issues they consult their respective group members and represent their opinion to the managing committees.

III. Board of Directors: Nine board members are elected from the representative general body. President, Vice-President and Treasurer and six board members constitute board of directors and this board is responsible for day-to-day decision-making and overall management.

IV. Manager: He/she is a full time employee paid by the society and responsible for the job chart delegated by the governing body.

The unit has extended into a land area of 2.5 Acres with abundant facilities. The unit consists of Machinery Hall, Packing room, Storeroom and an office room. In addition to this, chemical and quality testing laboratory is also setup with a Rs.10.00 lakh grant from the Spice Board, Kochi.

The Project proved that women have developed abundant self-confidence and self-esteem through SHG movement. Not only economic poverty but also social and gender issues can be tackled effectively through this process. Government and Non-Government agencies can play a proactive role in mobilizing, organizing and sustaining SHGs. Necessary managerial, technical and marketing skills can be imparted to groups to enhance their livelihood opportunities.

A drying yard is also constructed and Mango and Lemon plantation is done in unused area to derive additional income from the land apart from adding beauty and greenery to the area.

A vermin compost unit is also established to treat the waste material and converting it into organic manure.

Facilitation & Process Moderation

An NGO, MARI has played a vital role in mobilizing women and forming Srujana MACTS and bringing governmental agencies together to access financial and other resources for establishing the unit. This has also become a model for Government and Non-Government organization partnership in development process. NGO can mobilize and motivate people to come together and Government Agencies can extend necessary financial, technical, managerial and marketing support to establish an enterprise.

Procurement, Production: The chilli is procured from shareholders as well as from other farmers. Parvathagiri, Narsampet, Nallabelli, Duggondi, Parkal, Eturunagaram and

Mangapet Mandals are identified as having good production of Warangal Chapata Chilli. G4 and Sannam Chilli variety production is abundant in 50 kms radius of the unit. Primary processing of whole chilli is done by the members at their houses. The processed whole chilli is procured in bulk and the same is kept in cold storage. As per the production demand material is transported to the unit. Powdering of chillies can be done meeting highest quality standards. Per shift (8 hours) one-ton chilli can be powdered. Packaging machine for automatic pouch filling of 50 and 100 grams pouches and electronic weighing and packing of higher quantities can be done ensuring the best quality and hygiene standards.

Quality:- This unit is linked to a project of organic cultivation of chilli in 300 acres. Thus, the product of the unit is very safe in terms of pesticide residues levels. Samples of raw material will be analysed in the laboratory to ensure required oleoresin, pungency and colour value. Laboratory analysis also helps in eliminating dust and filth particles in the final product. Work force is educated and provided with necessary hygiene & safety ware for ensuring product quality. Storage of raw material in cold storage also helps in protecting the quality. The producers have already been provided with tarpaulin sheets and drying yards to protect quality in post harvesting processing.

Marketing Strategy:- Multi pronged strategy including local marketing to export has been contemplated. The product will be thoroughly popularized among all the SHGs in the district and channels for distribution of product to all the strategic marketing locations will be developed. Networking with other marketing enterprises of SHG women in neighbouring districts will be established. Consumption points under the control of Government like hostels, Devastanams (temples) would be approached for bulk orders. Product will also be marketed through PDS and Gruhamithra supply channels. For exporting Chapata Chilli product, opportunities would be explored through Spices Board, Kochi. Private marketing agencies will be involved for pushing the product into the mainstream market. Cleaned and Dried whole mirchi will be supplied to the oleoresin extracting units in Kerala.

Uniqueness of the Project

1. First women SHG's initiative and entrepreneurship in the state.
2. Quality product with Agmark from Government of India.
3. Participation by SHGs, Government organization, NGO & Bank. A successful intervention by all the development partners.
4. Total construction of the project is done by women groups only.
5. An innovative project to utilize the local resources to create sustainable employment opportunities and providing reasonable market rates to producers of chillies and spices commodities of the area.
6. Transforming the consumption based SHGs into entrepreneurship oriented SHGs leading to employment generation and empowerment of women.
7. Value addition to the agriculture products.

Experience in the Project

The project proved that women have tremendous energies to start their own enterprises given the right opportunities. They have developed abundant self-confidence and self-esteem through SHG movement. Not only economic poverty but also social and gender issues can be tackled collectively through this process.

Government and Non-Government agencies can play a

proactive role in mobilizing, organizing and sustaining SHGs. Necessary managerial, technical and marketing skills can be imparted to groups to enhance their livelihood opportunities.

This is a classic example of convergence of all stakeholders for achieving the anticipated common goal. The differences, if any, between Government organizations and NGOs may be resolved for further development agenda and then we can expect our energies becoming synergies.

Further, Govt. of India/financial institution, while releasing any grant to NGOs can also involve stake-holding institutions for achieving better results. NGO, alone cannot achieve substantially without the active support from Government agencies.

This is a successful experiment but the requisite coordination and convergence is required in marketing the products and making it a viable enterprise.

16

Role of DWCRA in Empowerment of Women

Development of Women and Children in the rural areas is a national programme (DWCRA). We include here a case study of DWCRA in empowerment of women in Andhra Pradesh since we have data pertaining to the State. The essential elements of DWCRA's programme all over the country are same with some variations from State to State.

INTRODUCTION

Government of Andhra Pradesh has given basic impetus for women's empowerment as the starting point to tackle rural poverty and socio-economic issues. Through self-management technique women are brought together to shape their future destiny by forming into Self-Help Groups. These groups have started basically with thrift and savings. But with the passage of time, these groups have evolved into a force by their numbers, unity and solidarity. Today they are in the forefront for lobbying and advocacy for their justifiable demands throughout the state. Approximately there are 4.53 lakh Self-Help Groups in Andhra Pradesh covering 60.95 lakh women. They could mobilize Rs. 1494.04 crores corpus fund. These women groups are basically engaged in micro-enterprises as the main source of income generation for which the critical input, i.e. capital is made available by Self-Help Group.

After attaining economic development, women groups have taken up the path for social development and they are marching fast in this direction. A recent study of 1000 groups in three districts of Andhra Pradesh has shown changes for better in the following areas: sending the girl child to school, providing better nutritious food to the children, reducing family size, frequent interface with the Government officials, self management of the group, etc., there is considerable improvement in the women's participation. Similarly women's participation in local self-government and community based organizations (CBOs) like Vana Samrakshana Samithi, Water Users Associations, Village Development Committee and Village Education Committee has shown an increase over time. In the household affairs also, there is an improvement in the decision making by women from these Self-Help Groups. As a consequence women are planning of occupational mobility due to their awareness, skills acquired, availability of capital and channels for marketing. In addition, family members of the women belonging to Self-Help Groups are also planning for better social mobility.

WOMEN SELF-HELP GROUPS OF ANDHRA PRADESH

Self-Help movement through savings has been taken up as a mass movement by women - a path chosen by them to shape their destiny for better. Development agenda of the State in the last few years of placing the people, especially women, in the fore -front has enabled formation of a large number of Self-Help Groups (SHGs) throughout the State where the women are saving one rupee a day.

A Women's Perspective

- To enjoy equal status with men in the family
- To live in dignity (freedom from humiliation)
- To meet basic needs like drinking water, fuel for cooking nutritious food for the family, safe livelihood and adequate shelter.

- Self-sufficiency
- Health & Education
- Government within the reach
- Decision-making capacity within and outside the household.
- Leisure
- Freedom from violence, conflict.
- Mobility
- Ability to make choices

Another motivating factor and key to mobilization was the "Kalajatha" - a powerful medium that packed its messages in the popular cultural idiom and forms, messages also linked literacy with basic problems of livelihood and enable them to question the exploitation of the poor and the women in the society. The final message was to escape from poverty, and resist oppression. These messages struck a chord of sympathy amongst women of the weaker sections.

Simultaneously the call for becoming literate by the District administration was not perceived as a threat by the local vested interests. Women participated in the massive environment building, met daily for evening classes and participated in the discussions with men on various social issues. The presence of District Collector and other Government Officials and Non-Governmental Organisations gave the campaign legitimacy and comfort in the eyes of conservative sections of the Society.

WHO IS A SELF-HELP GROUP MEMBER

She is

- An agriculture labourer in the field;
- A fruit, vegetable, fish vendor in the street;
- A stone crusher in the quarry;

- A basket maker working under a tree;
- A petty shop keeper in a bunk;
- A brick maker;
- A construction worker;
- A farmer working in the fields;
- A manager of milch cattle at home;
- A weaver;
- A potter and
- A provider of her family
- A woman like you and me
- A worker

Availability of credit is the basic requirement to any citizen, more so, to a poor person. Credit, should be timely as well as easily available. Formal institutions, including nationalized banks are unable to meet the micro credit requirements of the poor people, as normally credit for income generation has been institutionalized rather than micro credit for various purposes. This has left poor persons with no option except to depend on moneylenders for credit. Moneylenders with abundant common sense offer timely - but an exploitative credit, which acts as a poverty trap to the poor. Various studies have proved that in rural India, a person taking credit from money lender for health or for a ritual like marriage forever goes the below poverty line.

Poverty, as we understand, is a complex phenomenon and it cannot be solved only by providing income generation assets but through comprehensive personality development of poor person enabling him/ her to meet various needs.

Self-Help is the Best Approach

Experiments in various developing countries proved that the poor can be helped by organizing them into small self-help groups. To touch the core of poverty, women are the best agents. Hence women self-help groups (SHGs) have become the ray of hope to the developmental practitioners. Government of Andhra Pradesh having realized the power and potential of Self-Help groups in alleviating the poverty has started mobilizing the poor women into Self-Help groups. It is the unique phenomenon where government has taken the role of NGO and started mobilizing poor into Self-Help groups.

A typical SHG constitutes 10-15 like-minded poor women living below poverty line. Often the women belonging to neighbourhood communities, sharing thoughts and problems with one other form into SHG. Members of SHGs save equal amounts as decided in their groups. The movement of SHGs started with a slogan 'save a rupee a day'. Of course there are a number of groups today who are saving more than Rs.2/- or Rs.3/- a day.

There are about 4.53 lakh women SHGs in Andhra Pradesh covering nearly 60.95 lakh rural poor women. Andhra Pradesh alone has about half of the SHGs existing in the country. Up to 1994, only 10,000 groups were functioning and in the last seven years, there was a massive scaling up in SHG activities. The SHGs are not only resorting to thrift but are also taking small loans out of the corpus available with the group. An amount of Rs. 1494.04 crores is mobilized as corpus with these groups so far and it is estimated that it would increase to Rs.2000.00 crores.

DWCRA SCHEME

Development of Women and Children in Rural Areas (DWCRA) Programme was introduced in Andhra Pradesh in 1982-83 with UNICEF Cooperation with the primary objective of focusing attention on the women members of the rural families living below the poverty line with a view to provide them with opportunities of self employment on a sustained basis. The women members of DWCRA form groups of 10 - 15 women each for taking up economic activities suited to their skills, aptitude and locally available resources. This programme also aims to improve women's access to basic services like Health, Education, Child-Care, Nutrition, Water and Sanitation. There has been a phased extension in the coverage of districts every year and by the 1994-95, DWCRA has been extended to all the 22 rural districts in the State. Spread of the programme in the State is as follows:

1983-84-Srikakulam, Cuddapah, Adilabad,
1986-87- Mahabubnagar, Anantapur,
1988-89- Medak, Vizianagaram,
1989-90- Prakasam,
1990-91- Karimnagar,
1991-92-Nellore, Nizamabad, Kurnool,
1992-93-Chittoor, Nalgonda, Warangal,
1993-94-Khammam,Rangareddy, Visakhapatnam,
1994-95-East Godavari, West Godavari, Krishna, Guntur.

DWCRA aims at women because when resources are scarce and services are few, it is always the women who are most affected, there by children. Merely bringing in outside aid is not enough, there should be a lasting impact on the quality of life of rural poor women.

1. Aims and Objectives

- Improving the Status and quality of life of poor women and children in the rural areas.
- Enabling women to improve their earning capacity.
- Improving the impact of ongoing development programmes by stimulating, supplementing, strengthening and integrating them.

- Involving the community in planning and implementing the programme so that need based development activity will be carried on by the communities even after outside assistance is withdrawn.

2. Recommends

The selection of like-minded poor women living in the neighbourhoods.

3. Provides

- Group support to individuals.
- Access to resources and credit for purchasing income generating assets or working capital for an economic activity.
- Awareness about political and social situation.
- Information required for better living and environment.
- Build capacity of women to improve their status and quality of life.
- Access to service like safe drinking water, housing, preventive and curative health care, education, functional literacy, applied nutrition, pre school education and child care.
- Access to appropriate technologies and skill upgradation.
- Self-esteem/self-confidence - Face the society and the world confidently.
- Self-help and self-governing capacity.

SALIENT FEATURES

1. Group Approach

DWCRA programme focuses on organisation of women

into groups to foster a collective approach to their problems and improve their lot by enhancing their bargaining power and also to resist exploitation. These organised women can pull many of the resources of the Governmental Programmes into the village for their benefit. Hence they will be in a position to harvest the opportunities from schemes, resources, services and the laws meant to help them.

2. Participatory Approach

Government Staff and women groups work as partners.

3. Revolving Fund

Under DWCRA Rs.25,000/- is provided to the group as lumpsum grant. The members can use it collectively or share it on prorata basis and it can be used for any income generating activity. This is a common fund which is recouped and revolved periodically. Over and above this, if needed IRDP subsidy and bank loans can also be availed.

4. Not Target Driven

DWCRA programme is not target oriented in the conventional sense of the term. It has targeted coverage all the women living in BPL (Below poverty line) families in 5-6 years depending on the availability of funds.

There are no sectoral targets since the groups themselves decide on the work they will undertake. Generally the poor women only feel the necessity of group organization with savings as a base to provide a platform for them to stand together and muster strength.

5. Thrift and Credit

DWCRA recognizes that banks do not cater to the consumption needs of rural women, hence they selected 'Thrift and Credit,' for self-reliance. Within the group, women are encouraged to save their own money (Rs.10, Rs.20, Rs.30 per month) as a common fund. Rules are made, money is loaned and recovered - managed by women themselves. DWCRA helps to keep the women out of the grip of the moneylenders who often keep the poor "poor" for generations. In this way DWCRA helps the women to take action on the root cause of poverty.

6. Income Generating Activities

Women's income is found to have a positive correlation with the nutritional and educational status of the family and enhancement of the positive attitudes towards the status of women inside and outside the households. Cash income in the hands of mothers reach their children for improved living standards. If women become economically independent, their status in the family and the society improves.

7. Training and Awareness

Unskilled and illiterate women have lesser employment opportunities and low wages. This confines women to marginal categories of work or even unpaid work. Training in leadership, attitudinal changes, skills for income generation is an integral part of DWCRA Scheme. Training provides an opportunity to learn from their sisters who are better of than these women.

Progress of Group Formation

In a village, like-minded women living in neighbourhoods get together and select an organiser and a treasurer for the group. Such a group contacts Gramasevika/Village Development Officer (now Village Panchayati Secretary) and seeks his/her guidance to form as a self-help group. The members take a decision to save either a rupee per day or Rs. 10-20 per month based on their capacity. Members meet in their own habitations once in a fortnight or a month. During these meetings, Group leaders collect the saving amount. The amount so collected is deposited either in the nearest bank or in the post office in a joint account operated by the organiser and the treasurer of the group.

Success of a DWCRA Groups Depends on Five Variables

1. Groups of women in poverty with a purpose,
2. Savings as an, entry point for the members to get together,
3. Democratically managed and collective decision-making groups,
4. Sustainable income generating activities,
5. Least dependence on external marketing support.

Common Features of Group Dynamics

1. Starting point need not be the same for different DWCRA groups. It could be around a theme which holds maximum appeal to its members. Savings and credit could be one of the starting points.
2. Group trajectory need not be the same for different groups. After all group dynamics has several routes and multiple options available and hence trajectory differs from group to group.
3. Speed at which the group proceeds need not be forced from outside agencies. Gentle force and moderate acceleration is welcome - but abrupt shock and resultant jerks are quite capable of hastening collapse of group dynamics altogether.
4. Who exercises power to decide is extremely important for encouraging self-esteem of all group members. It is not "we" who decide for "them" however well intentioned the move may be. It must be "they" and "they" alone to decide about themselves.
5. As the group survives and moves forward, several issues are taken up by them not exactly sequentially

but in totality. End results have been almost identical. Each members of a DWCRA group has better income than a non-DWCRA member from her own community in the same village. Awareness about hygiene and nutrition has gone up. Urge for literacy, especially for daughters and acceptance of family planning has shot up; and the most important of all self-esteem of individual members and "we can do it" syndrome has become a part of their psyche.

6. There may be a few commas but no full stop for a DWCRA group. Starting from a nucleus of 10-20 women clustered around a theme which brought them together, it develops into a micro social organism ever evolving and embracing a wider spectrum of activities of their choice over a period of time.

District-wise SHGs, Members and Corpus

Sl. No.	*District*	*Total groups*	*Members*	*Corpus (Rs.in lakhs)*
1	2	3	4	5
1.	Srikakulam	22824	348291	5274.08
2.	Vizianagaram	14436	240369	3978.06
3.	Visakhapatnam	18930	272405	5135.09
4.	East Godavari	48154	607290	21193.17
5.	West Godavari	22330	293800	13509.17
6.	Krishna	25032	325420	6301.96
7.	Guntur	21062	246526	6506.42
8.	Prakasam	22010	288000	5056.00
9.	Nellore	17749	266285	5041.26
10.	Chittoor	19154	206874	5866.73
11.	Cuddapah	14473	154237	4653.94
12.	Ananthapur	18740	243620	6644.83
13.	Kurnool	19083	248580	5550.56

14.	Mahaboobnagar	25720	386000	8000.00
15.	Ranga Reddy	13102	182512	4968.92
16.	Medak	18000	269650	6800.00
17..	Nizamabad	14990	181125	2913.30
18.	Adilabad	14510	176553	2972.51
19.	Karimnagar	21602	325935	8691.00
20.	Warangal	24526	343364	7639.31
21.	Khammam	19055	209605	4707.91
22.	Nalgonda	17577	279045	8000.00
	Total	453059	6095486	149404.22

Groups are Disciplined

The basic pillar for success of SHGs is their discipline. Every group decides the frequency of group meetings, when and where to hold meeting. Best SHGs meet once in a week, but normally any SHG should meet atleast once in a month. The frequency of meetings strengthens the group processes, higher the frequency, the better it is. Best groups exert their discipline through fining the absentee members and late coming members. The thrift as well as credit operations take place in the group meetings. The meetings have specific agenda and the discussions go on as per the agenda.

A poor woman coming out of her house and attending meeting as a stakeholder itself is a step towards empowerment.

In the meetings, various issues are discussed at length and members decide who should be given the loan. The discussions take place in a democratic and transparent way. In the best SHGs, each meeting is presided over by members in rotation and this helps to impart leadership qualities to all the members.

Accounts are written in the meeting itself. The standard account includes attendance register, savings and loan ledger, cashbook and individual passbooks. The accounts are written either by members themselves or by a person employed by the SHG.

Best practices in SHG are being evolved continuously based on experience, to illustrate a few, following are mentioned:

- Regular meetings.
- Continuous savings
- Internal rotation of savings.
- Conduct of meetings with specific agenda.
- Thrift and credit operations taking place in the group meeting
- Rotation of leaders
- Transparent and democratic decision-making
- Non-exploitation of members' needs
- One for all and all for one
- Urge for increase of corpus
- Determination towards economic and social development

Training and Capacity Building

It is not sufficient to promote SHG but the group has to be sustained. Constant inputs of training and capacity building are required to sustain SHGs. District Rural Development Agencies are striving towards this goal by constantly organizing training programmes. Apart from DRDAs, number of NGOs (National as well as International), organizations like NABARD, are actively associated with the training and capacity building of SHGs.

It has been of general observation that any group requires atleast four days of training in a year. The groups are to be given inputs intensively in group management, best practices in group management, conduct of group meetings, accounts and book keeping and mode of accessing to government schemes and bank finance. Training is conducted to the following functionaries.

1. *Group Members/Group Leaders*

Group members are trained to understand the need for a strong group. Generally the trainings is informal conducted by Gramasevikas and A.P.O.(DWCRA) at the mandal level. Video films, posters and field visits within the district and to the other districts are found to be more effective. At least once in a month, a bus load of DWCRA women go out to see successful programmes like Podupulakshmi in Nellore, DWCRA groups in Anantapur. They also visit Hyderabad, Tirupati, Visakhapatnam and Vizianagaram to increase their worldly knowledge. Women are able to leave their villages, homes and families for one or two weeks and travel the length and breadth of the State. To the extent that mere physical mobility is an indicator of empowerment for women normally trapped in the Treadmill of life; It was remarkable that so many women of varying ages are able to undertake such tours. This was a tremendous confidence booster, after all they were confined to kitchen and home for generations! Women get back from these tours fully charged and resolve to work for the group with renewed vigour. For a young programme this is important.

2. *Gramasevikas and Field Training Officers*

Gramasavikas and F.T.O.s are trained to understand the philosophy of DWCRA, process of group formation, problem solving, and maintenance of Accounts. Gramasevika Manual in Telugu was published and was supplied to all. One or two weeks pre-service training is imparted in Andhra Pradesh Academy of Rural Development, Hyderabad. NGOs also train Gramasevikas and FTO at the district and regional level.

A.P.O.s, P.D.s, Bankers and NGOs

Workshops organised by NABARD, Banks and DRDAs at the District and State level provide an forum for DRDA staff and bankers to understand each other's view point. Conducted tour of bankers to the pre-selected enable Bankers recognise the strength of SHG/ DWCRA groups. Seminars / workshops organised in APARD for Project Directors, APOs., NGO and Line Department staff helped facilitation of Team work in the women's empowerment process.

Training of Trainers

10-15 dynamic and energetic group leaders willing to work as Volunteers / animators are selected in every Mandal. These animators are trained at the block/district level institutions through methodologies like lecture cum discussions, Field visits, video film and case studies. These trainers tour within the Mandal and district and explain DWCRA concept organically to other women.

Annual calender of training is prepared by DRDAs. It is proposed to conduct training in 4 phases.

Syllabus for training cluster volunteers is as follows: (4 days training and 2 days field visits). The following topics are discussed.

I. First Round of Training

1. Group formation through process approach
2. Self-Help concept
3. Team building and leadership
4. Group dynamics
5. Book keeping and accounts maintenance as well as preparation of minutes
6. Collection of information and group meetings schedule (model schedules should be filled by the volunteers)

7. Savings and credit management
8. Presentation and communication skills
9. Marketing skills

II. Second Round of Training

1. Information and knowledge of various Government programmes
2. Community participation and initiation
3. Potential of skill up-gradation and income generation Activities
4. Importance of literacy to mothers and children
5. Gender sensitization
6. Marketing skills

III. Third Round of Training

1. Importance of small family and family welfare schemes
2. Immunization of pregnant women and new borne children
3. Enrollment of children in the Primary Schools
4. Safe drinking water and sanitation
5. Tips on nutrition and kitchen garden
6. Health and personal hygiene including reproductive health care
7. Awareness on environment and tree planting
8. Energy conservation, use of alternate sources of energy
9. Sanitation
10. Marketing skills

IV. Fourth Round of Training

Women's time: Collecting firewood and water are tasks carried out by women who are already over worked and the time available for these activities is limited. Thus over exploitation of resources of fuel wood is linked more to the time available to women than their poverty status. There is a gender dimension, but not necessarily an income dimension.

1. Planning for self employment programmes
2. Group lending schemes

   (Approach banks and awareness on documentation and procedures for accessing credit, knowledge on watershed development programmes for effective participation in ecology regeneration programmes.
3. Rural economy and importance of domestic poultry, dairy, cottage industries - Modern technology & tools.
4. Marketing skills

Poor are Bankable

Once the SHG completes six months and members practice thrift continuously, rotating the corpus generated, then it becomes eligible to get bank loan. The loan amount ranges from two times of savings amount (including amount under rotation) to four times. Leadership of NABARD in Andhra Pradesh, today made bankers very positive towards SHGs. Bankers are viewing SHGs as a bankable option. Constant orientation programmes to bankers, and also positive attitude towards the groups on repayment has helped to scale up the SHG-bank linkage programme. During the last Three (3) years 1.76 lakh SHGs have got bank loan to the tune of Rs. 255.00 crores.

Government Assistance

To encourage SHGs, government is also providing incentives. Apart from centrally sponsored of SGSY, Government of Andhra Pradesh is also proving matching grant which is equal to the savings made by SHG. The amount of matching grant ranges from minimum Rs.5000/- to a maximum of Rs.10,000/-.

Convergence

The SHGs are sustainable only if they are more broad based and various services are converged at their level. Members in long run should not see SHGs only as micro credit provider but for providing various services like insurance, information etc. Government is also making conscious efforts to converge various services with SHGs.

A large number of the women from SHGs participate in Janmabhoomi (a government programme envisaging overall development of villages) regularly as active partners for their village development.

Various services / Programmes of Government are getting converged at SHGs level. Under deepam scheme 11.4 lakh women SHG members have been given LPG connections. In addition to the above, 15 lakh LPGas connections are proposed by Government under Deepam scheme this year to the members of women SHGs. Government is giving Rs 1000/- subsidy for each connection and power to select the beneficiaries is given to the groups.

Rural permanent housing programme of state government is being entrusted to the SHGs on pilot basis. Raising of nurseries, management of watersheds is also entrusted to women in some districts. In addition to the above, construction of individual sanitary latrines has been entrusted to women in various places. Women SHGs are actively participating in literacy programme "Akshara Sankranthi". Women SHGs had very good impact on reducing the influence of moneylenders in rural areas. Similarly there is impressive impact on SHG members of other Government programmes like family welfare, education, girl child education, immunization of children etc.

Marketing

Marketing support is provided to the SHGs through

DWCRA Bazaars (Market outlets), which have been set up in all the districts, and permanent DWCRA Bazaar is nearing completion at Hyderabad. Products worth more than Rs.100 crores were sold through DWCRA Bazaars in the last two years. Training and Technology Development Centres (TTDC) have been established in each district to introduce innovative technologies for the qualitative improvement of products made by the SHGs.

The SHGs are assisted in many districts to develop branding of their products ex: Stree Prakasham in Ongole district, Mahila in Adilabad district etc., Women are encouraged to participate in fairs taking place at national level and in other states. Collaboration with Hindustan Lever Ltd., has been secured by SHGs of Nalgonda district where MACS have been appointed as stockist points and groups as sales points for marketing DWCRA products. Leading super bazaars like Food World, Thrinethra super market came forwarded to tie up with SHGs to market DWCRA products.

Some DWCRA products have very good demand in pickle producing SHGs of Guntur district got orders worth Rs 6.00 lakhs, lace groups of West Godavari district got export orders.

Till late 1996, marketing of DWCRA products through Govt. intervention and initiatives was one of the weak linkages. Most of the D.R.D.As., in the State have District Level Market outlets like ADRAMS (Anantapur), HAMPI (Prakasam), RAMSONS (Nellore), DSMS (Srikakulam) etc., Enterprising DWCRA groups participated in Gramashree Melas, State Level and District Level Exhibitions. These groups had a very limited opportunity to expose themselves to the markets and expand activities.

DWCRA Mela 1997 is a unique event conceived and organised at Hyderabad from 22nd December, 1997 to 2nd January, 1998 by the Commissionerate of Rural Development,

Government of Andhra Pradesh to demonstrate and display the entrepreneurial skills and economic empowerment of women groups across the State. The Mela was first of its kind and had participation by DWCRA and SHG Women members from all the 22 rural districts. The Stalls and Sales were managed by Women themselves and Men were there to assist them.

OBJECTIVES

The major objectives in the organisation of DWCRA Mela are to:

- expose the skills of rural women to the Urban High class and middle class consumers;
- enable DWCRA to access wider and larger urban markets to understand consumer preferences;
- facilitate inter group interaction across the different districts in the State for exchange of information, ideas and promote net works of women who will be taking marketing of products in future;
- facilitate interface between producers and consumers without intermediaries;
- expose women to better manufacturing and production technologies, improved tools and implements;
- promote self-esteem among women through interaction with VVIPs such as Chief Minister, State Ministers, officers and the Elite of the Society.

Micro Markets and DWCRA Bazaar

Micro markets form is an important aspect of the socio-cultural fabric of the rural people, especially women. These markets are conducted once in a week on a fixed day in a village covering cluster of villages. Generally these markets are conducted the whole day and they provide an important platform for their social interaction.

Most of the DWCRA women sell their products and buy essential goods from these micro-markets. Business tricks are learnt by doing. More than 75% of the DWCRA products are sold in the micro-markets. Some women are producers and others are producers-cum-sellers. Traders constitute 20% of the women in these groups.

DWCRA Bazaar is an innovative approach to promote sale of DWCRA products. At the District and Mandal Head Quarters, a prominent place in a busy market place is selected to establish a Bazaar.

Women groups or their representative sell their products on definite days in a month (special sales).

DWCRA BAZAARS

Sl. No.	Name of the district	Location	Address
1.	Srikakulam	Near Rythu Bazaar,Srikakulam	Near Rythu Bazar, Srikakulam
2.	Vizianagaram	MPDO's office premises	MPDO, Vizianagaram
3.	Vishakhapatnam	R.K. Beach	Vishakhapatnam
4.	East Godavari	KNF Road, Amalapuram	KNF Road, Amalapuram
5.	West Godavari		
6.	Krishna		
7.	Guntur	Bradipet, Guntur	MRO's office, Guntur
8.	Prakasam	1. Near HPO, Ongole	
		2. Near RDO's office, Kandukur	
		3. SC, BC Colony office, Markapur	
		4. Kanigiri	
9	Nellore	1. MPDO, Gudur	
		2. MPDO's office, Venkatagiri	
		3. MPDO's office, Sullurpet	
		4. MPDO's Kavali	
		5. MPDO's office, Atmakur	
		6. MPDO's office Udayagiri	

10.	Chittoor	Mandal H.Q.	Chittoor
11.	Cuddapah	1. MRO's office Proddutur 2. Collector's office, Cuddapah	
12.	Ananthapur	1. Penukonda 2. Puttaparthi	
13.	Kurnool		
14.	Mahabubnagar		
15.	Ranga Reddy		
16.	Medak		
17.	Nizamabad	LIC X Roads	Nizamabad
18.	Adilabad	Adilabad	Adilabad
19.	Karimnagar		
20.	Warangal	Near TTDC, Hasanparthi	Near TTDC, Hasanparthi
21.	Khammam	Wyra Road, Khammam	SC. Corporation shoping Complex, Khammam
22.	Nalgonda		

Socio-economic survey of such SHGs conducted by District Rural Development Agency (DRDA) in different districts has indicated that the scheme has helped women earn additional income of around Rs.2000/- per month depending on the economic activities taken up. In addition, women have taken initiative in improving their socio-economic status by participating in governmental programmes such as family welfare, promoting their nutritional and educational status, awareness on environment, public health through sanitation and clean drinking water.

Special programmes have been designed for training and capacity building of the SHGs. Training for skill development and awareness generation through exposure visits was taken up in all the districts. Around 10,000 volunteers in the state have been working and guiding the SHGs.

Marketing support is provided to the SHGs through DWCRA Bazaars (market outlets) which have been set up in all the districts and permanent DWCRA Bazaar is completed in Hyderabad. Products worth more than Rs.100.00 crores were sold through DWCRA Bazaars so far.

It has been planned by the government to bring all the rural poor women under SHGs in the next 4 to 5 years. It is programmed to cover at least one woman from a BPL (Below Poverty Level) family as a member of SHG in next two years. So far, all the habitations in the State have at least one SHG.

DWCRA/SGSY

SHG Groups have been assisted under DWCRA/SGSY scheme in the form of Revolving Fund @ 25,000/- to each group. DWCRA scheme was in implementation w.e.f. 1983-84 to 1998-99 and ultimately merged in SGSY w.e.f. 1999-2000. Groups assisted with Revolving Fund so far are as follows:

S. No.	*YEAR*	*No.of groups covered*	*Expenditure (Rs.in lakhs)*	*Total women covered*
1	2	3	4	5
1.	1983-84	283	9.83	4484
2.	1984-85	712	69.05	12288
3.	1985-86	330	83.99	4618
4.	1986-87	65	85.66	794
5.	1987-88	280	70.56	5005
6.	1988-89	356	70.94	5885
7.	1989-90	504	100.73	8321
8.	1990-91	477	87.15	7705
9.	1991-92	601	91.71	8586
10.	1992-93	935	88.23	6694
11.	1993-94	5647	553.29	61517
12.	1994-95	25071	4306.52	378460
13.	1995-96	17164	2735.43	246923
14.	1996-97	17737	3544.99	277319
15.	1997-98	7178	1288.34	100876

16.	1998-99	3828	938.08	59753
17.	1999-00 Special Assistance	20867	5015.17	292138
	TOTAL	102035	19139.67	1481366
18.	1999-2000 (SGSY)	10698	2674.50	160470
19.	2000-01	9393	2348.28	140897
20.	2001-02	7043	1760.75	105645
21.	2002-03	6091	1522.75	85274
22.	2003-04 (May'03)	275	68.75	3575
	TOTAL	33500	8375.03	492286
	STATE TOTAL	135535	27514.70	1973652

(b) State Revolving Fund

For ensuring financial viability of SHGs, the state government has been releasing State Revolving fund from 1998-99. The progress under this is as follows. During 2002-03, an amount of Rs. 40.00 crores has been released to assist 40,000 groups covering 6.00 lakh women @ Rs.25,000 (Rs. 10,000/- subsidy + Rs. 15,000/- loan) as revolving fund to each group. In this year 39134 groups have been assisted utilising Rs. 39.26 crores out of the releases and Rs. 58.89 crores credit has been mobilised. This is in addition to Government of India grant under SGSY.

STATE REVOLVING FUND

S.No	Year	*Financial (Rs. in lakhs)*			*Physical (Beneficiaries)*	
		Allocation	*Releases*	*Expenditure*	*Target*	*Achievement*
1.	1998-99	1900.00	1900.00	551.98	19000	5719
2.	1999-00	4400.00	1100.00	1514.55	11000	18656
3.	2000-01	4400.00	4400.00	5207.85	44000	63808
4.	2001-02	4400.00	4400.00	4474.30	44000	51752
5.	2002-03 (upto 1/03) Credit	1500.00	4000.00	3926.01 5889.02	15000	37339
	Total Credit	16600.00	15800.00	15674.69 5889.02	133000	177274

(b) SHG Bank Linkage

NABARD, Commercial Banks and Regional Rural Banks are providing direct assistance to the SHGs under the " SHG Bank Linkage". 3.89 lakh groups have been assisted so far and average assistance per group ranges from Rs.20,000 to Rs.1 lakh. Around Rs.936.23 crores have been provided by banks under the scheme so far. During 2002-2003 an amount of Rs. 364.37 crores is mobilised as credit covering 135237 groups.

SHG BANK LINKAGE

S. No.	*Year*	*Groups covered including repeat finance*	*Loan mobilised (Rs. in lakhs)*
1.	1998-1999	12270	4189.05
2.	1999-2000	43568	8862.77
3.	2000-2001	103606	17338.17
4.	2001-2002	117352	26195.31
5.	2002-2003 (upto1/03)	135237	36437.52
	Total	412033	93622.82

4,12,033 groups cover repeat finance also.

Institution Building

SHGs are encouraged to come together as Cooperative Societies at the village level and mandal level by federating them under Mutually Aided Cooperative Societies Act 1995. Nearly 250 societies have been formed so far. These societies will be accessing credit from financial institutions, donor agencies, DRDAs and Voluntary organizations and help the members of women SHGs in availing bigger loans for economic activities and also help in collective bargaining in marketing of products, purchasing raw materials etc. Due to this massive Self-Help movement, there is perceptible improvement in socio-economic status of rural women. Due to constant efforts of the government, women have become very active, assertive and are concerned with the issues relating to them and their surroundings.

Non-Governmental Organizations' Efforts

Right from the beginning, NGOs in Andhra Pradesh are working for the cause of women and more than 200 committed NGOs have been involved in facilitating formation of SHGs and in the efforts for their sustenance. NGOs are working in close coordination with DRDAs in training and capacity building, skill development training programmes building SHG centred organizations etc.

Financial Resources

Upto 1994-95, cash support to revolving fund of Rs.15,000/- per each group was shared equally by Government of India, State Government and UNICEF. During 1995-96, revolving fund for each group was enhanced from Rs.15,000/- to Rs. 25,000/-. Government of India, State Government and UNICEF shared @ 40:40:20 respectively. During 1996-97, UNICEF withdrew its support. Government of India and State Government shared the revolving fund on 50:50 basis. UNICEF provided support to administrative staff cost for a period of 5 years initially for each district. Later it will be met from IRDP administrative staff cost. UNICEF also provided a vehicle for APO (W) in each district. From 1.1.1996, UNICEF withdrew totally from DWCRA.

Financial Support During 2000-2001

The Government released Rs. 44 crores during 2001-02 to assist 44,000 groups covering 6.6 lakhs women @ Rs. 10,000 as revolving fund to each group. This is in addition to Government of India grant of Rs. 4.5 crores. NABARD, Commercial Banks and Regional Rural Banks are providing direct assistance to the SHGs under the "Self-Help Linking Scheme " of NABARD.

The achievement under SHG-NABARD linkage scheme during the last 3 years and target for 2001 - 02 are as detailed below.

Year	*Amount (Rs in crores)*	*Groups (in lakhs)*
1998-1999	41.90	0.12
1999-2000	88.63	0.44
2000-2001	173.38	1.03
Total	303.91	1.59
2001-2002 (Target)	255.00	0.75

STATUS OF DWCRA / SHG

TOTAL GROUPS	*395233*
DWCRA	150414
SGSY (Revolving Fund)	17687
State matching grant (Groups)	140833
Groups formed in 200-01	60441
Eligible SHGs for assistance	86299
Women Covered (Rs. in Lakhs)	53.59
Women Savings (Rs. in Crores)	550.00
Govt. Assistance (Rs. on crores)	493.00
Total Corpus (Rs. in Crores)	1043.00

DWCRA

S.No.	*Year*	*Financial (Rs. in lakhs)*			*Physical (Groups)*	
		Allocation	*Releases*	*Expenditure*	*Target*	*Achievement*
1.	1995-96	3244.50	2728.75	2735.43	12875	17164
2.	1996-97	2520.00	3392.88	3544.99	11440	17737
3.	1997-98	724.50	724.50	1288.34	2875	7178
4.	1998-99	869.90	938.08	938.08	3828	3828
5.	Special Assistance		5000.00	5000.00	20000	20867

SGSY: This Scheme Came into Implementation w.e.f. 1.4.1999

S.No.	*Year*	*Financial (Rs. in lakhs)*			*Physical (Groups)*	
		Allocation	*Releases*	*Expenditure*	*Target*	*Achievement*
1.	1999-00	8292.75	8281.34	10044.08	237388	335318
2.	2000-01	7070.69	5853.88	7082.46	199110	206886
3.	2001-02	4091.08	5282.45	6240.76	115211	177519
4.	2002-03 (upto 1/03)	4091.08	4217.73	4009.38	115205	102000

LIST OF PRODUCTS MADE BY SHGS

Srikakulam	Mesta Products, Food items, Handlooms, Candles, Agarbarthis, Wooden toys, Home toys, Grooms, Brass, Bell metal, Papads, Tamarind, Groundnut, Kernel, Cashew nut, Dry Fish, Pottery
Vizianagaram	Mango jelly, Leather & Rexene Bags, Wire Bags, Embroidery, Bobbili Veena, Banyans, Adda Leaf, Honey, Wool, Lace, Khadi, Soft Toys
Visakhapatnam	Food items, Mesta, Etikoppaka Wooden Toys, Plam Leaf, Handlooms, Pickles, Coir, Tamarind, ginger, Mirabulum, Brass, Leather, Detergent Powder, Mango jelly, woolen Carpets
East Godavari	Kalankari, Coir Products, Wooden Toys, Sea Shells, Zari Sarees, Handloom Sarees, Lace Products, Dry Fish, Pickles, Coconut Products, Coir, Soft Toys, Seakoi, Soap Nut, Cane Products, Plaster of Paris, Non Veg. Pickles, Cloth bags, Candles, Croatia bags
West Godavari	Lace products, Food items, Pickles, Lungies, Blankets, Carpet, Kalankari, Soft toys, Mats, Printed sarees, Paper sweet (pootarekulu), Coconut brooms, Coconut oil, Readymade garments, Wire bags
Krishna	Dry Fish, Kalankari, Pickles, Wool items, Baniyans, Detergent powders, Plam Leaf, Rexene Bags, Ties, Pop corn, School Bags, Ready made Dresses
Guntur	Eatable items, pickles, Note books, Pads, Detergent Powder, Paper pulp toys, Leather Lampshades& Puppets, Peteru Sarees, Kalankari, Rold Gold Ornaments, Wire bags, Honey, Ghee, Wool items, Decorative articles, Hair Oil, jute bags, Khuresha wire bags

Prakasam	Leather bags, Pickles, Sarees, Dress material, Eatables, Croatia bags, Eatables, Fish & prawn, Readymade garments, Masala powders, Agarbathi, Dry Fish, Crotia wire bags, Zukad Sares, Chilli Power
Nellore	Zari Sarees, Sea shells, Modern dress making, Kalankari, Croatia bags, Banana wire bags, Palm leaf, Cushion covers, Leather& Rexene bags, Leather chappals, Wooden cutlery, Carpets, Agarbathi, Massala powder, Pickles, Paturi sarees, Readymade garments, Soft toys
Kurnool	Eatable, Soft toys, Embroidery, Wool items, Leather goods, Wool blankets, Sculptures, Furniture, Leather goods, Kalankari, Khadi, Fabri printed sarees Dyeng & Painting sares, Silk sarees, Pickles, Bed sheets & towels, Rexene bags
Anantapur	Leather lampshades & Puppets, Readymade garments, Dress material, Pickles, Masala powders, Gem stones, Agarbathi, Bamboo products, Eatables, uit cases, Nylon mats, Bags, Sarees, Soft toys, Kalankari products, Wool products, Silk cloth, Dress material
Cuddapah	Basket making, Wire bags, Broom sticks, Sweets, Ghee, Wooden sculptures, Sweets, Pickles, Masala powder, Mosquito net, Towels, Cotton Sarees, Handlooms
Chittoor	Terrakota pottery, Kora toys, Leather goods, Wire bags, Zaree sarees, Lungies, Agarbathi making, Ariveni Handicrafts, Sea shells, Pen refill making, Copper vessels, Brass idols, Plaster of paris, Furniture (windows), Wooden toys, Readymade dress material
Ranga Reddy	Banjara needle work, Pochampalli sarees, Dress material, Soft toys, Pot painting & wood painting, Palm leaf, Eatables, Pickles, Detergent powder, Napkins, Bed sheets, Petticoats, Photo lamination & paints, Decorative articles, Agarbathis, Candles
Nizambad	Soft Toys, Food items, Readymade Dresses, Leaf plates, Ornaments, Pottery, Embroidery, Gollabhama Sarees, Chappals, Blankets, Toys, Medicine, Papads, Wool products, Jute items, Lambadi ornaments, Banjara toys, Eatables, Dry Fish, Cow Therapy medicines
Medak	Embroidery, Wool, Leather, Rexene item, Blankets, Toys, Medicine, Papads, Pearls, Jute items, Readymade

	garments, Camphor, Naphthalene, Incense sticks, Hindi crafts, Eatables, Detergent powder, Chappal, Leaf plates
Mahbubnagar	Cotton & Silk sarees, Gadwal Sarees, Towels, Pickles, Hats, Kalankari bed sheets & towels, Soft toys, Readymade garments, Eatables
Nalgonda	Bed sheets, Handlooms, Chudidars, Pillow covers, Diwan sets, Frocks, Cushion cover, Petti coats, Blouses, Plaster of paris toys, Lambadi ornaments, Fish Pickle, Leather chappals, Brass items, Turmeric, Chilli powder, Cloth bags, Bakery products, Food items
Warangal	Lungies, Towels, Kalankari, Sarees, Carpet, Chappals, Durries, Baniyans, Candles, Turmeric powder, Leather bags, Greeting cards, Honey, Ghee, Bakery products, Detergent powder
Khammam	Handlooms, Sarees, Carpets, Brass items, Leaf Plates, Greeting cards, Dry Foods, Mats, Pickles, Readymade Garments, Kalankari, Candles, Eatables, Pickles
Karimnagar	Silver Filgree items, Rexene bags, Velvet bags, Decorative items, Petti coats, Sarees, Shirts, Eatables, Pickles, Soft toys, Rexene Bags, Luggage bags, Papads, Bamboo products, Pillow covers, Purses, Towels, Baniyans, Detergent powders
Adilabad	Handlooms, Agarbathi, Bamboo items, Brass articles, Mondas, Pickles, Adda Leaf Plates, Chappal, Toys, Paints, Cement products, Wooden furniture, Baskets, Petty coats, eatables, Lace items, Leather Chappals, Wool products, Chilli & Turmeric powder

TRAINING & TECHNOLOGY DEVELOPMENT CENTRES (TTDCS)--AN INNOVATIVE APPROACH

A nodal Agency to integrate all training programmes for the beneficiaries of various departments of State Government & Government of India, banks, NGOs education institutions and user groups was initiated in the last two years. TTDCs were established in all the 22 Districts with the following objectives:

- Training for skill formation / upgradation
- Technology transfer to rural areas through adoption, adaptation, development and dissemination
- Technology display centre
- Training at doorsteps through distance mode
- Repository of district level data on resources, extension services
- Planning for sustainable development
- Interface platform for experts and artisans
- Fostering and nurturing SHGs

Functions of the TTDCs are:

- Acting as a clearing house for information on technologies suitable for the establishment of micro-enterprises;
- Technology training for skill development, i.e., for organising Skill Development Programmes
- Technology display and demonstration
- Acting as a source of information on the SGSY (Swarnajayanthi Gram Swarojgar Yojana) and other rural development schemes of government of India and the state.
- Technology dissemination, improvisation, modernization
- Technology extension services like, counselling on newer technologies, providing access to information, making available the services of experts and other professionals for advise and problem-solving, market intelligence and on-line help through internet
- Providing interface with bankers, Government functionaries, and other line agencies

- Networking with similar institutions, both public and private, including reputed NGOs actively engaged in the area of rural development
- Maintaining a data-base on the resources of the region serviced by it
- Maintaining conference facilities for facilitating active interaction amongst SHGs
- Arranging technology melas periodically

In short, the Training and Technology Development Centres are the most important media for technology adoption, assimilation and innovation.

DWCRA/Women Self-Help Groups in Nalgonda district in the Telangana region manage agriculture service units and take up activities like fertilizer retail sale, hiring of agricultural machinery etc. Agriculture produce transport is taken up by youth groups in several parts of the state as self-employment venture. Chief Minister Empowerment of Youth (CMEY) and Prime Minister Rojgar Yojana (PMRY) beneficiaries established units like courier services, restaurants, hotels, retail outlets for consumer goods, veterinary services, repairs to equipments like radio, television, refrigerator, agriculture pump sets etc. Under the scheme, supply of improved tools kits to rural artisans, carpentry, pottery, laundry service etc., are proved to be useful in enhancing employment and income opportunities.

Training for the skilled manpower in service sector activities must be prioritized. Local polytechnics and Training and Technology Development Centres can impart skill training. Women groups (DWCRA) groups can take up activities related to tourism - for eg., Cookery, Catering, house keeping, lighting and restaurants.

Service sector in the state contributes 43% of GSDP. Future

economy will be service led economy, which will an ideal sector since the state is having large work force.

Employment Opportunities for SHGs

Specific targeted anti-poverty programmes started in right earnest from the sixth five-year plan did not yield desired results. As poverty is a complex phenomenon and it manifests itself in a myriad ways, the poor not only suffer from low incomes and high unemployment but also low life expectancy, low levels of literacy and poor health. Women's poverty is more complex as it is reinforced by social factors.

The State Government recognized self-help approach as an effective strategy to tackle socio-economic poverty especially amongst women. Nearly 3.3 lakh self-help groups, covering 48 lakh women could mobilize Rs.650 crore of corpus fund. Every habitation in the State has at least one women SHG.

Similarly 1.0 lakh youth groups having 5 lakh membership and 7.96 lakh youth have taken up various self employment ventures under IRDP, SGSY, PMRY and SSI units which require upscaling of finances, technologies and marketing. 6600 SHGs have been formed in JFM (Joint Forest Management) committees in-charge of forest protection, conservation and utilization. 20,000 SHGs in watershed committees and 10 lakh practicing artisans will have to find a direction to move forward and maintain sustainable level of activity.

Employment for the SHGs (2000-2001)

Department	*No. of Units*	*Assistance by Banks (Rs.in Crores)*	*Persons employed (in lakhs)*
Rural Development/ DWCRA	1,31,260	242.00	19.69
S.C. Corporation/SHGs	1,073	2.68	0.161
Youth Services/CMEY	60,000	300.00	9.00
Minorities/ DoMUA	469	0.70	0.07
Tribal Welfare	495	0.58	0.05
TOTAL	193297	545.96	29.42

Particulars of Functioning of Technology and Training Development Centres (TTDCs) in Districts

Sl. No	Name of the District	Location	Address	Technologies Installed Particulars of M&E Procured
1.	Srikakulam	Etcherla	Near MRP's office, Etcherla	1. Packing machinery 2. Philips Multi Media Projector 3. Philips Digital Camera 4. Solar Dryer with Solar TV path 5. Pulvariser 6. 2 1/2 size cupid round knife with cutting machine 7. MP-1150 single needle sewingg machine 2 no. 8. Frame loom - For Durries - Furnishings 9. Decortications 10. Low cost brick making
2.	Vizianagaram	Vizianagaram	Near Govt. Girls ITI, V.T.Agraharam	1. Chips making 2. Fibre separated 3. Plastic Packing machine 4. Pottery machine 5. Rope making machine 6. Potato chips making machinee 7. Pottery wheel power operated 8. Rope making cherka
3.	Visakha-patr.am	Mahila Pragati Kendram	Pendurthi	1. Turmeric Powder Pulveriser 2. Potato chip making 3. Adda leaf plate making 4. Ready made dress making fashion designing & Embroidary 5. Industrial Sewing for Rexine bags and hand gloves making **Model displayed** 1. Vermiculture ponds 2. Biogas plant 3. Smoke less chulhas 4. Low cost sanitation model 5. Soil & Moisture conservation norms 6. Loose boulders 7. Dug out ponds
4.	East Godavari	Samalkot	Samalkot	1. Rexine bag making machine 2. Packing machinery 3. Plastic Packing machine

			4. Kalamkari Dyeing printing equipmentipment 5. Wooden toys making machinee 6. Coir rope & Mat making machinehine 7. Machinery Medlery Cherka 8. Potato Wafer making machinee 9. Coconut chiller 10. Zigzag embroidery machine 11. Cream separator 12. Mini Flour mill 13. Soft Toy making equipment 14. Power Pottery wheel 15. Radha ground nut digger
5. West Godavari	Government ITI Premises	Sathrampadu, Eluru	1. Coconut chiller 2. Medlery cherka 3. Papad making 4. Adda leaf making 5. Carpentry power tool 6. Blacksmithy power tool 7. Plastic Chips making 8. Potato chips making 9. Pottery powder tool 10. Solar cooker 11. Nylon rope making proposed another 12. Technologies installationring the year
6. Krishna	TBMPP,	TBMPP, Nimmakuru	1. Coconut chiller 2. Popcorn making machine 3. Cream Separator 4. Hawai Chappal making 5. Vermicelli making 6. Leaf plate making 7. Papad making
7. Guntur	Kotappa-konda	Kotappa-konda	1. Medlery Charka 2. Coconut chiller 3. Broomstick polishing machinee 4. Solar cooker 5. Sisal fibre extraction 6. Pottery power tool 7. Nylon rope making 8. Cream separator 9. Bio gas stove 10. Carpenter equipment 11. Toy making machine

8. Prakasam	ONGOLE	S.No.82/183, Mamidipalem, Ongole	1. Cotton stitching machine 2. Popcorn making machine 3. Potato chip making 4. Leaf plate making 5. Key chain making machine 6. Sisal fibre making machine 7. Rope making machine 8. Pottery wheel power operated 9. Coconut chiller 10. Leather stitching machine
9. Nellore	MPDO'S OFFICE	Udayagiri	1. Carpentry equipment 2. Printing & Binding machinery 3. Leather goods making machinene 4. Footwear making machine 5. Offset printing 6. Dress making equipment 7. A.C. & Refrigerators 8. Computer
10. Chittoor	MPDO'S OFFICE Bypass Road Autonagar Tirupathi	Indukurpet Naidupet Nellore	Tiruchanur Road, Tirupathi 2. Nylon rope Charka 3. Leaf cup & plate making 4. Sisal fibre extraction 5. Papad press machine 6. Coconut Chiller 7. Coir fibre Spinning 8. Salem type cherka with woodn frame 9. Single mat weaving 10. Tamarind pressing machine 11. Motorized coir yarn spinning yarn machine 12. Broom stick machine
11. Cuddapah	Vanam, Har- ita Cuddapah	Chinnachar(v), Cuddapah	1. Soft Toy makingent of Rs. 26000/- process]
12. Ananthapur	Besides Nirm- ithi Kendra	Rathadu	1. Sisal Fibre extraction machinee purchased 2. Chips making machine purcha-sedased 3. Plastic moulding machine purchasedroposed 4. Gem cutting - proposed 5. Low cost building fixtures purchasedoposed 6. Micro concrete roofing titles proposed

13. Kurnool	B. Thand rapadu	B. Thand rapadu, Kurnool	1. Sisal Fibre extraction machinee 2. Agarbathi Sticks splitting machineachine 3. Medlery wool spinning machinene 4. Medlery Slide spinning machinee 5. Coir rope making machine 6. Papad making machine 7. Potato chips making 8. Broom stick leaf splitting machinechine
14. Mahabub-nagar	Bandimi-dipalli	Bandimidipalli	1. Carpentry power tools 2. Electrician power tools 3. Stone cutting power tools 4. Rope making machine 5. Packing machine 6. Leaf cut & plate making machinehine 7. Wool turning lathe 8. Soft toys making equipment 9. Sisal Fibre extractor machine 10. Papad press machine 11. Polythene bag sealing machinehine
15. Ranga Reddy	TBMPP	Chilkoor	1. Leaf plate making 2. Soft Toys making 3. Chalk piece making 4. Candle making 5. Book binding 6. Potato chip making 7. Pottery machine (power operated]tor) 8. Medlery wool Cherka 9. Fodder cutting machine 10. Solar cooker & Dryer 11. Bicycle water pump 12. Bicycle Modern spray pump
16. Medak	Sangareddy	Near Collectorate	1. Leaf plate making 2. Jute bags making 3. Rope making machine 4. Packing machine 5. Papad press machine
17. Nizamabad	Ghanpur	Ditchpally(M)	Proposed to procure machinery
18. Adilabad	Dasnapur	Dasnapur(v)	1. Procuring Technologiesr process

19. Karimnagar	Karimnagar	Besides Dr. B.R. Ambedkar stadium	Machinery is to be installed
20. Warangal	Samskruthi Vihar	Hasanparthi	
21. Khammam	Mahila Pranganam	Tekupalli(V)	1. Lace cost housing & Sanitary 2. Biogas plant 3. Smokeless chulhas 4. Solar system of street light, water heater procurement of machine Domestic light and
22. Nalgonda	Ramnagar	Nalgonda	1. Papad pressing machine 2. Potato wiper making machinee 3. Popcorn making machine 4. Leaf plate making machine 5. Pottery machine [power] 6. Sanitary napkin knitting 7. Book binding 8. Pan mixer for Hash

COMMUNICATION STRATEGY

DWCRA is a social development project requires communication between members of a group and development functionaries, credit institutions, field workers and so on. Communication involves the sharing and exchange of ideas, information, emotions, hopes and fears and it is a part of every group's activity.

Available channels of communication in the groups are as follows:

> Oral or interpersonal, an intimate communication was made possible among the members of the groups through weekly / fortnightly monthly meetings. Informal chitchat enables the members to understand one another and appreciate their strengths and weaknesses.

Village / Mandal / block / district level meetings of group leaders and members provide a platform for these women to articulate their problems and remove the barriers with Government officials. Inter personal communication through group contact by N.G.O provides a base for good environment building. Services of ICDS staff, Women Development and Child Welfare Department, Village level officers, Gramasevikas, literary volunteers, Field officers in Banks, Teachers are utilised for interpersonal communication with DWCRA groups. Public representatives, especially women are involved in workshops and training programmes conducted for group leaders and members. It is not uncommon for the Ministers and Members of the Legislative Assembly to attend motivation training programmes for DWCRA leaders. Sensitization workshops for various Government officials bring in attitudinal changes to motivate them to take active part in the scheme and develop positive attitude towards women's development issues.

Print Media

Though a large number of women are illiterate in the villages, impact of Print media can not be under estimated. Every group has at least one or two members either literate by themselves or they have educated sons/daughters who read news papers/magazine/pamphlets for them. Yojana a monthly magazine published in Telugu from Hyderabad allotted center page to publish pictures and messages to DWCRA Women. 5000 copies of Yojana are distributed to equal number of DWCRA groups during 1996-97 for about 10 months.

Eenadu, a Telugu daily publishes a separate page for women every day entitled "VASUNDHARA" publishes success stories of DWCRA/women groups. Good work done by the group organisers, women's collective action on savings, empowerment processes are highlighted.

Monthly magazines for women groups provide an effective means of communicating success stories, appropriate messages to the groups. Information is provided on various Government schemes to the groups. Pamphlets and posters on district specific programmes like Podupulakshmi (Nellore and Kurnool) SAMBHAVANA (Nalgonda), Podupu Jyothi (Rangareddy) Grama Laxmi (Chittoor), Malakshmi (Mahboobnagar) Sapta Sutralu (East Godavari) Pragati Prakasini (Prakasham district) are used to provide communication with people at large on the process of savings, credit, self help leading to empowerment of women.

Electronic Media

All India Radio and Doordarshan broadcast/telecast several programmes on DWCRA / Women movement in Andhra Pradesh. Interviews with Group leaders and members, Government Officials, N.G.Os and public representatives, meetings and visits of dignitaries to the districts are covered these programmes.

Group singing and dancing is very common when these women meet in workshops and training programmes as an emotional bond to hold them together!

Multimedia Campaigns

Information and Public Relations department of Govt. of India conducts multimedia campaigns in selected districts every year through Field Publicity Offices Project positive aspects of DWCRA scheme.

Kalajathas

A team of artists are trained at the district level and sent to villages to propagate the idea of savings through songs and drama performances. Such teams play an important role in social mobilisation and environment building for the formation of new SHGs.

Eradication of Information Poverty - First step in women's empowerment process

Existence of development schemes does not automatically lead to the development of people. A properly functioning delivery system should be in place. The people for whom these schemes are meant should know about the objectives of the schemes. What they intend to achieve, what procedures involved, which officials are to be approaches and how to take the benefits of the scheme. If this is to happen, the group of women should have the relevant information. However the dispossessed and the have-nots of our villages are not only have-nots in respect of lands, houses, education, they are have-nots in respect of information also! They do not have correct information about why they are in such a situation! What should be done to improve their lot, what Government is doing for them and in what manner the benefits of these schemes are reaching them. Power of Information is the power of the Government hierarchies and the power of the middleman ! As the eminent economist and media expert Dr. P.C.Joshi said "Eradication of Information poverty is a pre requisite to the eradication of economic poverty". Before a change in their material condition could take place, first of all there should be a change in their mindsets. Electric Media is an effective means to provide information to a large number of illiterate women in the SHGs.

MANAGING DWCRA/SHG

Good management is often no more than common sense, but common sense is far from common and there is an enormous need for training in basic management skills particularly for the staff at the gross roots, NGOs who are quite unfamiliar with financial services and for bankers who until recently have not been free to manage.

However the manual of best practices of which there are many. The aim is to promote diversity through & discussion and debate rather than to impart specific skills.

There is a need to promote more number of Self Help Groups, ultimately to reach all the poor families within the State and in each and every habitation. At present only half of the poor families have adopted self help processes and the efforts needs to be massified / mass marketed.

In the task of scaling up, Government alone cannot perform all the activities. Environment building, social mobilisation, Managing and guiding, monitoring and evaluating needs to be done by different actors. Large number of voluntary organisations, staff of the Financial Institutions, especially Regional Rural Banks, Community Based Organisations, UNDP, DFID and other Donar agencies can play a vital role. Youth groups, (CMEY), Water User Associations (WUA), Watershed Committees (WC), Vana Samrakshna Samiti (VSS) and Village Education Committee (VEC) have to supplement one another's effort.

Should DWCRA / SHG institutions try to retain those of their members whose enterprises grow and need larger loans and different services or should they encourage such women to 'graduate' to other institutions such as the existing Commercial Banks / Co-operative Banks / Regional Rural Banks / Mutually Aided Co-operative Societies (MACS), so that they can remain focussed on their core business, the micro enterprises of the poor?

Different groups have different starting points, it could be around a theme which holds maximum appeal to all its members. Speed at which the group proceeds need not be forced from outside agencies. Abrupt shocks and resultant jerks are quite capable of hastening the collapse of group dynamics altogether.

A Self-Help Group starting with savings & internal group lending activity becomes eligible for assistance under DWCRA scheme depending on the availability of Revolving fund.

Since the number of groups is much more and DWCRA can only cater to the needs of a few groups, Banks extend loans under NABARD SHG scheme with or without intermediation of NGOs.

Some of the DWCRA and SHGs are also assisted under Group lending schemes under IRDP. Some members in a group are assisted under individual IRDP schemes leaving others behind. Sometimes this also adversely affect the group dynamics altogether. There were instances in which IRDP intervention resulted in defunct group due to wrong signals of staff stating that the loans need not be repaid. However it is noticed that all the members in a group do not have the same levels of literacy, economic status and enterprise levels. Needs of women having higher level of enterprise need to be addressed separately under IRDP. However it is advisable to carefully maintain group dynamics by encouraging savings habit and self help nature of the group. It is not desirable to invest the entire corpus fund in business activity, leaving nothing for the group an opportunity to interact.

In some of the defunct groups it was observed the women invested entire corpus in a single scheme and the scheme failed due to reasons beyond their control.

Compared to men, women are more reliable borrowers and savers. They use profits of their business for their families rather than for themselves. Women's business tend to remain small, however because their owners have other commitments; they do not grow and create jobs for others

SHG / DWCRA groups have been able to charge almost interest rates they wish because these rates are lesser than those charged by moneylenders. In the federated women societies organised by NGOs they are able to offer life insurance and coverage against specific losses such as the death of livestock or even crop failure.

In some SHG / DWCRA groups members are compelled to make substantial savings before they could borrow and while they are repaying. It is not uncommon for the members losing interest in the savings activity as they could not see any immediate benefit. It is essential for the members to make use of their own limited resources. Some times Banks which lend to SHG / DWCRA groups demand that the groups deposit as much as half of the amount of their loan with the Bank, and do not allow any of it to be withdrawn until loan is totally repaid. After the half-way point of repayment schedule, the groups are effectively paying the bank in order to borrow back their own money.

Loan repayment schedules in most of the groups are rigidly standardised and the borrowers were made to repay as soon as their loan is disbursed, to clear the loan completely within the predetermined period irrespective of the house hold cash flows or timing of the income from the asset for which the loan is used. This method is easy for the organisers and members to calculate and understand and it simplifies record keeping but it also causes hardship. In these groups flexibility in repayment schedules need to be introduced. DWCRA groups repay loans as and when they have cash flows from the income generations activity. They do not necessarily repay once in a month / quarter / half yearly.

WOMEN'S VOICE: (MAHILA VANI)

A unique way of eliciting information about the opinion of SHG and DWCRA group members on the functioning of Government departments, was initiated in June 1998 by the Chief Minister. A questionnaire containing 41 questions was designed to elicit responses from Women groups on their impressions about the DWCRA scheme, Co-operation from officials and Public representatives, their opinion on adequacy and quality of rural infrastructure like roads, electricity, School,

Hospitals, Drinking Water etc. Questions were designed to elicit Women's opinion about the corruption in Government Departments public representatives and functioning of various Village level institutions.

This Questionnaire was printed on Optical Micro Record (OMR) sheets and were distributed to all the Districts. Women group leaders and members were instructed to assemble at Mandal Head Quarters and the Questionnaire was explained to them. Women leaders Opinion was collected, computed and analysed.

It is heartening to note that more than 94% of the members assemble once in a month and 92% of the groups have Joint Savings Account and 88% of the Women have knowledge about the Financial transactions in the Bank accounts.

88% Women members respond to social problems and 95% of the members are aware of small family norms and adopt these methods.

85% of the Women expressed that they repay loans regularly. Almost 33% of Women felt that 'corruption' is a big problem in their area. 20-30% of the women are not satisfied with the functioning of Village institutions like roads, electricity, Schools Hospitals, Drinking Water, Police and other Government functionaries. Responses collected from one lakn Women groups are shown.

ORGANIZATION EVALUATION CONSULTANCY ON STRENGTHENING OF SELF-HELP GROUPS IN ANDHRA PRADESH SWOT ANALYSIS OF THE GROUPS SURVEYED IN ANDHRA PRADESH

ORG-MARG Research Limited, Hyderabad

Strengths

- Groups are homogeneous and cohesive

Group membership based on Income, Caste and Neighbourhood.

- Member composition

  SC = 22% ST = 4% BC = 49% Others = 25%

- High percentage of Women in fertility group

  Mean age of members - 35years

- Flexibility in group management

  The Group decides independently on Interest Rate, Prioritizing Loan, and Social Pressure

- Purpose of Group Formation

  Savings = 56% Future Security = 25%, Self-Help = 25% Loans=8%

- Group exercises social pressure to inculcate thrift and regularity in attendance

  Action taken against chronic absentees - 24%

  Non-conformity leads to expulsion from group

- Regularity in savings (saving from necessity and not always from surplus)

  Defaulters in the last three months 8%

- Purpose of saving

  Future security 68% Self-Help = 16% Avail loan = 15%

- Necessity guides decision on loan

  Criteria for sanctioning loans Necessity of loan = 84%

  — Loan application appraised by group as a whole (75%)

  — Creditworthiness assessed

  On the basis of Income and occupation = 49%

Past Repayment Record=30%; Property owned=27%; Faith in member=17%

- Issues discussed in Group meetings

  Health / Sanitation = 50%; Janmabhoomi = 29%; Village problems = 22%; Household problems/need = 14%; Family Planning = 12%

- Active participation in pulse polio immunization & Janmabhoomi Programme

  Participation in Village Dev. Works - Janmabhoomi 84%,

  Pulse polio = 73%,

  Anti Child Labour activities = 6%

- High rotation of group corpus

  Corpus on rotation (Internal Loans) 78%

- Gradual shift from consumption loans to productive loans

  Purpose of Loans Productive Loans = 82%

  Consumption Loans 18%

- Dependence on moneylenders among members is declining

  Members would have gone to moneylenders had there been no SHG 61%

  Members would not have started the activity had there been no SHG 7.5%

- Loan recovery rates are high

Loan Period	% Repayment Bank Loans	Group Loans
1997-1998	100%	89%

Weaknesses

- Participation of widows and destitutes

  Widows /destitutes in the group 9%

- Group over dependence on the leader

  The leader manages all activities regarding Accounts, loan and attendance, etc

  Members' involvement in mobilisation of savings - 4%

- Development of leadership among other members is lacking Leadership Rotation In 13 % Groups

- Poor growth of leadership

  84% of leaders and 93% of members are not part of other institutions including local bodies.

  -- High illiteracy among women resulting in poor book keeping and maintaining records.

     Illiterate group members 75%

  -- Mobilisation of savings outside group meetings 25%

- DWCRA Bazaar awareness

  Not aware Leaders - 37% Members - 60%

- Marketing efforts need strengthening

  Branding of products and Placement.

Threats

- Overburdening of Additional Gram Sevikas (AGS) & Animators

  An AGS manages about 250 groups

- Inter group conflicts

  Lack of transparency in selecting groups for providing aid/loan - Member's perception

- Training and capacity building has not been given due importance

  Limited Training that too to Leaders only

  — Limited inter linkages between various organizations involved in group formation
- Inadequate external support for identification of micro Enterprises
- Resistance of men folk in group formation

Opportunities

- Channelling various development schemes particularly concerning women and children - Convergence of development activities
- Networking amongst the group - Mahila Banks
- Provides a platform for women to discuss common problems
- Improves awareness level of rural women - on various
- Development schemes and government agencies implementing them.
- Improves socio-economic well-being of the rural women through micro credit.
- Marginalizing the role of moneylenders in the rural areas through access to credit.
- Instill a sense of self-confidence among rural women

ACRONYMS

DWCRA	Development of Women and Children in Rural Areas
UNICEF	United Nations International Children's Emergency Fund
D.R.D.A.	District Rural Development Agency
P.D.	Project Director
A.P.O.	Assistant Project Officer.
I.R.D.P	Integrated Rural Development Programme.
TRYSEM	Training of Rural Youth for Self-Employment.
N.G.O.	Non-Governmental Organization
T.L.C.	Total Literacy Campaign
I.R.D.A.S	Institute of Resource Development and Social Management.
A.S.C.I.	Administrative Staff College of India
Y.F.A.	Youth For Action
V.D.O.	Village Development Officer
V.A.O.	Village Administrative Officer
C.B.C.S.	Community Based Convergent Services.
F.T.O.	Field Training Officer
A.G.S.	Additional Grama Sevika

Source:- http://www.ap.nic.in/dwcra

17

DWCRA and Janmabhoomi for Empowerment of Women and Family Planning*

For quite sometimes since independence, women in our country, rural women in particular, were not organized to promote any welfare programmes for themselves and the society. However, in urban areas, there are isolated and small groups formed by women in the name of 'Mahila Mandals', Women Teachers' Associations and so on. On the other hand, men in urban areas, have had their associations, clubs, trade unions and similar group formations to serve various purposes. Culturally, women were not encouraged in the past to form similar associations, parties, groups, etc., like men, although they did have pressing problems and issues to be solved. The advantages of forming groups, even among the illiterate, are many. They help for periodic interaction among different people and provide opportunities for informal learning for all participants, literate or otherwise. Periodic meetings help the members of groups to interact with one another frequently, discuss and debate among themselves the problems and issues facing them, and thereby enrich their awareness, deepen their knowledge and clarify to themselves their own ideas, attitudes and concepts. All these enable them to reinforce ideas wherever necessary and bring about necessary behavioural changes among them, for development all-round.

In Andhra Pradesh, the massive organization of all people under Janmabhoomi and women in the name of DWCRA have been functioning with commendable success leading to all-round holistic development. Women in families in general have been repeatedly benefited by the DWCRA. How awareness among women in the state has increased and become sharpened was demonstrated when they organized a big way in the early 1990s a movement to protest against arrack/ liquor consumption in the state and demanded total prohibition. This was a historic movement of women, begun and sustained largely by rural women. In the pages that follow women's opinion on the following welfare programmes initiated through the DWCRA and Janmabhoomi are presented: (1) Health Education, (2) Health service programmes, (3) Sanitation-cum-clean and green, (4) Immunization of children, (5) Family Planning, (6) Literacy and Education, (7) Overall women's development programmes and (8) Suggestions given to improve these programmes in future. An index of their opinion regarding the implementation of the programmes is also given.

DWCRA is the abbreviation for 'Development of Women and Children in Rural Areas', initiated by the Ministry of Rural Development at the Centre. As the name indicates, the emphasis in this programme is on the development of women and children. Seventy-two per cent of the country's population dwells in rural areas, of which 60% are women and children. This programme is designed for the development of women and children of those families below the poverty line.

The focus of DWCRA is chiefly on women, rural poor women in particular should organize themselves into groups and derive the benefits of development through their own efforts, combined with the efforts of society as a whole. That is why the emphasis is on 'women', An all-round improvement in the status of women is at the centre of its goal. Improvement in the ability and understanding of women in relation to the many roles they have necessarily to play will lead to an improvement in their status. The development of children will happen 'indirectly', so to speak, as a result of their mothers' development. Children develop through their mother's care, awareness and action on their behalf. The development of both women and children are intertwined. That is why the two are specially emphasized in the very name of the scheme DWCRA.

This programme is for the 'poor' and 'the poor' are the officially selected families below the poverty line, selected by the 'gram sabhas' or village meetings at the Gram Panchayat level. These lists are available at the village panchayat, block and district offices. The selection is based on the survey of income resources of the families. Only those included in the list are called 'chaynit pariwar' or 'selected families'.

Key Features of the DWCRA Programme

The DWCRA is not merely a welfare scheme. It provides opportunities to women and children to benefit from various kinds of services and facilities. The specific programme activities will be formulated in each village group on the basis of local needs. Therefore, the implementation of the DWCRA programme is not uniform throughout the nation and varies from area to area.

The DWCRA is a flexible programme, based on the needs of the area. Its programmes emphasize the principle that planning and implementation should be decentralized, with both activities taking place at the village level. The planning and responsibility of implementation should be as close to the group as possible.

The DWCRA lays stress on the principle of participation as the root of decentralization. So, the effort is to enlist the participation of people right from planning through evaluation to implementation. Participatory planning means that the women's groups decide on the kind of work they will undertake. Generally, when a community service is organized by the government, without direct participation of the rural people, they do not feel responsible for its full use or maintenance. Therefore, the objective of the DWCRA programme is that people in the group would decide what programme they need, how it is to be implemented in their village and thus really become a part of the programme.

Objectives of DWCRA

The following objectives have been generally considered for the promotion of DWCRA.

1. To help women to organize themselves into groups in order to work collectively for solving their manifold problems like employment, economic improvement, educational betterment, improvement of health, prevention of diseases, adoption of Family Planning and overall betterment of the quality of life for women and children;
2. To develop skills and ability in their avocation and improve the efficiency of their work through self-employment.
3. To promote income generating activities to supplement their personal needs and for the well being of the family;
4. To promote self-confidence, awareness about all the developmental programmes and the benefits available for women through Government Programmes, familiarize them with the rights and responsibilities in a changing society;
5. To provide appropriate care for their children through crèches and Balvadis to develop their health, personality and education.

Organizational Set-up

At the national level the Rural Women's Programme Division in the Ministry of Rural Development Plans, administers and monitors the programme. At the state level, the Women's Programme Cell of the Department of Rural Development is responsible for the implementation of the programme. At the district level, the Assistant Project Officer (A.P.O.) and Field Training Officer (F.T.O.) under guidance of the Project Director (DRDA), and at the block level, the Gram Sevika (G.S.) under guidance of F.T.O. and Mandal Development Officers (M.D.O.) are responsible for programme implementation.

National level	--	Ministry of Rural Development (Rural Women's Programme Division)
State Level	--	Rural Development Department (Women's Programme Cell)
District Level	--	Assistant Project Officer
Block Level	--	Gram Sevika
Village Level	--	Group OrganizerGroup members

Identification of Beneficiaries

The scheme identifies women below the poverty line in rural areas, the poverty line was defined as a family having an annual income of rs.6,400 or less (IRDP Manual, 1987). But the "cut-off" line for selecting the beneficiaries under the DWCRA scheme is a family having an annual income of less than Rs.3,400 and these families get priority in selection. While the target group of DWCRA is the same as IRDP, the methodology of reaching is through a group rather than individual beneficiaries. The financial provisions under the DWCRA are available only for the group. Individual income generation projects will be financed on the IRDP pattern from the IRDP budget.

Formation of Group

A group of 15-20 women of homogenous category come together for an activity of mutual interest to all. The group must be linked to collective economic programmes. The process of group formation should also be a process of building rapport between the women, on the one hand, and the grassroot level Government functionaries, on the other. Through the organization of groups, women improve their participation in various programmes of rural development and economic well being. With this, women improve their earnings, acquire new skills, reduce their daily workload, and have better accessibility to credit and other inputs of development.

The assistance available to a group is the following.

Rs.15,000 as a one-time grant contributed in equal measure by Central and State Government and the UNICEF, which can be used as:

(i) Revolving fund for purchase of raw materials and marketing.

(ii) Honorarium to the group organizer, which may not exceed Rs.50/- per month for a period of one year.

(iii) Infrastructure support for income generating activities; and

(iv) One-time expenditure on childcare facilities.

Interaction Within DWCRA

Discussions in the DWCRA groups focus on several aspects concerning women. The principal deliberation in the monthly DWCRA group meeting centres on different aspects of financial management. The membership fee collected is pooled and deposited along with the matching grant from the Government in a bank in the name of the DWCRA leaders. The profits made through the organized sale of commonly produced materials are equally shared by the members as their take home family benefit. Loans are given to the members for several productive schemes of self employment such as buying milch cows/ buffalos, making garments, tailoring, plastic/ jute bag making, running petty shops, vending, skirt-making, sheep-rearing, agricultural promotion of sericulture, raising vegetable gardens and so on. In addition, loans are also given for the education of children, construction of toilets, repairs of houses, marriage expenses, meeting the emergency health needs and so on. These loan facilities have liberated many rural people from the clutches of Shylock like moneylenders who generally exploit the poor and the middle class people. What is more, many women members, for the first time in their life, individually handle money, save money without the interference of the husband. This is a big revolution, not merely financial, among women through the DWCRA programme. Whenever members do not pay the loan installment for clearing the loan obtained from the DWCRA, other members put pressure on them and realize it. There is also a definite understanding not to allow the husband to meddle with the finance of DWCRA through the wife. This is a positive development for women's economic emancipation.

During the monthly meetings of the DWCRA, in addition to deliberating on financial matters, the members discuss several other issues concerning women and their families. For instance, they share the problems created by husbands through alcoholism. They encourage such women sufferers to face boldly their husbands and threaten them if necessary that they would report the matter to the police for justice and thus admonish the husbands. In fact, there are instances of a decrease in the harassment of wives by husbands through alcoholism, owing to the impact of the DWCRA and the consequent empowerment of women. The DWCRA members and the two leaders of their group help other members in several other ways. The leaders of the DWCRA accompany the members for procuring raw materials. They individually and together work for the marketing their products. They also periodically discuss issues like the health problems, family planning adoption and programmes like the education of their children in future and so on. In fact, the enlightened and educated members of the DWCRA share their experiences with other members of the group. All these interactions within the group provide non-formal education to the members and help in the empowerment of women.

Opinion of DWCRA Members on Welfare Schemes

As stated earlier, several health, family planning, environmental, economic and social problems are tackled through the Janmabhoomi and DWCRA programmes. While the Janmabhoomi programme is implemented once in 3-4 months, the DWCRA meeting taken place at least once in a month. During the Janmabhoomi programmes and the DWCRA meetings, special sessions are arranged for skill development, and for education. However, such interventions have not been adequate, although they have rendered great service by disseminating of knowledge among the DWCRA members, who in turn have passed on the same to their friends and relatives, the benefits they have received. In the following, we examine the opinions of the DWCRA members regarding their response to the Janmabhoomi programmes, their friends and relatives, the benefits they have received. In the following pages, we examine the opinion of the DWCRA members regarding their response to the Janmabhoomi programmes, their several components, and the benefits derived from them.

Health Education and Services

Under health education three aspects were prominently discussed during the Janmabhoomi and DWCRA meetings. During the Janmabhoomi programmes experts on health from different institutions were involved to impart education on several aspects of health to the members of the DWCRA and other participants. When their opinion was sought regarding such health education, an overwhelming proportion (84%) of them said that they found it useful. While half of them felt it really useful, one-third of them felt it somewhat useful. However, one-third of the respondents felt that it was a waste. About 40% of them were not able to express any opinion. Therefore, there is a need to strengthen the health education programme by repeating it frequently with more audio-visual aids and encouraging question - answer sessions in the meetings, besides involving as many people as possible in such group meetings. The benefits generated through health education did not differ much in the different regions (Table 1).

TABLE 1

Percentage Distribution of Women According to Their Opinion on Discussion of Health Matters at Janmabhoomi

Opinion on Health topics discussed	*Districts*		*Total*
	Chittoor	*Krishna*	
Useful	52.5 (105)	51.5 (103)	52.0 (208)
Somewhat useful	29.5 (59)	35.0 (70)	32.3 (129)
Waste	12.5 (25)	11.5 (23)	12.0 (48)
Don't know	5.5 (11)	2.0 (4)	3.9 (15)
Total	100.0 (200)	100.0 (200)	100.0 (400)

The mothers were also asked to give their opinion regarding the immunization programme for children. Nearly a quarter of the women (24.0%) said that they did not get the benefit of immunization. Another quarter of them did not appreciate the coverage and service done for immunization. However, nearly 50% of them were satisfied with it. Therefore, there is need for a thorough review of the on-going immunization programme under Janmabhoomi to avoid wastage and make it really useful in future.

Sanitation-Cum-Clean and Green

The clean and green programme including sanitation formed a major component of the Janmabhoomi programme. It is very appropriate to include this programme because drainage and sanitation are very poor in most places and there has been a reckless destruction of trees and forests all over the state. In this context, it is good to know that in Sweden even private tree cannot be cut without the permission of local government and in all the Scandinavian countries, the government extends all encouragement for tree planting. In India, tow states, Gujarat and Tamil Nadu, have taken the lead in social forestry. Thanks to the visionary social forestry programme adopted in Tamil Nadu by the late MGR, all along both sides of the road in the state, there are rows of trees grown. It is some comfort that Andhra Pradesh has adopted the social forestry programme in earnest. However, Planting new trees and assuming their uninterrupted growth has not been keeping pace with the callous destruction of trees in the State.

TABLE 2

Percentage Distribution of Women According to Their Opinion on Clean and Green Under Janmabhoomi Programme in Chittoor and Krishna Districts in Andhra Pradesh

Opinion on Clean and Green	*Districts*		*Total*
	Chittoor	*Krishna*	
Useful	52.0 (104)	51.5 111)	54.0 (216)
Somewhat useful	28.0 (56)	39.5 (79)	34.0 (136)
Waste	14.0 (28)	3.5 (7)	8.5 (34)
Not Applicable	6.0 (12)	1.5 (3)	3.5 (14)
Total	100.0 (200)	100.0 (200)	100.0 (400)

A very high percentage of the women (88%) expressed appreciation of the clean and green programme. While more than half of them were very happy about it, one-third of them felt that it was only somewhat useful. Only negligible percentage of women regarded it as a waste. In these opinions the two regions did not differ much (Table-2).

Family Planning: A Spectacular Success and a World Record

The family planning programme in Andhra Pradesh did not progress satisfactorily till about a decade, unlike Kerala, Tamil Nadu, Goa and Punjab. It was probably because of the massive illiteracy of women in the state. Further, road transport facilities in the state were poor. When the infrastructure is poor and clients are illiterate, naturally family planning cannot flourish despite special efforts made through World Bank aided UPP projects. Under such circumstances, the population grew very high in Andhra Pradesh till 1991. In fact, the average annual growth rate in the state was 2.1% till 1991. Since then, however, during the last one decade (1991-2001) the annual growth rate has declined to 1.30%. Such dramatic decline of the annual growth rate can be explained largely as due to the positive impact of the Janmabhoomi and DWCRA programmes. The family planning programme was there in the state during the last four decades, and the massive IPP programme had been funded by World Bank during the 1981-91 period. However, such extra input was not there to promote the reduction of the growth rate of population during the 1991-2001 period. Therefore, it seems logical to argue in the absence of any special family planning programme like the IPP during the 1991-2001 period, what other programmes could have caused the rapid decline in the growth rate both in rural and urban areas in the last one decade compared to all the other states in India. Such rapid and steep decline of growth rate during the last decade did not happen in any other state. Interestingly, such a revolutionary and dramatic decline of growth rate of population happened in China (Mahadevan and Taun, 1994). The decisive impact, both direct and indirect, made by the massive community movement through the periodical Janmabhoomi and DWCRA programmes, on eligible couples and the interaction among the group members, would have contributed to improvement in knowledge of family planning development of favourable attitude towards it and increased acceptance of contraception to raise it as high as 70% in several districts, barring the backward areas in the state (see details in F.P. Chapter).

OPINION ON FAMILY PLANNING THROUGH JAANMABHOOMI

Family planning is discussed among the DWCRA members during their monthly meetings and they in turn frequently discuss it with their friends and relatives later on. Through the Janmabhoomi programme additional family planning (FP) education has been carried out on a quarterly basis during the last five years. Therefore, the respondents were specially asked to mention their view of the usefulness of F.P education imparted through Janmabhoomi per se. According to Table 3, a significant proportion (64%) of women admitted the usefulness and benefits of F.P education periodically impart5ed to them through the several Janmabhoomi programmes. There is no major region-wise variation in such education. Therefore, it may be summarized that statewide large-scale benefits of the IEC programme have permeated among the women in general. Since most of the adopters are women (see F.P.chapter) their opinions mentioned above reflect the positive impact of the F.P. education through the Janmabhoomi and DWCRA programmes. It is in addition to the interaction effect and diffusion of knowledge resulting from these programmes. Although one-third of the women expressed the view that the F.P. education through

Janmabhoomi was a waste, it does not reflect the negative aspect of the programme because most of the earlier adopters mentioned it as a waste.

Thus, the principal causal factor for the rapid and extensive adoption of F.P in Andhra Pradesh and the consequent steep decline of the growth rate of population can be the direct impact of the Janmabhoomi and DWCRA programmes and the indirect impact of the interaction and diffusion effects operating from the participants of themselves and with others.

TABLE 3

Percentage Distribution of Women Regarding Opinion on Health and Family Education Through Janmabhoomi Programmes in Chittoor and Krishna Districts in Andhra Pradesh

Opinion on Clean and Green	*Districts*		*Total*
	Chittoor	*Krishna*	
Useful	45.5 (91)	47.5 (95)	46.50 (186)
Somewhat useful	19.5 (39)	16.0 (32)	17.75 (71)
Waste	29.0 (58)	35.0 (70)	32.00 (128)
Not Applicable	6.0 (12)	1.5 (3)	3.75 (15)
Total	100.0 (200)	100.0 (200)	100.0 (400)

LITERACY AND EDUCATION OF WOMEN

Literacy and education constituted one of the components of Janmabhoomi programme. In fact, 77% of women expressed appreciation of it. However, the remaining were either not expressed appreciation of it. However, the remaining were either not ex posed to it or found it not necessary for them. In the context of the prevailing high illiteracy among women in Andhra Pradesh, this programme deserves very high priority. When literacy increases and adult education spreads, women become well informed, and knowledgeable and empower themselves. As a result they also quickly adopt F.P.

OVERALL OPINION ON WOMEN ORIENTED WELFARE PROGRAMMES

Certain Janmabhoomi programmes were exclusively devoted to the development of women, for instance, the programmes which were focused on the girl child, girl's education, etc, An index was prepared covering all the welfare programmes promoted for women through the several Janmabhoomi programmes. All the questions were trichotomised into 'less useful', moderately useful' and 'very useful' categories. The scores of these questions were quantified and classified into three categories (Table 4).

TABLE 4

Percentage Distribution of Women by Index on Their Opinion About the Implementation of Various Welfare Programmes Under Janmabhoomi in Chittoor and Krishna Districts in Andhra Pradesh

Opinion on Health topics discussed	*Districts*		*Total*
	Chittoor	*Krishna*	
Very Useful (Score 14-18)	50.5 (102)	49.0 (98)	49.8 (216)
Moderately useful (Score 10-12)	21.5 (43)	18.0 (36)	19.8 (79)
Less useful (Score 6-9)	27.5 (55)	33.0 (66)	29.3 (121)
Total	100.0 (200)	100.0 (200)	100.0 (400)

It is interesting to note that 70% of the women found these programmes very/moderately useful, less than one-third of them found them 'less useful', perhaps because they had been already exposed to such information and therefore did not find relevant to them. Since a high proportion of women found the programmes beneficial, and several others are oriented towards the welfare programmes through Janmabhoomi, this programme deserves to be expanded, diversified and repeated for a few more years till women in the state are fully educated, modernized and the quality of their life is improved.

SUGGESTIONS FOR IMPROVEMENT OF DWCRA AND JANMABHOOMI

The women respondents were asked to give their suggestions. Several suggestions were put forward by them. They are as follows. Active and regular participation of the government officials concerned is mentioned as major recommendation. This recommendation implies that certain officials have been irregular on their participation and shown poor commitment to the DWCRA AND Janmabhoomi programmes. Therefore, it suggested that special region-wise diagnostic studies of the extent of the participation of government officials in DWCRA and Janmabhoomi may be strengthened to enforce discipline among them in executing the DWCRA and Janmabhoomi programmes successfully. Other suggestions given by the women were : Need for expansion of all awareness programmes on (1) Health, (2) Child welfare, (3) Health promotion, (4) Clean and green, (5) Special programmes on girl children, (6) Programme for raising girl's age at marriage, (7) Dowry eradication, (8) Reproductive health promotion, (9) Prohibition, (10) Old age security and (11) Care of destitute women.

Regarding the DWCRA programme, an overwhelming percentage of women demanded more revolving fund to be provided to them by the Government, which may enforce a proper utilization of this fund for productive use. There is the need for better official co-operation and co-operation among the members of DWCRA themselves for marketing their products on a remunerative basis. Another important suggestion is that they need diversified skill development programme through periodic training to enable them to produce attractive and competitive products in future. Therefore, by and large, most of the women are enthusiastic about the DWCRA and want to expand, diversify and improve the functioning of the DWCRA in future.

FACETS OF EMPOWERMENT OF WOMEN

The assumption here is that through their active participation in the DWCRA and Janmabhoomi programmes, women would develop several facets of empowerment because interaction with one another regarding the growth and development of women enables them to get rid of shyness and withdrawal tendency. Further, they would develop awareness of several aspects of their life which may improve their self-confidence, aspiration, world-view, etc., and enable them to achieve autonomy in decision-making. Added to these factors, the economic gains they make through self-employment in the DWCRA programme would add to their empowerment. All these positive developments will pave the way for greater participation of women in decision-making on a number of issues in the family. Therefore, in the present study, women's empowerment has been assessed through their autonomy along with their level of aspiration, role in decision-making regarding the education of children, transaction of property, health utilization, family planning and so on. All these facets of change in women together can indicate their present level of empowerment, which has improved through the DWCRA in particular.

INDEX OF AUTONOMY IN DECISION-MAKING

Traditionally women have little autonomy in taking decisions in most aspects of day-to-day affairs, more particularly in serious matters like property transaction, education of children, seeking medical treatment, family planning and so on. To assess their cumulative autonomy in decision-making, a number of questions relating to the items mentioned above were posed to the women in order to assess the level of their autonomy as low, moderate and high. A score value of 1-3 was assigned to the tripartite classification of five such questions on different themes, The cumulative score was graded to represent the hierarchy of autonomy, which is presented in Table 5. The findings conclusively confirmed that majority of women developed very high level of autonomy in both the districts. Another quarter of them also developed moderate level of autonomy. These findings reveal a revolution in empowerment of rural women in Andhra Pradesh now.

Table 5: Percentage distribution of women according to the Autonomy enjoyed by them in various aspects of decision - making in Chittoor and Krishna Districts of Andhra Pradesh.

Opinion of Autonomy of Women	*Districts*		*Total*
	Chittoor	*Krishna*	
Low	25.0 (50)	11.5 (23)	18.3 (73)
Moderate	24.5 (48)	26.5 (53)	25.1 (10.1)
High	51.0 (102)	62.0 (124)	56.6 (226)
Total	100.0 (200)	100.0 (200)	100.0 (400)

AMBITION OF CAREER FOR DAUGHTER

Traditionally, in most developing countries, except China, most rural women prefer to remain at home as housewives. In fact, Chinese women are even far ahead of women in the developed countries in terms of their employment outside home, and notably in the field of sports. It is well-known that China ranked second in the recent Olympic games next only to the USA and Chinese women dominated in several sports events. However, Indian women lag far behind the Chinese women except in the field of politics and basic academic field. Now, let us see the changing ambition of mothers regarding the careers of their daughters in future, according to the women respondents.

The data given in Table 6 shows a contrasting scenario

regarding the daughter's career. In fact, 57% of women in all preferred a career life outside home for their daughter's career. In fact 57% of women in all preferred a career life outside home for their daughters and their number is significantly more in the Krishna district (69.0%) than in the Chittoor district (46.0%). Therefore, based on the development of the region, women tend to prefer jobs for their daughters outside home mostly because of their educational advancement. In addition, it is likely that periodic interaction with others, outside home mostly because of their educational advancement. In addition, it is likely that periodic interaction with others, debate among themselves on issues concerning their formal and informal education received by the rural women through the DWCRA in particular and to a certain extent through the Janmabhoomi programme, would have strengthened in a majority of them their ambition of a career goal for their daughters. Therefore, another dimension of empowerment is manifested in these findings.

TABLE 6

Percentage Distribution of Women Expressing Career Ambition for Their Daughters in Chittoor and Krishna Districts of Andhra Pradesh

Career ambition for Daughters	*Districts*		*Total*
	Chittoor	*Krishna*	
Housewife	54.5 (109)	31.5 (63)	43.8 (172)
Employment outside home	45.5 (91)	68.5 (137)	57.0 (228)
Total	100.0 (200)	100.0 (200)	100.0 (400)

Other Dimensions of Empowerment

In order to identify the improvement in the empowerment of women on other dimensions, a few other questions were put to the respondents. When their opinion was sought regarding their family life, 69% of them wished for several changes in family life deviating from the traditional patterns, which reflects their empowerment. Their number is significantly more in the developed Krishna district (82.0%) in the Chittoor district. In fact, the development of this dimension of empowerment is at least in part through the DWCRA (Table not given). Yet another dimension of empowerment was assessed in terms of their participation in decision-making concerning (1) education of children, (2) seeking medical aid and (3) acceptance of family planning. As for the education of children, 77% of the women respondents confessed that they generally involve in decision-making along with the husbands ion the past and/or in the future. Regarding seeking medical aid, a similar trend emerged for acceptance of family planning (see Table in Chapter on F.P.) In all these three decision-making patterns significantly more women in the Krishna district preferred to involve themselves in decision-making along with the husbands. Once again, these three aspects of decision making in the family manifest a modern trend and improvement, which in all likelihood resulted with the impact of the DWCRA programme.

Thus, the foregoing discussion of autonomy, ambition of mothers for their daughters' future and their involvement in decision-making together indicate a significant change from the traditional set-up to an enlightened modern pattern of empowerment of women. All these changes together would have considerably improved the empowerment of women through the DWCRA programme. In fact, the above-mentioned findings may be rare in rural areas and therefore, the impact of DWCRA commendably would have contributed for improvement in empowerment of women in Andhra Pradesh.

(Authors: K.Mahadevan, P.Sumangala, P.J.Reddy, M.Lalitha & R.Varalakshmi

Source: www.ap.nic.in/dwcra)

18

Efforts of NGOs in Promoting Mini-Enterprises among Women in Andhra Pradesh

Right from the beginning, NGOs in Andhra Pradesh have been working for the cause of women and more than 200 committed NGOs have been involved in facilitating formation of SHGs and in the efforts for their sustenance. NGOs are working in close coordination with DRDAs in training and capacity building, skill development training programmes building SHG centered organizations etc.

Apart from the consistent efforts made by the government through several programmes especially organising Self-Help Groups under national programme DWCRA, some of the NGOs have initiated helping women groups enter into mini entrepreneurial activities. The spur for this movement is provided by the NGOs and in the case of Hindustan Lever Limited (HLL) though on one hand it may look like boosting their products in rural areas, it has created employment and considerable earning to the women more especially who fall under below poverty line (BPL).

PROJECT SHAKTI[4]

Hindustan Lever Limited (HLL) and its constituent companies have been in India since 1931. Over these decades, HLL has benefited from the developments in the country. The company equally, in its own way, has contributed to these developments. HLL has consciously woven India's imperatives with the company's strategy and operations. These areas have been developing and using relevant technology, stimulating industrialization, exports, adding value to agriculture and generating productive employment and income opportunities.

Project Shakti is HLL's latest initiative, in keeping with this purpose of integrating business interests with national interests.

The objectives of Project Shakti are to create 'Income generating capabilities' for underprivileged rural women by providing a sustainable micro enterprise opportunity, and to improve rural living standards through health and hygiene awareness.

HLL's vision for Project Shakti is to scale it up across the country by 2010, creating about 11000 Shakti entrepreneurs, covering 100,000 villages and touching the lives of 100 million rural consumers.

Following the pioneering work carried out by Grameen Bank in Bangladesh, several institutions, NGOs and governmental bodies have been working closely over the last 4 to 5 years to establish Self-Help Groups (SHGs) of rural women in villages across India. Their experiments clearly show that micro-credit, when carefully targeted and well-administered, can alleviate poverty significantly. Importantly, success depends not only on infusion of credit, but on investment opportunities.

This is where HLL is playing a role in creating such profitable micro enterprise opportunities for rural women. For the SHG women, this translates into critically needed sustainable income contributing to better living standards and prosperity. For HLL, it provides access into hitherto unexplored rural hinterlands. Armed with micro-credit, women from SHGs become direct-to-home distributors in rural markets. This micro enterprise is relatively risk-free and high on return. HLL provides the necessary training inputs to these groups on the basics of enterprise management, which the women need to stabilise their enterprises. Under the project, HLL offers a range of mass-market products to the SHGs, which are relevant to rural consumers.

This model was piloted in Nalgonda district of Andhra Pradesh in 50 villages in 2001. The Government of Andhra Pradesh took the pioneering step of supporting the initiative by enabling linkages with the network of DWCRA groups of ruiral women, set up for women development and self-employment. It has since been extended to over 5000 villages in 52 districts in Andhra Pradesh, Karnataka, Gujrat and Madhya Pradesh. Project Shakti, as of date, has 1000 woman entrepreneurs in its fold. HLL is being assited in the rollout by Marketing & Research Team (MART), an organization engaged in the social sector.

State Governments as well as NGOs are actively involved with HLL in the implementation of this project. The response has been encouraging. Most SHG Women have seen this as a powerful business proposition and are enthusiastically participating in it. A typical Shakti entrepreneur conducts business of around Rs.15,000 per month, which gives her an income in excess of Rs.1000/- per month on a sustainable basis. As most of these women are from below the poverty line, and live in extremely small villages (less than 2000) population), this earning is very significant, and is almost double of their past household income. For most of these families, Project Shakti is creating opportunities to live in conditions of dignity, with real freedom from want.

The most powerful aspect about this model is that it creates a win-win partnership between HLL and its consumers, some of whom will also draw on the organization for their livelihood, and builds a self-sustaining virtuous cycle of growth for all.

To improve the business skills of the SHG women, extensive training programmes are being held. Such workshops have already covered over 1000 woman entrepreneurs in Andhra Pradesh and Karnataka.

Additionally, as a part of their training programme, HLL Management Trainees are spending over 4 weeks in rural areas, providing business consultation to nascent SHG enterprises engaged in the manufacture of various products such as spices, hosiery items, etc.

HLL is now in the process of piloting 'i-Shakti' an IT-based rural information service that will provide solutions to key rural needs in the areas of agriculture, education, vocational training, health/hygiene, etc. in Nalgonda district. Plans are being drawn up to bring in partners involved in agriculture, health, insurance and education to catalyse overall rural development.

Step by step, Project Shakti is unleashing the potential of rural women and thus changing their lives. It is ushering in prosperity and, more importantly, self-respect. As one of the Shakti entrepreneurs, Rojamma, says, 'It is more important than money. When they see me, they crowd around me and call me 'Shaktiamma'. I am someone today.'

Fast-moving consumer goods (FMCG) major, Hindustan Lever Ltd, is picking up where the Grameen Bank of Bangladesh left off. Leveraging the micro-credit model to expand its rural market, it is piloting 'Project Shakti' - its five-month-old marketing initiative involving women belonging to micro-credit self-help groups (SHGs) in the Nalgonda district of Andhra Pradesh.[5]

Willing to experiment, the company followed the growth initiative suggested by HLL's Project Millennium last year that drew upon the Grameen Bank concept.

The project, with an obvious 'win-win' partnership potential, involves women from SHGs turning into direct-to-home distributors for HLL in their area, thus helping the company expand its rural market from its existing 40 per cent penetration in villages with population of over 2,000.

For the women, it means income generation without the headache of starting their own venture and becoming vegetable vendors, fish vendors, pan shop owners, etc., which has generally been the micro-credit model to date.

The products being sold through this unique direct marketing initiative are HLL's leading brands including Clinic Plus shampoo, Lifebuoy, Wheel, A1 tea and Nihar coconut oil.

In fact, due to customer demand for other HLL products, Three Roses tea, Fair And Lovely cream and Pond's talcum powder have been added to the inventory. At the grassroots level, the project is being coordinated and implemented by Marketing and Research Team (MART).

Andhra Pradesh was obviously chosen for the pilot project as 20 per cent of its rural population is covered by the micro-credit model. The micro-credit concept, that impacts 45 lakh women belonging to 3.33 lakh SHGs in the State, creates wealth for the members of the groups and helps them better their lives and alleviate poverty. The micro-finance collected in the State, through savings as well as institutional loans, is around a whopping Rs 800 crore.

For the project, 50 SHGs closest to the highway in Nalgonda district were identified. These are covered by three Mutually-Aided Credit Thrift Societies (MACTS), which act as semi-distributors in the project. MACTS, which generally consist of 14 to 15 SHGs, are federated into a co-operative and work in close tandem with the SHGs.

In fact, the project has had several interesting spin-offs. One of the MACTs distributing HLL products has started its own supermarket, while another is shortly purchasing a vehicle for its distribution network.

"The investment opportunity is relatively risk-free and high on return. HLL is committed to providing the necessary training inputs to these groups on the basics of enterprise management which the groups can then use to enlarge their initiatives," says an HLL spokesperson. But it plans to upscale the pilot only after its analysis and evaluation is completed.

"The challenge has been to move from micro-finance to micro-enterprise," says Mr. Kashyap whose organization has also carried out a feasibility study for the Andhra Pradesh Government on the micro-enterprises that can be taken up by SHGs. It is, in addition to, training of district functionaries and the women themselves on how to run such micro-enterprises.

Some of the ventures being implemented are superbazars run by the women, sanitary napkin units and the traditional dairy and handloom initiatives. But for the corporate world, it's Project Shakti to look out for.

While speaking of the success of the efforts made by HLL in organizing and providing opportunities to women to become self-employed and also emerge as mini-entrepreneurs, here we have in brief a few interesting profiles of individual women who had the benefit of support from the HLL.

1. Ms. Rojamma
   Village: Kurumurthy
   District: Mahabubnagar, Andhra Pradesh

Ms. Rojamma was married off when she was 17. After two daughters were born, her husband abandoned the family.

She heard of Project Shakti, at a meeting at the District Rural Development Authority's office, and took a loan of Rs.10,000 from her Self-Help Group (SHG).

Today, the turnover of her enterprise is about Rs.20,000 a month. Her net earning is approximately Rs.1500 a month, which is double what she earned before becoming a Shakti entrepreneur.

Ms. Rojamma says that today she has the confidence of educating her two daughters -- and she has self-respect. 'When they see me, they crowd around me and call me 'Shaktiamma'. I am someone today - It is more important than money," adds Ms. Rojamma.

2. Jella Sujathamma
   Village:- Peddakaparthy
   District:- Nalgonda

Ms. Sujathamma's spouse is a weaver. But the income was not enough for the family, including their daughter and two sons.

Five years back, she joined a Self-Help Group (SHG), formed under the aegis of the District Rural Development Authority. She came to know about Project Shakti in January, 2001, and became one of the first Shakti entrepreneurs of the State.

Ms. Sujathamma did not have enough funds of her own. So, she took a loan of Rs.10,000 from her SHG to start the enterprise. Today her turnover has grown from Rs.10,000 a month to Rs.25,000. Besides, she now also sells staples, sugar, edible oil and a variety of other household items.

Her income over the past two years has brought about a sea change in her family's standard of living. Ms. Sujathamma now wants to buy a moped to extend her overage area and increase the scale of her enterprise.

3. Ms. Jayamma
   Village:- Basireddypalem
   District:- Prakasam

Ms. Jayamma is a widow, with two daughters and a son. Her son has dropped out from school, while the two daughters are students of Class X and V respectively.

Her son used to be engaged in agriculture, but stopped work some time back as the earnings were poor. She was finding it difficult running the household, and meeting the educational expenses of her daughters.

It was at such a stage that she heard about Project Shakti, and decided to become a Shakti entrepreneur. She was trained by the Company on how to run her own business. Today she runs a successful micro-enterprise and is happy with her earnings. She hopes that the future will see her enterprise expanding.

4. Ms. Pogaku Anitha
   Village:- Areypally
   District:- Warangal.

Ms. Anitha used to be a part-time anganwadi teacher but lost her job. Her father's income is just about Rs.1400 a month, which was not enough to run the household.

The potential of Project Shakti attracted her to join the

initiative. Today she does a business of Rs.18,000 to 20,000 a month, and her personal earning is over Rs.1500 a month. She says that she and her family are very happy with her new business and the regular monthly income generated.

Her dream is to grow her enterprise beyond Rs.50,000 per month.

5. Ms. Sundaramma
   Village:- Bhimanapalli
   District:- East Godavari

Ms. Sundaramma is 50 years old. Marrying the three daughters left the family in deep debt. The couple's only son has separated from them. Her age did not permit her to engage in hard labour and there was not much else that she could do.

She heard about Project Shakti through a meeting at the MDO office. She became a Shakti entrepreneur and today, she has expanded her operations to her village and neighbouring villages. Her income out of the enterprise is about Rs.1200 to Rs.1500 per month. In addition, she prepares and sells pickles.

She says that though she is 50 years, Project Shakti has ensured that she is not dependent on anyone. Rather it is she who is helping out her children. She believes that if the bank were to increase the loan, she can expand the enterprise.

6. Ms. Narayanamma
   Village:- Mangapatnam
   District:- Kadapa.

Ms. Narayanamma's husband is a farmer. They have two children, studying in Classes IV and III.

There was a pressing need for Ms. Narayanamma to supplement her husband's income, as agricultural earnings were poor due to vagaries of rainfall. It was at this point that she came to learn of Project Shakti from the Assistant Gram Sevika.

Ms. Narayanamma says that her earnings have not only helped the family tide over present financial difficulties, but also that they are now able to save some money for the future.

Ms.Narayanamma wants to build her Shakti enterprise further. With the confidence that she has gained from the initiative, she also wants to take up new projects.

7. Ms. Padmavati
   Village:- Chirumarri
   District:- Khammam.

Ms. Padmavathi's husband is a carpenter, but earnings have been sparse in the last one year. Though a housewife, she wanted to support the family with additional income. That is when she heard of Project Shakti at a meeting at the Mandal Development Office. She decided to become a Shakti entrepreneur, and took a loan of Rs.10,000 from her SHG. With a helping hand from Hindustan Lever through the initial days of transition into an entrepreneur, her turnover today is about Rs.15,000 a month, and her net earning out of it about Rs.1000 a month.

With her confidence and her acquaintance with the wider world, she is now starting an entirely new enterprise -- an Internet Kiosk in her village. HLL is helping her in this pursuit. She says she has herself become self-reliant and has endowed her family with greater financial strength, all because of Project Shakti.

CASE STUDY OF TWO SUCCESSFUL NGO'S IN ANDHRA PRADESH[6]

Further, the initiatives taken by the Mahila Abhyudaya Podupu Sangam, Tirupati, Rashtriya Seva Samithi (RASS) and Swayamkrushi Mutually Aided Cooperative Thrift Society Limited in Andhra Pradesh are quite interesting. The contribution by the NGOs mentioned above is really paving the way and motivating other non-governmental organizations to work towards developing entrepreneurship among women. The role played by the NGOs in this respect is rather a stimulant and an encouraging factor to the government to further their schemes and efforts to cover larger population of women help themselves become self-employed as entrepreneurs.

THE 'PADMAVATHY' EXPERIENCE

The women in Tirupati were mostly migrants from nearby areas backed by illiteracy, poverty and lack of basic amenities. They were involved in odd activities with fluctuating incomes. Against this background, women had major responsibilities of maintaining their families. This necessitated the need for a regular source of credit. The efforts were to identify and promote income-generating activities among women through a credit delivery system. The banks were initially persuaded to provide loans at Differential Interest Scheme. Despite good repayments, banks could not meet the growing demands for credit on a continuous basis and there was no scope for repeat loans.

The Mahila Abhyudaya Podupu Sangam is a self-managed group which generates financial resources through their own savings. Each sangam consists of 10 to 15 members belonging to a particular slum. The primary source of funds is from the savings of members and interest earned on loans extended. Each sangam creates a common fund in order to meet the operational cost. The repayment rate is 100 percent because of individual responsibility of each member. Apart from financial functions, sangam is a platform for women to interact and address many of their day-to-day problems. The interactions between sangams resulted in the formation of an association called 'Cluster Association'. Each sangam became a member of the same. The activities of the Association include; promotion of new sangams, resolution of conflicts within and between sangams, address to the common issues etc.

The 'Padmavathy' which is a legal entity has certain objectives:

- To mobilize funds from formal financial institutions to meet the larger credit needs of its members.
- To promote formation of new sangams.
- To motivate the members to manage financial requirements independently without external subsidies.
- To promote unity among women of different sangams to give them collective identity for collective action.

Besides the above objectives, 'Padmavathy' functions as a forum for information and exchange of ideas among different sangam members. It also has the responsibility of reaching out to more and more of poor women by expanding its activities.

IMPACT OF 'PADMAVATHY'

'Padmavathy,' which started its operations a decade ago, had 221 sangams and 2647 members by July 1996. The sangams have mobilized Rs.38.58 lakhs as savings 'and Rs. 8.31 lakhs as common fund after having met their operational costs. The sangam members with their own savings have a sense of security and confidence.

'Padmavathy' sangam is the first organization linked under the informal banking programme of SIDBI. Initially, It availed a soft loan of Rs.4 lakhs from SIDBI with the purpose of promoting micro enterprises by women. This assistance had encouraged 200 women to start their own income generating activities. Because of a good repayment experience, SIDBI had sanctioned a second loan of Rs.5 lakhs also a grant for training members for better credit utilization.

It is true that sustainability of any development initiative is possible only when the participants change their role from passive recipients to active own managers. The 'Padmavathy' experience has proved it through commitment to work, sincere efforts to share the benefits of development and active involvement of several sangam members. The model further proves the fact that poor are bankable and the timely access to credit can bring about changes in the lives of thousands of poor women. The sangams have been successful in obtaining loans on reasonable terms with simple procedures. They have also been instrumental in motivating many members who were earlier idle, in taking up some economic activity. Thus, the experience of this model is a source of inspiration for many other poor women with similar socio-economic conditions.

THE RASHTRIYA SEVA SAMITHI (RASS) BACKGROUND

The RASS was established in 1981 at Tirupati. The activities and programmes of RASS were designed for the development of poor in the drought prone Rayalaseema districts of Andhra Pradesh. This region has a high percentage of population who belong to scheduled castes and the backward castes. The region does not have any major industries except a few agro-processing units. It also lags behind other regions of the State in terms of basic amenities. The rapid growth of population has aggravated poverty, unemployment and environmental degradation in the Rayalaseema region. Some of the anti-poverty programmes proved ineffective, as it was more on target achievement rather than human development. Moreover, the rural poor were not involved from the stage of planning to the stage of implementation and evaluation of programmes meant for their upliftment.

OBJECTIVES

The main objective of RASS was to adopt such a strategy, which would bring into fold the poor in the development process .The RASS, believes in the following:

1. Involvement of poor in the entire process of development from planning to monitor.
2. Identification of priorities by the poor themselves.
3. Empowerment of women as a key to self-sustained development of the poor.
4. Provision of community infrastructure as an essential pre-condition for self-sustained growth.
5. Development of agriculture and related activities using local knowledge and local resources apart from modern techniques to reduce the incidence of poverty and unemployment.

The RASS considers the following four interventions as crucial for the poor to reach a stage of social consciousness and empowerment.

Human resource development (by way of massive education, skill upgradation, health services, safe drinking water, sanitation etc. for the disadvantaged groups)

Economic development (through propagation of modern agriculture and technology, family based asset creating activities and waste land development)

Attitudinal changes (to promote greater gender equality, self-reliance and environmental sensitivity)

Self-management and momentum (for the promotion of saving and credit, community management of infrastructure, leadership and self-help).

AREA OF OPERATION AND GROWTH

The core area of operation of RASS includes the districts of Cuddapah, Anantpur, Kurnool and Chittoor. The initial activities of RASS were concentrated in Chittoor district, which accounts for an estimated population of 4.3 million. Subsequently, these activities were spread to other districts of Rayalaseema.

Over a period of eighteen years, RASS has been successful in building up a large administrative infrastructure and reaching out to the rural poor in the backward areas within Andhra Pradesh and in the States of Orissa and Tamil Nadu. Because of its involvement in multi-faceted activities, several funding agencies at the national and international level have shown interest and confidence in RASS. Starting with three program activities in eight villages with 15 staff members, RASS has acquired the status of a national level organization. During 1997-98, RASS had 32 programme activities with 3695 programme staff in 3540 villages operating in three States. The budget of RASS which was Rs.0.08 million 1981 had gone up to Rs.72.08 million during the year 1998. Thus, RASS has recorded a phenomenal growth for the past eighteen years.

WOMEN CENTERED ACTIVITIES

To tap the potentialities and managerial capacities of rural women RASS has implemented several activities. RASS has been instrumental in organizing rural women to show their strength and defend themselves for their rights with the formation of Mahila Mandals. These Mandals work under the direct supervision and guidance of RASS and also, get regular information about Government programmes, bank financing, marketing trends etc. The successful working of Mahila Mandals has resulted in the formation of a large number of Self-Help Groups (SHGs).

For women to get gainful employment especially belonging to SC, ST and BCs, RASS provides training facilities and generates innovative programmes. The vocational skills, thus acquired, help women to be self-reliant.

GROWTH AND PERFORMANCE OF SHGS

The successful working of Mahila Mandals has resulted in the formation of a large number of Self-Help Groups (SHGs). In 1990 with the help from RASS, 30 SHGs were formed involving 10-15 women members. Within a year, there were 123 SHGs with a total membership of 1559 women. A significant feature of this system was that a large number of women shifted their borrowing from traditional moneylenders to SHGs at reasonable rates of interest. Moreover, RASS has linked with Rasthriya Mahila Kosh (RMK) and NABARD to mobilize funds. RASS has borrowed about Rs.7million from RMK and lent it to informal women groups. Along with the loan from RMK and their own savings, women groups have generated credit to the extent of Rs.11million. Some of the notable features of this scheme are a high percentage (96) of repayment, utilization of funds for income creating activities and generation of savings by women members in the SHGs.

CONSTRAINTS

- Lakhk of support from male members (of the families) as well as banks
- Large magnitude of the target group of poor people

- Attitudinal rigidities
- Difficulty in creating awareness among people
- Limited resources with the NGOs
- Large requirements of training and sensitization of issues
- Limited number of experienced intervention agencies
- Diversities of situations due to wide coverage

OVERALL IMPRESSION

- Use of resources (credit) for income generating activities
- Adoption of non-traditional activities
- Improvement in the income levels of SHGs members
- Nearly 100% recovery of loans
- Generation of small savings in the rural sector among women
- Use of local knowledge and resources in productive activities
- Reduction in transaction cost for both banks as well as SHGs
- Maintenance of minimum records in the form of registers.
- Maintenance of proper accounts by the SHGs.
- Regular meetings of the SHGs members to tackle problems among themselves.
- Healthy relation and coordination between SHGs, NGOs and banks.
- Grant assistance by banks to NGOs for capacity building (towards strengthening and monitoring of SHGs, training, computerization, etc.).

- Support services to NGOs by banks for networking with other smaller NGOs.

SWAYAMKRUSHI MUTUALLY AIDED COOPERATIVE THRIFT SOCIETY LIMITED[7]

The formation of a women's savings and credit system...

Swayamkrushi was formed for women. Poor women generally need small amounts of credit at frequent intervals. Repayment schedules have to be adjusted to their earning cycle. There is a need to build a micro-credit system, as the poor in the area are otherwise wholly dependent on private moneylenders. To understand the formation of Swayamkrushi it is important to understand the history of another organization - the Youth Charitable Organization (YCO). Revolving loan schemes and team action groups. In 1984 YCO worked with 15 villages to establish a revolving loan programme to finance income generation activities through women's savings and credit groups (known locally as TAGs). Each TAG has an average of 10 members and the TAGS in each village made up a Mandal. At this stage loans were extended with no interest rate and no fixed repayment time.

The loans were used to purchase dairy animals and to invest in agriculture, fish vending, sheep rearing, palm fibre processing and other small businesses. The use of a revolving loan fund motivated the women's TAGs to increase their saving activities. Between the TAGs a decision was made to save on a uniform basis. These savings were used to support further lending and also helped the groups, via YCO, to access external lines of credit. In particular external credit was received, via local banks and YCO, from NABARD, a national agricultural credit programme run by the Government, and from RMK a department of the government focused specifically on supporting women's economic activities. By 1993, 90 villages were involved.

THE DEVELOPMENT OF SWAYAMKRUSHI

By 1996 it was clear that some TAGs were able to save at faster rates than others were. Groups therefore established their own monthly savings targets. At the same time the groups' capacity to record and manage savings and loans had improved. A decision was made by YCO to support the formation of an independent mutual cooperative which would be fully owned by the women who were members of the savings and credit groups. As a result Swayamkrushi (self-help) Women's Development Mutually Aided Cooperative Credit Society came into existence. Swayamkrushi currently has 5,450 members each of whom has paid a Rs10 membership fee and provided Rs.10 share capital. The way Swayamkrushi works and the women who are members of Swayamkrushi and who save on a regular basis for 6 months are eligible for loans financed by the members' savings.

Each time a member takes a loan, she must provide 10% of the loan amount as additional share capital. If a woman wants to leave Swayamkrushi she must first ensure that her loan is fully repaid. Her savings and share capital are returned to her although she has the option to leave her share capital with Swayamkrushi if she wants to. In this case she remains eligible for payment of share dividends. All members also pay an annual premium of Rs 100 towards a group life insurance scheme. At the moment external lines of credit are still managed by YCO at the request of external financiers. However it is anticipated that Swayamkrushi will begin managing external credit during the next 12 months and that there will be a gradual transfer of savings and credit management responsibilities from YCO to Swayamkrushi. YCO has committed personnel support to Swayamkrushi for the first three years of its operation but the organization is expected over this time to gradually begin to provide partial remuneration for the staff involved and to be fully self-sufficient in a couple of years.

LEGAL STATUS OF SWAYAMAKRUSHI

The Co-operative is legally constituted under the 1995 Andhra Pradesh Mutually Aided Cooperative Societies Act. There are currently 8900 members. The Cooperative is managed by a Board that meets monthly and is composed of 9 individuals elected by the Membership. The Chief Executive Officer attends Board meetings as an ex-officio member but with no voting rights.

SWAYAMKRUSHI LOANS

Current outstanding short and medium term loans amount to Rs 15,930,208 (US $ 331,879) out of the total loans of Rs. 44,433,900 (US $ 925,706). All payments are made in cash. The current sources of capital used by the Cooperative to support its loan portfolio are shown in the table below. All members are required to save a minimum of Rs30 per month. Where lines of credit are provided by agencies such as RMK, that restrict the interest rate at which funds can be on lent, additional savings are required from members taking out loans from these lines. The additional savings are used, in effect, to harmonise the interest rates applied to medium term loans and ensure a consistent charge of 18% across this part of the loan portfolio. A 24% interest rate is applied to short-term loans (12 months or less).

However to date only 2 of these have been taken out. Housing loans attract a 12% interest rate with terms ranging between 5 and 12 years. Members of the Cooperative receive 6% on their savings, a rate that is competitive with other local financial agencies (commercial banks 3.5%, other local cooperatives 4.5% - 5%). If a member wishes to resign from the Cooperative she must provide one month's notice.

Members receiving loans have an option to pay back the loans sooner than the term agreed (i.e. to prepay). 10 people have done this in order to be able to take out a further loan. However, no payments lower than the monthly repayment are allowed. If a member has problems in repayment this has to be dealt with at TAG and/or Mandal level. Under the Co-operative Act there is provision for default to be dealt with rapidly in the court.

CRITERIA FOR SHORT & MEDIUM TERM LOANS:

- The borrower must be a member of the Cooperative. (i.e. Have contributed Rs. 100 for 10 shares, paid a membership fee of Rs. 10).
- The borrower must have saved regularly for at least 6 months. (Minimum monthly savings currently set at Rs30/month).
- The borrower must provide 2 guarantors who are also members of the Cooperative.

CRITERIA FOR HOUSE LOANS

Rs. 35,000 for 10 years repayments of Rs. 400 per month. As for short and medium term loans but also:

Land deed or patta in the applicant's own name or House or land deed in the name of the member's father or brother together with a letter authorising transfer in the case of default. In the case of land or house being used as collateral valuations and lien searches are carried out by the Government sub-registrar in the relevant area and appropriate certification provided to the Cooperative.

DIVIDEND

Members have agreed that the Cooperative should retain all dividends for the first 3 years of its operation.

THE FUTURE DEVELOPMENT OF SWAYAMKRUSHI DEVELOPING AUTONOMY

Over the next 2 years it is anticipated that the Cooperative will take over entire responsibility for management of the savings and loan portfolio associated with the village Mahila Mandals. Major external credit lines will be managed during this time by YCO, until Swayamkrushi has established a financial management record. Staff who are currently on secondment from YCO will be permanently employed by the Cooperative by the end of the period at which time their salaries will be the sole responsibility of Swayamkrushi. A three-year business plan has been developed for the Cooperative along these lines.

INCREASING THE HOUSE LOAN PORTFOLIO

At the moment the number of house loans extended by the Cooperative is extremely limited. It should be noted that at the moment, in theory, families with title deeds could apply for house loans directly from commercial banks. In practice this would be extremely difficult. The standard term for individual mortgage financing from these agencies is 3 to 4 years and the repayment structure means that repayments in the early stages only reduce the capital loan marginally. Processing time is also much shorter in the case of the cooperative - 15 days compared to 3 or 4 months in the case of the commercial lenders. In any case few families in the area could, at the moment afford commercial house loans delivered outside of the Guarantee initiative which offers considerably longer repayment terms.

One of the ideas being explored at the moment is the establishment of a separate house savings scheme within Swayamkrushi with provision being made for investment in share capital specifically linked to house loans. The aim is to encourage families to save 5%-10% of the house loan they will require and for this amount to be maintained as a hedging fund, reducing the vulnerability of the Cooperative to defaults on house loan repayments.

INCREASING THE CAPITAL BASE BY ATTRACTING RICHER VILLAGERS

Swayamkrushi is considering offering larger loans to better off villagers in order to increase its capital base and hence its long term financial viability. However security in the form of land and/or gold and jewelry would have to be provided. At the moment gold cannot be accepted as security as the offices are not sufficiently secure. The intention is to require gold to the value of four times the loan size.

KEEPING SWAYAMKRUSHI IN WOMEN'S HANDS

The Cooperative has considered the issue of men's participation in the savings and loan scheme. In some villages there are men's associations but no mahila mandals as the men have resisted their formation. The co-operative has taken a clear decision to exclude men's associations from Swayamkrushi. They believe that men's inclusion would only strengthen the exclusion of women from financial management at village level

REFERENCES & SOURCE

1. India, 1991, Publications Division, Ministry of Information & Broadcasting, Govt. of India.
2. www.ap.nic.in/dwcra
3. T. Chiranjeevulu, Empowering Women through Self-Help Groups, Kurukshetra, New Delhi, March, 2003, pp.16-19.
4. Hindustan Lever Limited - Project Shakti Brochure
5. http://www.blonnet.com/businessline/2001/05/21/stories/14210204.htm
6. http://www.gdrc.org/icm/wind/rass.html
   - RASS, 1998. 'Partners in Progress - Organizing Communities for Development'

- RASS, 1998. Awakening Gender Potential - The SHGs Way.
- SIDBI, 1999. Annual Report 1998-99'.
- SIDBI, 1997. Development Report, October 1997.
- Sri Padmavathy Mahila Abyudaya Sangam, 1996. Community Banking - Our Gurthimpu.
- Sri Padmavathy Mahila Abyudaya Sangam, 1996. Training Manual for Community Banking.

7. http://www.ycongo.org/women's_coop_.htm

Index

J

❑❑❑

①

270